FABERGÉ'S EGGS

Toby Faber

FABERGÉ'S EGGS

The extraordinary story of the masterpieces that outlived an empire

MACMILLAN

First published 2008 by Macmillan
an imprint of Pan Macmillan Ltd
Pan Macmillan, 20 New Wharf Road, London N1 9RR
Basingstoke and Oxford
Associated companies throughout the world
www.panmacmillan.com

ISBN 978-1-4050-5388-4

1 3 5 7 9 8 6 4 2

A CIP catalogue record for this book is available from
the British Library.

Printed and bound in Great Britain by
Mackays of Chatham plc, Chatham, Kent

To

my father, Tom

my wife, Amanda

and

my daughter, Lucy

Picture Acknowledgements

First picture section

Armoury Museum, Kremlin, Moscow: p. 6 (bottom, left); p. 7 (bottom).
Armoury Museum, Kremlin, Moscow / The Bridgeman Art Library:
 p. 6 (bottom, right).
Faber, Toby, Ltd: p. 6 (top); p. 6 (centre).
Images courtesy of The Forbes Collection, New York: p. 3 (top); p. 3 (bottom, left);
 p. 5 (top, right); p. 5 (bottom). All photographed by Joseph Coscia, Jr.
 Copyright © All rights reserved.
Getty Images: p. 4 (top, left); p. 5 (top, left); p. 8 (bottom, left).
PA Photos: p. 3 (bottom, right).
Tillander, A.: p. 2 (bottom).
Wartski, London: p. 1 (bottom); p. 2 (top); p. 8 (top).

Second picture section

Armoury Museum, Kremlin, Moscow: p. 3 (bottom).
Images courtesy of The Forbes Collection, *New York*: p. 3 (top; photographed
 by Josh Nefsky, New York); p. 8 (bottom, left); p. 8 (bottom, right).
 Copyright © All rights reserved.
Getty Images: p. 1 (top, left); p. 1 (top, right); p. 4 (top); p. 4 (bottom, left);
 p. 5 (top); p. 8 (top).
Katamidze, Slava, Collection: p. 5 (bottom, left).
Mary Evans: p. 4 (bottom, right).
PA Photos: p. 6 (top); p. 6 (bottom); p. 7 (bottom).
State Archive of Film and Photographic Documents, St Petersburg: p. 2 (top, left);
 p. 2 (top, right).
Studio C. E. Hahn & Co., Tsarskoye Selo: p. 1 (bottom); p. 2 (bottom).

Every effort has been made to contact copyright holders of photographs reproduced
in this book. If any have been inadvertently overlooked, the publishers will be
pleased to make restitution at the earliest opportunity.

Contents

Because it's fun. It's a hunt. I get a certain joy
out of finding rare works, out of learning
the stories attached to them.

ARMAND HAMMER
The Armand Hammer Collection,
Allbright-Knox Art Gallery

Romanov family tree, showing selected descendants of Nicholas I and their spouses

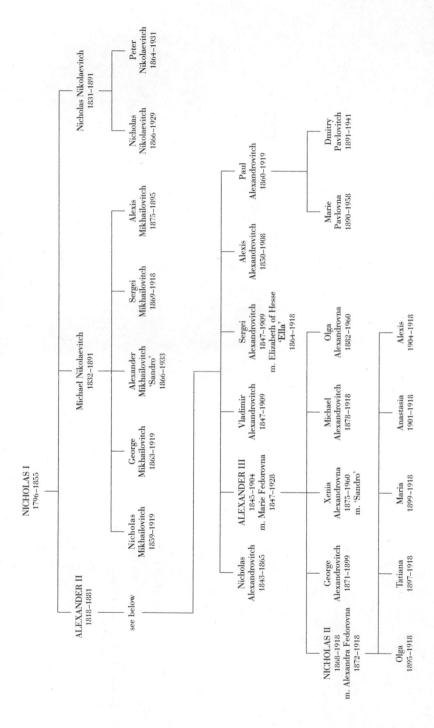

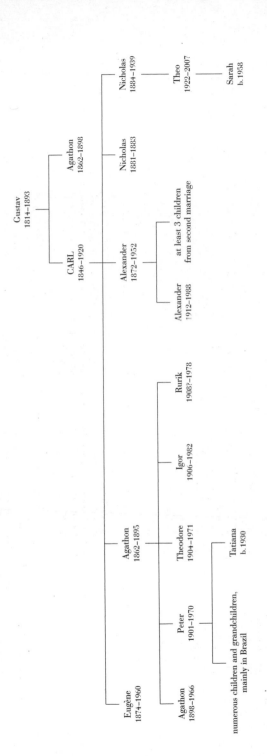

Fabergé family tree

Introduction

Theo Woodall first looked at his birth certificate in 1969, when he was forty-seven years old. An elderly aunt had suggested he do so. 'You should have been told earlier,' she added. The document told Theo why. His 'parents', Philip and Linda Woodall, were really his aunt and uncle. Linda's sister, Theo's glamorous Aunt Dorise (she had added the final *e* some years earlier), was his true mother. That's the kind of news that would shake any man, but what really struck him was the name of his father – on the birth certificate, despite Theo's illegitimacy – Nicholas Fabergé. Theo's paternal grandfather had been the world's most famous jeweller, supplier to the Romanovs and half the nobility of Europe, Carl Gustavovitch Fabergé.

For the previous thirty years Theo had been a production engineer. In 1967, two years before he discovered his true parentage, he had co-founded a coil-winding firm, Theobar Engineering. It was the culmination of a technical career that had started with an apprenticeship at General Aircraft at the London Air Park in Feltham. The information on his birth certificate, however, changed everything. Within a few years Theo had sold his share of Theobar and found a new vocation as a woodturner and, eventually, jewellery designer. Reclaiming his father's name, he died in August 2007 as Theo Fabergé; his daughter, born a Woodall, is now known as Sarah Fabergé. Her St Petersburg Collection is sold from a shop in London's Burlington Arcade, around the corner from Tiffany's and Asprey's. Its limited edition pieces sell for thousands of pounds. As a family, they've come a long way from coil-winding.

How can the discovery of a birth certificate make such a difference to a life? What is it about the knowledge of descent from
Carl Fabergé that could wreak such a change? It is not as though
the goldsmith's products are universally admired as icons of good
design. Some may have been copied and admired by successive
generations of jewellers, but others, even the deepest aficionados
would admit, are fabulously over-the-top concoctions. An elaborately decorated parasol handle or rhinoceros-shaped match
container may make you laugh, but that is no reason for the
respect, even semi-deification, that their maker now enjoys.

A typical piece of Fabergé is not particularly rare; Carl was
no lone artisan; his workshops employed hundreds of workmen
turning out thousands of objects every year. Nor is it usually the
diamond-studded ornament of popular imagination. Fabergé's
creations may have come to symbolize the enormous wealth of
his clientele – the aristocracy of Europe's golden age – but they
were made with relatively unexciting materials. Carved hard-
stones and enamel were Fabergé's stock-in-trade, not fabulous
diamonds or enormous rubies.

Even the name Fabergé is hardly redolent of unambiguous
luxury. For fifty years it has been most commonly used as a name
attached to – at best – mid-market toiletries. For Britons of a certain age it is indelibly linked with a brand of aftershave, whose
television advertisements, fronted by a boxer who had once
knocked down Muhammad Ali, advised users to 'Splash it all over.'

Nowadays, of course, the price of Fabergé alone commands
attention. It is difficult not to be impressed when an enamelled
silver desk clock made in 1903 and less than five inches high sells
for £100,000 at auction. Few investments outpace inflation by
something like a factor of forty. Yet price alone is no reason for
respect. In the words of one modern Fabergé dealer, 'There's only
really one price that's significant with a work of art and that's
what the patron pays; the rest is just completely ephemeral.'
Besides, value is surely a consequence, not the cause, of whatever makes this particular jeweller's works so special.

One reason for the mystique attached to Fabergé's name can be found in the sheer quality of his work. As Queen Mary, wife of Britain's King George V and one of the jeweller's most fervent admirers, once put it, 'There is one thing about all Fabergé pieces, they are so satisfying.'[1] The click of a well-closed case, the perfection of a flawless surface, the sense of solidity when holding even the most apparently ethereal piece: all speak of an attention to detail and devotion to quality that demands admiration. But Fabergé's craftsmanship is hardly unique. Several of his contemporaries maintained similar standards, and there is no ripple of excitement when their fabrications appear in the saleroom.

No. If there is one reason why we have all heard of Carl Fabergé, it is because we have all heard of his most famous creations. He is, to put it bluntly, the 'egg guy', famous above all for the eggs made by his firm for Russia's tsars to give as Easter presents to their tsarinas. In a little over thirty years, fifty of these 'Imperial' eggs were completed – each one unique. And now their reputation is legendary, enough to overshadow all the jeweller's other pieces, but also to give them lustre.

Even modern imitations benefit from the originals' reflected glory. In March 2006 the story that supermodel Kate Moss smuggled the drugs Ecstasy and Rohypnol in a '£65,000 gem-encrusted'[2] Fabergé egg – clearly a replica – made headlines around the world. And the St Petersburg Collection's most sought-after products, by far, are its eggs, notably those designed by Sarah Fabergé to celebrate footballers like Jimmy Johnstone and George Best.

As for the original Imperial eggs, each tells a story. Their individual designs inevitably reflect something of what was then happening in the lives of the tsarinas. Fabergé's relentless search for novelty, for something that would interest his royal Romanov patrons, makes certain of that. And, since the fall of the tsars, they have accumulated anecdotes. Eggs have been smuggled past border guards, used to repay favours among communist sympathizers and stolen from exhibitions – only to be recovered months later in a high-speed car chase. Most tantalizing of all, perhaps, are the eggs for which there is no history, those which disappeared in the Revolution or soon afterwards. They raise the possibility, however remote, of eventual discovery, of the classic attic treasure trove. It is no wonder that in films from *Octopussy* to *Oceans Twelve*, a Fabergé egg has acted as immediate short-hand for desirability, glamour and intrigue.

As a group, too, the overall history of the Imperial eggs is equally fascinating. Whether fairly or not, their opulence and occasional vulgarity mean they have come to symbolize the decadence of the court for which they were made. 'Now I understand why they had a revolution' is the common remark of someone viewing these creations for the first time. They may be masterpieces, but they also embody extravagance that even the Romanovs' most ardent supporter would find hard to justify. After 1917's inevitable cataclysm, the eggs disappeared in the chaos of the times. Most eventually emerged, carefully preserved in the Kremlin's vaults, only to be earmarked for sale in Europe and America by communists eager for foreign exchange. Since then they have been bought and sold by monarchs, entrepreneurs and collectors. And they have acquired a new status: immensely personal, yet gloriously flamboyant, they have become perhaps the most tangible surviving symbols of the last tsar and his family, and of the gilded lives they led before their final tragic end in a Siberian basement.

Now, apparently closing the circle, the eggs have begun returning to post-communist Russia, bought back by an oligarch who might be considered a modern-day successor of the Romanovs. Their narrative illustrates the development of Russia's relationship with the West, from tsarist cosmopolitanism through communist insularity to its current ambivalent embrace of capitalist freedoms. It is a remarkable story, and it begins in 1885, with the first egg that Fabergé made for Tsar Alexander III.

1. 'Christ is risen!'

FOR RUSSIAN Orthodox Christians in the nineteenth century, no date in the religious calendar was more important than Easter day. The long fast of Lent would have been strictly observed – no meat, milk, butter or eggs for over seven weeks – until the solemn celebrations of Holy Week built steadily to their joyful climax at a midnight service finishing early on Easter Sunday morning. Throughout the day itself, friends and family greeted each other with the traditional three kisses, and responded to the jubilant 'Christ is risen!' with a reply of equal certainty: 'He is risen indeed!' And then, in a ritual whose symbolism stretches back to pagan spring festivals, they would exchange eggs.

So Tsar Alexander III was simply following tradition when, in 1885, he gave his beloved Tsarina, the popular Marie Fedorovna, an apparently unexciting white enamelled egg. About two and a half inches high, it had the size and appearance of a large duck egg, but with a gold band around its middle. Only when the Empress opened the Tsar's present did it reveal its true nature: like an elaborate Matrushka doll it contained a perfect yolk, made of gold; within that was a golden hen, sitting on a nest of golden straw; and inside the hen was a diamond miniature of the imperial crown, concealing a tiny ruby pendant. Every detail was exquisitely rendered – the craftsmanship unparalleled, the creativity inspired. It was the first egg made by Carl Fabergé for the Russian court.

FABERGÉ was not even forty when his firm made that first egg for the Tsar, but his family had, in a sense, spent more than a lifetime preparing for this moment. Not only was his father, Gustav, a jeweller, but it is safe to assume that his more distant ancestors were craftsmen too. Their surnames alone give that away: Favry, Fabri and Fabrier all appear to have been used at some point and all, like Fabergé itself, are derived from the Latin word *faber*, meaning smith or maker. In the eighteenth century these ancestors had been living in France, but their Protestant religion marked them out for persecution by another absolute monarch, the Roman Catholic Louis XIV (1638–1715). At least two hundred thousand Huguenots, many of them skilled artisans, fled France following Louis's repeal in 1685 of the Edict of Nantes, which had until then guaranteed religious toleration. Carl's ancestors were among them, and chose to go east.

By 1800, Peter Favry had settled in Pärnu, in current-day Estonia, where he had taken Russian citizenship, a move that gave his family freedom from further religious intolerance. Gustav was born here in 1814, and by 1820 his surname was already Faberge. He seems to have added the accent to the final *e* in 1842. The gradual name change smacks of an attempt at social betterment. The aristocracy of nineteenth-century Russia still spoke in French and looked to Paris as the fount of culture. It would have done the former Favrys no harm to stress their Gallic origins.

Gustav's ambition is evidenced by his early move to Russia's capital, St Petersburg. Here he trained with some of Russia's most eminent jewellers, including I. V. Keibel, the firm which only a few years earlier had reset the crown jewels for Tsar Nicholas I. Soon enough he was ready to set up on his own as a master goldsmith, and in 1841 he had opened his own shop – only a basement, but located on Bolshaya Morskaya, one of the smartest streets in St Petersburg.

Five years later, on 5 May 1846,* Gustav's son Carl Gus-

---

* According to the Julian calendar in use in Russia until the Revolution. In the nineteenth century this was twelve days behind the Gregorian calen-

tavovitch Fabergé was born. He would become the vehicle for his father's dreams, not only attending one of the most fashionable schools in St Petersburg but also spending long hours in the workshop. Here he started to learn the basics of jewellery-making from his father's senior employee, Finnish workmaster Hiskias Pendin.

Then, in 1860, when he was still only forty-six, Gustav Fabergé retired. Leaving Pendin and a manager in charge of the business, he took his family to Dresden, the capital of Saxony. It seems a bizarre decision. Gustav was not apparently ill; he lived for another thirty years. It may be that he could no longer stand the marshy atmosphere of St Petersburg – the houses sealed tight against the cold of winter, the quagmires of spring and the baking heat of summer. Or it may be that he had become aware of his son's talent and realized that for it to flower Carl would need to be educated in a manner that Russian schools simply could not provide. If Gustav was to remain in at least nominal contact with his business in St Petersburg, there was no better place both to expand his son's horizons and to develop his skills than Dresden, the 'Florence of the Elbe'.

Certainly, Carl's education from 1860 bears the hallmarks of a carefully plotted trajectory. It began at Dresden's *Handelsschule*, literally, trade school. This was where the sons of Saxon merchants went to learn the rudiments of business administration. A subsequent grand tour gave Carl the opportunity to visit jewellers in England, Italy and, above all, Paris, where newcomers like Cartier and Boucheron were turning out designs that married traditional craftsmanship with creative flair. In Paris too Carl spent more time in a commercial college. Finally, he took up an apprenticeship with a goldsmith in

---

dar of western Europe and the US. So the Western equivalent of this date is 17 May. The gap increased to thirteen days after 1900. Throughout this book, unless otherwise noted, dates are expressed in the form used by the Russian government at the time.

Frankfurt, but it was only a short attachment, one that gave him the opportunity to see a master at work, not to perfect every technique. In short, Carl seems to have spent his years outside Russia in pursuit of two main aims: exposure to Western culture and preparation for a life in business. The son of Gustav Fabergé was destined to be the head of a firm: an employer, not an employee.

In 1864, four years after his father had taken him to Dresden, Carl Fabergé returned to work for the family firm in St Petersburg. He was only eighteen; his education continued. Partly this would have involved learning at the side of Hiskias Pendin, but Carl also did his best to seek out the works of earlier, more European, master jewellers. He found them in the Hermitage, the great museum attached to St Petersburg's Winter Palace. Here, treasures accumulated by previous generations of tsars had been on display to the public since the 1850s. Carl developed friendships with members of the Hermitage direc-torate and in 1867 began unpaid work there. The museum had started to receive items of ancient jewellery discovered during archaeological investigations; they needed someone to repair them and assess their materials; Carl volunteered.

By 1872, when he was twenty-six, Carl Fabergé was ready both to take over his father's business and to marry. His wife was also his cousin, Augusta Jacobs, the daughter of a cabinet maker. Three sons followed in quick succession, born between 1874 and 1877: Eugène, Agathon and Alexander. A fourth son, Nicholas, died aged only two in 1883; and a fifth and last son, again called Nicholas, was born the following year. Later employees of Carl Fabergé would tell of him welcoming his customers' children and setting out animals carved from semi-precious stones for them to play with, unconcerned with the fragility of a chosen toy. This suggests a kindly and inter-ested father, and his sons all eventually chose to join him in the company. Nevertheless, whatever the distractions of family life, Carl remained focused on the business entrusted to him by his own father. He moved it to larger premises, still on Bolshaya Morskaya, and began the changes that would transform what his eldest son Eugène later called 'a dealer in petty jewellery and spectacles' into the premier jeweller in Europe.

Fabergé's time in Europe and the Hermitage had inspired him; he wanted to make pieces of jewellery that were more than the sum of their parts – to elevate design and craftsmanship above mere materials. In his own words, much later, 'Expensive things interest me little if the value is merely in so many diamonds or pearls.'[1] In nineteenth-century Russia this was groundbreaking. Everyone knew the story of how Count Orlov had secured his position at Catherine the Great's court with the gift to her of a single massive diamond, smuggled from India. The purchase had bankrupted him, but favours from a grateful empress soon proved it a wise investment. Little had changed in the century since Catherine's death. According to an English diplomat, Lord Frederic Hamilton, who spent much of the 1880s in St Petersburg, 'A stone must be very perfect to satisfy the critical Russian eye, and, true to their Oriental blood, the ladies preferred unfaceted rubies, sapphires and emeralds.'[2] Carl Fabergé's great achievement was that he not only made beautifully designed jewellery, but succeeded in selling it to the Russian aristocracy. He changed the taste of St Petersburg.

Very few pieces of Fabergé survive from these early years, so it is hard to trace the development of Carl's ideas or of his skills as a designer. By 1881, however, he had achieved enough recognition among his peers to be appointed a 'master of the Second Guild'. In keeping with the commercial flavour of his education, the title marked him as a merchant or retailer, rather than a craftsman. It allowed him to use his own hallmark confirming precious metal content without submitting his pieces for official testing. It is probably no coincidence that this was the year that Hiskias Pendin died. The firm might still be called Gustav Fabergé, but its owner remained in Dresden. Carl was now formally acknowledged, by all, as its head.

   The business was already reasonably substantial, employing about twenty people, but it was the following year, 1882, that brought Fabergé his first major breakthrough – the attention of the Imperial family. The occasion was an exhibition in Moscow of artefacts from all over Russia. Fabergé had been invited to participate because of his work at the Hermitage Museum. The articles he had helped to restore included Greek and Scythian jewellery dating back to the fourth century BC, which had been found at Kerch on the Black Sea coast. Fabergé had obtained permission both to copy them and to incorporate their designs in more modern objects; he made the results the focus of his display at the exhibition. It was an inspired decision; Fabergé could show off creativity then unexpected in a jeweller, while rooting it in a tradition so ancient that no Russian could fail to be impressed. A notice in the magazine *Niva* was suitably ecstatic: 'Mr Fabergé opens a new era in the art of jewellery. We wish him all the best in his efforts to bring back into the realm of art what once used to be a part of it.'³ The same article carried a final, telling paragraph: 'Her Majesty honoured Fabergé by buying a pair of cufflinks with images of cicadas which, according to Ancient Greek belief, bring luck.'

   A decade after taking over his father's business Carl Fabergé had achieved royal recognition. Nevertheless, he was only one jeweller among many supplying the Russian court; at least five firms feature in the Imperial accounts for the following year, 1883, and the amount paid to Fabergé – just under 6,400 roubles (£640, £43,000)* – was by far the smallest. The next year his friends at the Hermitage tried to get him an Imperial warrant, formal acknowledgement of his position as a royal supplier and a hugely valuable affirmation of status in a capital city where life still revolved around the Court.

---

* Throughout the text, the first figure in parentheses gives the then sterling equivalent of the sum stated, and the second figure translates this into a modern equivalent, based on the UK Retail Price Index for 2006.

The request was refused; that sort of honour was not given away lightly.

Only one year later, however, in 1885, the Tsar gave his wife her first Easter present from Fabergé – the *Hen Egg*. He had given her jewelled eggs on previous Easters; he cannot have known that this gift would be the first of a series that would eventually span over three decades. Nor was the cost of this first egg – 4,151 roubles (£400, £28,000) – such that the decision to order it needed very much thought. It represented a tiny fraction of the Tsar's annual income – an estimated nine million roubles (£900,000, £70 million). Fabergé may simply have been chosen for the commission because it was his turn. Nevertheless, there is evidence that this year at least the Tsar wanted an egg that was designed to be more than just a collection of precious stones. It comes from a pair of letters, now in the Russian State Historical Archives, exchanged between the Tsar and his brother the Grand Duke Vladimir.

The first letter is from the Grand Duke. Sent on 21 March 1885, three days before Easter, it clearly accompanied the egg, which Vladimir must have picked up from Fabergé on his brother's behalf. The note contains detailed instructions on how to open each successive layer within the egg and gives his opinion of it as 'a complete success . . . praiseworthy for its fine and intricate workmanship'.[4]

In his reply, written the same day, the Tsar agrees: 'I am grateful to you, dear Vladimir, for the trouble you have taken in placing the order and for the execution of the order itself, which could not have been more successful.' There is enough here to suggest that it was the cosmopolitan Vladimir who had first conceived the idea to order an egg from Fabergé. It is the closing sentence of the Tsar's letter, however, that truly intrigues: 'I do hope the egg will have the desired effect on its future owner.' What 'effect' on his wife did the Tsar have in mind? What, in fact, was the nature of their relationship?

*

ALEXANDER III had taken the throne following the gruesome assassination of his father, Alexander II, a few weeks before the Easter of 1881. On Sunday 1 March the old Tsar was on his way back from the ceremonial changing of the guard at the Mikhaelovsky Riding School in St Petersburg when a bomb was thrown under his carriage. The explosion damaged the vehicle, killing and injuring part of the escort, but the Tsar himself was unharmed. Ignoring his driver's pleas to speed on, he stepped down from the carriage and began speaking to the wounded men, questioning the captured bomb-thrower and praising his good fortune at a lucky escape. Almost immediately a further assassin ran forward. Shouting, 'It is too early to thank God,' he launched a bomb that exploded directly at the Tsar's feet.

Alexander was still alive, but only just. His legs had been torn away and his stomach ripped open, yet he still had enough strength to whisper a last command: 'To the palace, to die there.' He was obeyed. Dripping blood up the marble staircase, his body, not yet a corpse, was carried into the Winter Palace. There the Imperial family gathered around his deathbed. Among them were the future Alexander III, his wife Marie Fedorovna, still clutching the ice skates she had been about to put on when the news of the bomb had reached her, and their son Nicholas, aged thirteen and dressed in a blue sailor suit. All were there when the surgeon made the expected announcement: 'The Emperor is dead.'

Russia had a new tsar: Alexander III. Hearing the surgeon's words, he turned from the window through which he had been staring, nodded and gave a few swift instructions to the chief of police. Then he and Marie walked out of the palace and stepped into a waiting carriage. In the words of his cousin Grand Duke Alexander Mikhailovitch, another witness to the deathbed scene, 'In less than five minutes he had acquired a new personality. Something much bigger than a mere realization of the Imperial responsibilities had transformed his massive frame.'[5]

Of all the nineteenth-century tsars, Alexander II had come the closest to being a modernizer. A pragmatic statesman, he had responded to Russia's disastrous defeat in the Crimean War by overseeing a series of reforms to its judiciary, censorship, education and the armed forces. Most famously, the emancipation of the serfs in 1861 had earned him the title 'Tsar Liberator'. Twenty years later, on the morning of his assassination, Alexander had signed a document convening an elected national council; it had been on its way to the printers when the terrorists intervened. By itself this 'manifesto' would have made little difference to Russia's constitution, but it would have been a first step down a road that might, eventually, have culminated in Alexander turning his empire into a parliamentary democracy.

None of Alexander's reforms was enough for his more radical opponents. In 1879 a small clique of students had formed Norodnya Volya – People's Will – a nihilist movement dedicated to revolution. Only by destroying all existing hierarchies, it believed, could a new, fairer society be rebuilt. The death of the Tsar, the man at the centre of the government, was at the heart of all its plans. For all his apparent liberalism Alexander remained an absolute monarch; aided by a vast bureaucracy, he wielded ultimate power over every Russian. He was the state, and therefore the ultimate target of every revolutionary. There had already been several attempts on his life before that final bloody success in 1881.

Alexander III, like his father, had been a liberal. If he had come to the throne in different circumstances he might have carried on with the reform programme. Assassination, however, was hardly likely to foster constitutionalism in the murdered man's son. Rumours circulated of a meeting at the Winter Palace on the evening of the murder. Supported by his younger brothers, the new Tsar determined to withdraw his father's last manifesto; only a weak tsar would ask his people for advice; the printing presses were stopped. Alexander deliberated for a few more weeks and then, on 9 May, issued his accession manifesto, firmly repudiating any hint of liberalization: 'The voice of God commands Us to place Ourself with assurance at the head of the absolute power. Confident in the Divine Providence and in His supreme wisdom, full of faith in the justice and strength of the autocracy which We are called to maintain, We shall preside serenely over the destinies of Our empire which henceforward will be discussed between God and Ourself alone.'[6] Alexander III would rule in the manner of his predecessors, with all power centred on himself as Tsar. His reign would be characterized by counter-reform and repression.

St Petersburg was not, however, a safe environment for the Tsar. He moved his family to the Gatchina Palace, about thirty miles south-west of the capital. The high wall surrounding the five square miles of its park gave the palace some security, which the permanent presence of a brigade of cavalry reinforced. By day, sentries patrolled the grounds a hundred yards apart; at night the distance between them shrank to twenty-five yards. Outside Gatchina's walls Russia turned into a police state, with conspiracies – real or imagined – around every corner. Constantly threatened and under permanent guard, Alexander frequently, and with justification, referred to his vast empire as his prison.

Gatchina itself was a fairy-tale castle, its extravagance typical of the man who commissioned it, the diamond-loving Count Orlov. In 1783 Catherine the Great had bought the palace from his estate, and subsequent generations of tsars had added wings so that by the time Alexander III came to occupy it, Gatchina had over 900 rooms. His youngest daughter, Olga, particularly loved the Chinese Gallery; the huge vases it contained, placed there by her great-great-grandfather, Paul I, were ideal for hide-and-seek. To her cousins it was Gatchina's special odours that were particularly memorable: a mixture of turpentine, Russian leather and cigarette smoke for Queen Marie of Rumania, and a scent 'like clean wood' for the Grand Duke Cyril Vladimirovitch.

Amid this magnificence, Alexander chose to live on a mezzanine floor, whose cramped rooms and low ceilings had little to do with the popularly imagined lifestyle of a tsar. Here, following a practice established by Peter the Great, the Imperial family lived in what seems like wilful simplicity. The children slept on army beds with hard pillows and rough blankets; they took cold baths in the morning and had porridge for breakfast. The theme was self-restraint; outward emotion was to be avoided as much as unnecessary luxury. Alexander treated himself little better: he rose at seven, splashed his face with cold water and, armed only with a pot of coffee, settled down to work at his desk. Later, he and Marie might share rye bread and eggs for their morning meal. Immensely strong, Alexander's party trick as a young man had been to tear a pack of cards in half. Now, as a middle-aged autocrat, he found nothing more relaxing than an afternoon spent chopping wood or a night fishing.

It is hard to know what the new Tsarina made of all this. By the time Marie married Alexander, her father was Christian IX, King of Denmark, her elder sister Alexandra was married to the Prince of Wales, the future Edward VII, and her brother Wilhelm was King of Greece. Yet when she was born in 1847 the young Dagmar, as she was then called, could have expected little of this glory. Her family lived in relative poverty in a small grace and favour mansion in Copenhagen, minor cousins of Denmark's King Frederick. Their situation only improved in 1852, when the childless King adopted Christian as his heir. For the first five years of her life, therefore, Dagmar was almost a commoner. She could hardly fail to be aware of the luck behind her sudden elevation. She revelled in her good fortune; her vivaciousness would eventually make her the most eligible bride in Europe.

So, in 1864, the sixteen-year-old Dagmar had become engaged to the Tsarevitch, heir to the Russian empire. Deeply in love, the young couple recited poetry to each other and scratched their names on the window of the castle in Denmark where they courted. Their future as Europe's golden couple seemed assured. Dagmar's fiancé, however, was not Alexander but his elder brother Nicholas. He had less than a year to live.

Early in 1865, while on holiday in Cannes, Nicholas was thrown from his horse. Meningitis set in, and it was soon clear that he would die. Hurrying to his side from Copenhagen, Dagmar was just in time, so the story goes, to accede to her dying fiancé's last wish: that she should marry his brother Alexander instead. Understandably, both parties to the new arrangement had considerable doubts. From Marie's point of view, the younger brother, by comparison with Nicholas, was a boor of little obvious charm. As for Alexander, he was in love with one of his mother's maids of honour, Princess Marie Mebtchersky. Gradually, however, duty asserted itself. More than a year after that deathbed promise Dagmar and Alexander announced their betrothal. In October 1866 Dagmar converted to orthodoxy, taking the name Marie Fedorovna,* and one month later she and Alexander married.

Husky-voiced, dark and petite, Marie was pretty rather than beautiful, but she charmed all who met her. From the moment of her arrival in Russia she was the queen of society. At Imperial balls she danced the high-spirited mazurka in front of two or three thousand guests, and showed off her jewels: tiaras, earrings, chokers, necklaces, brooches and bows of rubies and diamonds 'so large', according to the wife of the American envoy to St Petersburg in the 1880s, 'they would not be handsome worn by any other person, as in that case, they would not be supposed to be real'.[7]

The sense of responsibility that had begun Marie and Alexander's marriage would eventually deepen into something

---

* Russians take as their second name a patronymic derived from their father's first name, with the suffix -vitch for men and -vna for women. The patronymic Fedorovna can be roughly translated as 'Gift of God', and was traditional for foreign brides.

more. That he grew to love her was hardly surprising, but she came to appreciate his steadfastness and sense of purpose. The Anitchkov Palace in St Petersburg became both a glittering court-in-waiting and, according to a later letter from Marie, a 'beloved, cosy home'. After the birth of their eldest son, the future Nicholas II, in 1868, five more children followed: three sons, of whom one died in infancy, and two daughters.

By the time his last child, Olga, was born in 1882 Alexander III was already Emperor. Marie had lost her husband to the labours of autocracy far too early. She can scarcely have appreciated it, nor did she enjoy her semi-exile from St Petersburg to the cramped quarters at Gatchina. Whenever possible she escaped back to the capital, occasionally dragging her husband along, for the social functions that were to him a duty and to her a pleasure. Here, they could return to the Anitchkov. Even their son, Nicholas, noticed his mother's preference for this palace, writing in his diary there in 1893, 'We had tea with Mamma upstairs. Thank God, she is in good spirits. I believe that the height of the rooms does her a lot of good.'

Overshadowing any discomfort or frustration that Marie felt in Gatchina, however, there must have been fear. Those ice skates that she still held by her father-in-law's deathbed somehow symbolize the change in her that his assassination wrought. She had picked them up in happy anticipation of a morning spent skating with her family, but it was with horror that she continued clutching onto them, hours later. In the months and years that followed terrorist threats would be aimed at her as much as at her husband. Notes would be left for her to find. The threats they contained were alarming enough, while their locations – a coffee table in her private salon or a private photograph album – provided proof that even within the palace walls she could not consider her family safe.

In 1883, the year Alexander III was to be crowned in Moscow, Easter brought a particular shock. Among the jewelled eggs sent as gifts and awaiting his inspection was one that was

especially beautiful. Marie was the first to open it. Inside she
found a little silver dagger and two skulls carved from ivory.
The gilt-edged card beside them carried the usual Easter
message – 'Christ is risen!' – but also another: 'You may crush
us – but we nihilists shall rise again!' On the same day Moscow's
prefect of police received a basket of painted hens' eggs. Several
were stuffed with dynamite, although none exploded. This
time the accompanying note read, 'We have plenty more for the
coronation.'

Warned of the terrorists' intentions for the ceremony, the
Tsar's secret police justified its existence by uncovering a
number of conspiracies. One was intended to exploit one of the
more modern features of the festivities: a plotter had apparently
wired bombs into the lighting circuits that lined the route of the
procession. Another was more basic: revolutionaries were to be
given cloth caps stuffed with dynamite for throwing in apparent over-exuberance straight at the coronation coach. Although
the day eventually passed without incident, for many this was
little short of a miracle.

So we can start to imagine what kind of effect the Tsar was
seeking when he wrote that letter to his brother in 1885. He
wanted an Easter egg that would surprise and delight his wife,
one that would divert her, for a moment, from the cares of her
position. In looking to Fabergé, moreover, Alexander had made
the perfect choice. Here was a goldsmith with little interest in
'so many diamonds or pearls'. He could produce a design that
would provide the perfect bridge between the Tsar's taste for
simplicity and his wife's for ostentation.

The true brilliance of that first egg, however, was that it met
the Tsar's requirements by being both more and less than a piece
of brilliant creativity: less because it was not an original design,
but more because the model it copied is one that Marie would
have recognized. The Danish Royal Collection still contains
what must have been Fabergé's inspiration: an egg dating to
the early eighteenth century. It is made of ivory rather than the

enamel that Faberge used, and its final surprise is a ring rather than a pendant, but otherwise it is remarkably similar to the *Hen Egg*. The young Princess Dagmar would certainly have seen it; perhaps she was allowed to look inside. Marie had enjoyed a famously happy childhood. Even as Tsarina she returned to Denmark whenever she could, joining her brothers and sisters for summer holidays when her parents played host to half the royal families of Europe. The genius behind Fabergé's first egg was that it reminded the Empress Marie of a carefree past. It was the ideal antidote to the bad memories of recent Easters.

Six weeks after Alexander gave Marie the egg, on 1 May 1885, the Court issued the following announcement: 'His Majesty the Emperor has granted his Supreme permission to St Petersburg 2nd Guild Merchant jeweller Carl Fabergé, with a store at 18 Bolshaya Morskaya, to bear the title Supplier to the Imperial Court with the right to bear the State Coat of Arms in his shop's sign.'[8] Fabergé's formal relationship with the tsars had begun.

2. 'As precious as an egg on Christ's own day'

On 17 October 1888 the Tsar, the Empress and their five children were on their way back to St Petersburg from holidaying in the Crimea. The Imperial train that carried them was the last word in contemporary travel – multiple coaches dedicated to providing the royal family with every conceivable luxury. The family was in the dining car, working through a pudding prepared in the onboard kitchen. Suddenly, and to the accompaniment of a deafening crash, the train was lifted from the rails and plunged down the embankment, turning over as it did so.

With debris and devastation all around, it seemed clear to all that the terrorists had, once again, succeeded in striking at the heart of Russia's government. Even the realization that no member of the Imperial family had been hurt was scant consolation. Several attendants had been killed. Above all, it is the cry of the six-year-old Olga that still resonates, more than a century later: 'Papa, now they'll come and kill us all.'[1]

In fact, the train had probably just been travelling too fast on poorly maintained track, but it is understandable that Olga was nervous as the family waited for rescue on a remote stretch of Ukrainian railway. Eighteen months before, on the anniversary of the murder of Alexander II, another assassination attempt had been discovered only just in time, when the books of three university students on the route of the commemorative procession were found to be crammed with explosives.[*] Despite all the precautions, it seemed inevitable that one day the terrorists would be successful.

There was, however, one time of year when cares could be set aside: Easter. Many years later Olga would remember each year's festival as 'a busy, happy day. And how it reflected the truth of an ancient saying of ours, "As precious as an egg on Christ's own day." '[2]

That 'ancient saying' long predated Fabergé, of course, but there is no doubt that in the course of Alexander's reign an Easter egg from the jeweller became an integral part of his family's Easter celebrations. That first egg in 1885 had been good enough for the Emperor to commission a successor the following year. Questions went back and forth between the jeweller and the minister to the Court about design and materials, even deadlines – 'It is preferable to have it finished by Easter but not if this is detrimental to the quality.'[3] The archives describe the result as a golden hen, set with rose-cut diamonds, holding a sapphire egg in its beak, above a gold and diamond basket. It cost just under 3,000 roubles (£300, £22,000). There is no direct evidence that the gift was appreciated except that in 1887 the Tsar requested a third egg. At some point the reordering must have become automatic. A tradition had begun.

Apart from the 1885 *Hen Egg*, only one other Fabergé egg has survived from the 1880s: the 1887 *Blue Serpent Clock Egg*. It is a beautifully enamelled table ornament on which the tongue of the eponymous serpent points to the time on a band of roman numerals as they gradually rotate around the circumference of the egg. By comparison with its predecessor from two years before, it is remarkably elaborate, but there is little about it that makes it personal to Marie Fedorovna. Nor do the archival

---

[*] One of the conspirators, later executed, was Alexander Ulyanov, Lenin's older brother.

descriptions of the missing eggs make them sound particularly exciting. It is hard to escape the feeling that Fabergé's creativity was cramped by protocol, by having to communicate with his client through ministers and a committee.

With each year, however, the jeweller was given greater freedom in how he addressed his annual commission. The Tsar might have been an autocrat but he knew when to delegate. Only three rules were established: that each annual Easter gift should be egg-shaped; that designs should be not be repeated; and that each egg should contain a surprise for the Empress. Beyond that, not even the Tsar himself was allowed to know more. Fabergé would respond to enquiries with a smooth 'Your Majesty will be pleased.' Marginally less exalted interrogators would be met more sharply. An inquisitive grand duchess famously received the acerbic response: 'This year the egg will be square.'

The increase in Fabergé's autonomy may have been a gradual process, but by 1890 it was largely complete. That year's egg is so elaborate that it must have taken at least twelve months to make, evidence that by 1889 the following year's commission had become pretty much automatic. It is a glorious and flamboyant piece. About four inches high, the egg is made of coloured alloy gold covered with perfectly smooth enamel, whose milky-pink translucence sets off the rose-cut diamonds and emeralds that form a grid around the egg. At each end there is a medallion of gold leaves, of which one surrounds more diamonds and an unfaceted, or cabochon, sapphire.

It is the surprise, however, that shows how Fabergé was starting to understand his real client, Marie Fedorovna. The egg opens to reveal a gold screen with ten mother-of-pearl panels. Each carries an exquisite watercolour painted by the Court miniaturist Konstantin Krijitski. Five show Danish royal residences: Bernsdorff Castle, which became the young Princess Dagmar's home after her father was named King Frederick's successor; the Amalienborg Palace, to which she moved after her father's accession to the throne in 1863; Fredensborg Castle, where the extended family would gather each summer; and the villa on the same estate that Alexander bought for himself as a very necessary retreat from his in-laws. Only the fifth – Kronborg Castle at Elsinore – seems rather out of place. Although officially a royal residence and famous as the setting for much of Shakespeare's *Hamlet*, it had been an army barracks since the eighteenth century. Two further central panels depict views of the Cottage Palace at Peterhof, the summer residence given to Marie as a wedding present by her father-in-law, Alexander II. And one panel shows the Gatchina Palace itself, where Marie received the egg and where it would be displayed. Finally, the succession of views is bookended by pictures of the two imperial yachts – *Polar Star* and *Tsarevna* – on which the Imperial family would take Baltic cruises every summer.

Nowadays, the whole creation is known as the *Danish Palaces Egg*. Like the *Hen Egg* five years before, it referred back to Marie's childhood, but this time Fabergé had explicitly personalized the Tsar's Easter gift, making it a unique portrayal of its recipient – both of her origins in Denmark, and of the luxury she now enjoyed in Russia. Almost all its successors contain similar insights. Taken as a whole, they provide a magnificent perspective on the lives and preoccupations of Russia's last tsars.

IN THE SAME YEAR that Alexander gave Marie the *Danish Palaces Egg*, Fabergé was appointed Appraiser of the Imperial Cabinet. The position gave him a status at court above that of mere supplier; it was a formal recognition of an established fact: Carl Fabergé was now the royal family's favourite jeweller. The appointment underlined the honour he had received the previous year, the Order of St Stanislas, 3rd class. Overuse meant that this was the least prestigious of the various chivalric orders within the Tsar's gift, and the classification shows that Fabergé still had some way to go, but the award was a measure of the distance he had already travelled.* He must have worn its Maltese cross – red-enamelled, gold-bordered and pearl-tipped – with pride.

The recognition added lustre to what was already a flourishing business. The firm of Gustav Fabergé, still named after Carl's father, provided an ever increasing selection of objects – silverware, jewellery, trinkets, carved animals and decorative pieces – to customers that ranged from Russia's emerging middle classes to the highest strata of society. In 1887 the firm had opened a branch in Moscow. To manage it, Carl recruited a partner, Allan Bowe, an Englishman born in South Africa who had impressed the jeweller with his knowledge of the business. The Moscow branch would furnish the former capital's rapidly growing merchant class with objects that were more identifiably Russian than the westernized products sold in St Petersburg. Across the empire, families came to talk not of 'laying the table', but of 'setting the Fabergé'.

By now, the firm's output was far more than Carl Fabergé could oversee directly, even with the assistance of his younger brother Agathon, who had joined him as chief designer in 1882. Carl had established a system, however, that maintained quality even without his personal involvement. It was based around a system of semi-independent workshops, each headed by a highly experienced workmaster, often from Finland. The workmasters hired and oversaw the craftsmen and took personal responsibility for the most important objects. The *Danish Palaces Egg* carries the initials of Mikhail Perkhin, the work-

---

* Sir Frederick Ponsonby (*Recollections of Three Reigns*, p. 299) tells the following anecdote: 'A story went round Berlin about a General whose house was burgled. Everything of value was abstracted by the thief, and even all the General's decorations, with the exception of one, the Stanislas. This the burglar left behind, and when the detectives tried to unravel the mystery why the burglar had left this particular decoration behind they came to the conclusion that he already had it.'

master who would eventually produce more than half of the Imperial Easter eggs. Fabergé provided the designs, sourced the materials and marketed the finished product. It was a business structure that would prove remarkably flexible as the firm continued to grow.

The increase in Fabergé's sales allowed for almost complete specialization, as the firm took the artistry in its jewellery to a level that had never been seen before. The coloured gold in that 1890 egg, for example, was produced using a technique familiar to jewellers around the world, who rarely use pure twenty-four-carat gold in decorative pieces; it is simply too soft. Fourteen-carat gold (fourteen parts gold to ten parts base metal) is much harder and facilitates further creativity: the colour of the gold is governed by the base metal used in the alloy. So the *Danish Palaces Egg* contains red and green gold, made by using copper and silver in the respective alloys. Fabergé's French predecessors could produce four such colours – not just red and green, but white (using nickel or palladium) and yellow (copper and silver). They called the result *quatre-couleur* gold. As Fabergé's goldsmiths developed their techniques, they eventually doubled the range – adding blue (using arsenic as the alloy metal), lilac (zinc), purple (aluminium) and grey (iron) to the palette.

It was in their enamelwork, however, that the workshops extended the possibilities of jewellery-making most conspicuously. Enamel is applied by fusing a thin layer of powdered glass to a metal surface. It has to be heated to at least 600° Celsius to become soft enough to work; there is little margin for error, and the dangerously hot materials require absolute concentration. When the metal surface is curved – as with an egg – the complications are multiplied; simply achieving a smooth finish requires phenomenal skill. Yet the *Danish Palaces Egg* has five or six separately applied layers, giving depth to both its colour and its texture – the velvety feel that is one of the most remarkable characteristics of Fabergé's work.

While rivals were content to limit themselves to safe enamel colours – white, blue and pink – Fabergé eventually offered over a hundred, ranging from mauve to lime green. The choice of colour, however, was only the beginning. Frequently, a pattern would be engraved on the surface of the metal before enamelling began. The result was guilloche enamel. Again, this was known to earlier jewellers, but by using machine tools Fabergé was able to take it to new levels of precision and beauty. In another variation, a shape cut from gold leaf would be placed between applications of the glass, adding one more facet to the depth of decoration. Similarly, varying the colours of different layers meant that the appearance of a piece changed as it was turned in the light. Or, as with the *Danish Palaces Egg*, a single application of opaque enamel between other transparent layers would give an object the translucence of an opal or a pearl.

This all emphasizes that Fabergé's real genius lay in his ability to harness the creativity and talents of others. He set his craftsmen and designers challenges that spurred them to greater achievement, while his skills as a businessman ensured that they had enough financial headroom in which to flourish. Most impressively perhaps, he got the boring things right. The written systems that recorded the time each worker spent on an object, for example, may not gladden the hearts of many art historians, yet they anticipate by several decades the computerized costing operations of modern companies. The results fed directly into Fabergé's prices. He would be careful to make a profit, naturally, but would also ensure that it was not excessive. In fact it is possible that Fabergé's popularity with his Imperial paymasters began because he was able to undercut his rivals.

Most of all, however, there could never be any doubt as to the quality of every item sold. Despite all the specialization, each piece remained the overall responsibility of a single craftsman. At ten every morning Carl Fabergé would start his tour of the workshops. Occasionally he would examine an object that was nearly finished, put it on an anvil and smash it with a hammer with a rebuke that was all the more telling for the mild manner in which it was delivered: 'You can do better. Start again and do it right.'[4]

In October 1890 Alexander's heir, the Tsarevitch Nicholas, boarded a Russian naval vessel, the *Memory of Azov*,[*] for a nine-month tour around southern Asia. His parents had many reasons to send him on the trip. Nicholas was now twenty-two; it was time he broadened his outlook with an understanding of the peoples and countries to the empire's south. The voyage might also give him space to forget his incipient infatuation with Mathilde Kschessinska, a seventeen-year-old dancer with the Imperial Ballet. Nicholas's younger brother the Grand Duke George Alexandrovitch would accompany him on the cruise. George had developed a rather alarming cough, and his parents hoped that the sea air and warmer weather might do him some good. Lastly, there was a diplomatic aspect to the journey. Nicholas would be representing Russia, meeting foreign dignitaries at every stop. It was a chance for him to shine, to build new relationships and cement old alliances.

This last purpose for the voyage brought immediate profit to Fabergé. One of the corollaries of Carl's position as Cabinet Appraiser was that the Imperial household gave him priority when it needed to commission jewellery and other objects for state purposes. His firm was therefore asked to provide a selection of suitable gifts for distribution by the heir – snuffboxes, photograph frames, clocks and the like. Halfway through the voyage, stocks had to be replenished. In all, Fabergé's bill for the Tsarevitch's generosity came to 15,500 roubles (£1,550, £110,000).

To that one might add the 4,500 roubles (£450, £33,000)

---

[*] The original *Azov* was a Russian ship that had played a crucial role in the battle of Navarino in 1827, when Greece secured its independence from Turkey.

charged by Fabergé for the egg that Alexander presented to
Marie for Easter 1891, while their two sons were still away. It
is called the *Memory of Azov Egg* because of its surprise, a gold
and platinum replica of the cruiser in which the two young men
were travelling. Diamonds provided the portholes; the rigging
was exactly copied from the original, and the anchor chain
and guns were all movable. The model rested on a plate made
of aquamarine, representing water. The egg itself provided a
nice contrast to its *Danish Palaces* predecessor and a demonstration of the range of skills that Fabergé's workshops could
command. A little less than four inches high, it was carved
from a single piece of bloodstone, flecked with red and blue,
decorated with golden rococo scrolls. Marie must have liked the
result and the emotions it awoke in her: the following winter, as
she moved from Gatchina to St Petersburg, this jewelled objet
d'art travelled with her.

Whatever aims Their Majesties might have had for their
sons' trip on the *Memory of Azov*, it is doubtful that any of
them were achieved. The voyage had started in the Mediter-
ranean, where the brothers were joined by their cousin Prince
George of Greece. In Egypt the royal party transferred to a
riverboat. Here, belly dancers seemed to occupy rather more
of Nicholas's attention than the monotonous landscape of the
banks of the Nile. In India he complained of being surrounded
by the English. His mother immediately wrote back, warning
him to be civil. The tour went on to Ceylon, Indo-China, Hong
Kong and finally Japan. Here it was brought to an abrupt
halt by a sword-wielding policeman with murderous intent,
who attacked Nicholas on the streets of Otsu. The Tsarevitch
was hit hard enough to bear a scar for the rest of his life, but
the quick reactions of his Greek cousin saved him from worse.
Nicholas would swear that he bore his hosts no ill will for the
incident, but his private diaries from later life tell a different
story: 'I received the Swedish minister and the Japanese monkey,
the chargé d'affaires . . .' So much for his parents' hopes for a

broadening of the mind. When he returned to St Petersburg, Nicholas even resumed his liaison with Kschessinska.

Long before the attempted assassination Nicholas's brother had left the voyage. The intense heat of India seemed only to make his cough worse, and he developed a persistent fever. His parents ordered him to return home. When the *Memory of Azov* left Bombay for Colombo, the Grand Duke George was on a destroyer heading west. He had tuberculosis and would spend the remainder of his short life in the Imperial hunting lodge in the Caucasus, where the climate was thought to be healthier than the malign winters and uncomfortable summers of the Russian heartland.

As a child, George had been the family joker. Long after his death in 1899, aged only twenty-eight, Nicholas, by then Tsar, could be found chuckling as he recollected some particularly successful escapade. George's poignant exile, thousands of miles from his family, is remembered by Fabergé in the *Caucasus Egg*, given to Marie in 1893. Its top carries the Grand Duke's picture, visible through a flat-cut portrait diamond, and around its sides four panels open to reveal miniature views of the lodge where he spent his last years. Each panel is surrounded by half-pearls and together the panels have the year 1893 picked out in diamonds upon them. The egg itself is made of *quatre-couleur* gold, silver and platinum, and is covered in a ruby-red enamel. The contrast between its over-the-top vulgarity and the simplicity of the life portrayed in its pictures is striking. Perhaps it is claiming too much, but the whole concoction evokes the loneliness of its subject far more successfully than any plainer portrait could.

Compare the *Caucasus Egg* with the one Marie had received in 1892, one year before. The *Diamond Trellis Egg* takes its name from the lattice of rose-cut diamonds that surrounds its pale green shell, carved from jade. Its surprise has long since been lost, but recently found Imperial records describe it as a clockwork elephant, carved from ivory, carrying a gold tower and a black mahout. This was another subtle reminder

of Marie's happy childhood: an elephant appears on the coat of
arms of the Danish royal family. The surprise is also, however,
a toy, an object of frivolity, very different from the solemn
memento that Marie would receive in 1893. It was clearly a success. Fabergé would return to the idea of clockwork automata in
many of the Empress's subsequent eggs.

FABERGÉ and his craftsmen continued to use every opportunity
to learn from the designs of previous generations. In the
words of one designer, 'The Hermitage and its jewellery gallery
became the school for the Fabergé jewellers.'[5] Its collections of
items from pre-Revolutionary France provided the greatest
inspiration: the 1893 *Caucasus* and 1891 *Memory of Azov* eggs
imitate the jewellers of Louis XV's court; while the equally
opulent but more classical design of the 1890 *Danish Palaces
Egg* puts it in the style of Louis XVI. The attributions catch
the eye. It is impossible to ignore the parallels between the
eventual fate of the Russian monarchy and that of its French
equivalent, sent to the guillotine a century before. The elaborate forms that Fabergé copied seem to appear only in the last
years of dying regimes. His eggs in particular may be brilliantly
designed pieces in which the lavish materials are carefully bal-
anced with superlative craftsmanship but they are also examples
of meretricious vulgarity. They could only have been commissioned for a court that was disconnected from the country it was
meant to govern.

For the vast majority of Russians, even in the last decade
of the nineteenth century, life remained a grim struggle for
existence. Peasants might no longer be serfs, but their lives
were as circumscribed as they had ever been. Families lived in
one-room huts, in winter sealed tight against the cold, the air
inside rendered fetid by kerosene fumes, home-cured tobacco
and the warm, moist smell of the animals that shared their
owners' sleeping platforms. The brief summer months were a
race to plough, sow and reap, using technology unchanged since

the Middle Ages, before winter set in again. Poor yields and a system of communal field reallocation that rendered land improvement pointless combined to ensure that no farmer could raise himself above the subsistence level of his predecessors. Life expectancy was thirty-five years.

In the summer of 1891 famine struck Russia's Volga region; by the autumn it had spread across an area from the Urals to the Black Sea. Thirty-six million people faced the prospect of starvation. Refugees crammed the roads. Cholera and typhus followed. To many historians, these events mark the beginning of the process which made the Russian Revolution inevitable. The complacency with which the tsarist authorities regarded the onset of the crisis, and the incompetence with which they eventually tackled it, showed clearly the fallibility of the autocratic system. Even the regime's natural allies among the nobility started to question its legitimacy. Fabergé's eggs, of course, do not hint at the catastrophe among the Tsar's peasant subjects. Nevertheless, it seems grimly appropriate that as the workshops in St Petersburg were maturing – beginning to produce eggs that might reasonably be called masterpieces – events were occurring which foreshadowed the eventual destruction of the family for which they were made.

3. 'A continuation of the long funeral ceremonies'

IN 1894 THE IMPERIAL FAMILY's Easter celebrations took on an entirely different hue: just over a week before the festival, Princess Alix of Hesse, a tiny German principality, had finally agreed to marry the Tsarevitch Nicholas. It was entirely a love match; Nicholas had already spent ten years confiding in his diary first that 'we love each other' (this when Alix was twelve and he was sixteen) and then that his dream was 'one day to marry Alix H'.[1] All the evidence is that Alix returned Nicholas's feelings. Moreover, she had the royal blood that was a prerequisite for any future tsarina. Her older sister Ella had already married the Tsar's younger brother Serge. Nevertheless, right up until the engagement, Nicholas's pursuit of his future bride had seemed an entirely forlorn proceeding.

The initial obstacle to the match had been Alexander and Marie's disapproval. In previous generations there had been almost a tradition of marriage between the Romanovs and German royal families – enough for the *Almanac de Gotha* (the arbiter of status to nobility across Europe) to argue that the correct name of Russia's ruling house was Holstein-Gottorp Romanov. Twenty years later the French ambassador to Russia, Maurice Paléologue, would calculate that Nicholas himself was only 1/128th Russian. Marie's Danish ancestry, however, made her a committed Germanophobe. She had never forgiven Prussia for its forcible annexation of Schleswig-Holstein from Denmark soon after her father's accession to the Danish throne.

Of course Hesse was not Prussia, and its ruling family might declare, with some justification, that they had suffered from that state's aggression almost as much as Denmark. But that only highlighted another of Alexander and Marie's concerns: Hesse was insignificant. Surely the heir to an empire covering a sixth of the world could do better than that? And Nicholas's parents had one final cause for anxiety. They knew Alix, and what they saw was a shy and awkward young woman who spoke poor French and no Russian. Alix was undoubtedly beautiful – tall and delicately shaped, with a clear complexion and large grey eyes perfectly set off by golden hair so long that she could sit upon it – but, while she conformed to the popular image of a fairy princess, that alone would not make her a success as Empress.

At the beginning of 1894, however, Nicholas had finally received his parents' consent to ask for Alix's hand. He split with his ballet dancer mistress and began to press his suit, only for another impediment to emerge. Alix would not give up her deeply held Protestant beliefs for the Orthodox Christianity that the Tsarevitch's bride would have to espouse. This was no mere whim; Alix expressed her determination in sad but forthright letters to both Nicholas and his sister Xenia. Her refusal left no apparent room for argument.

Only the forthcoming marriage of Alix's brother Ernst to 'Ducky', a cousin of Nicholas, gave any cause for hope. The wedding was to take place in Coburg, one of the capitals of the Duchy of Saxe-Coburg and a traditional gathering place for Europe's royalty. Nicholas's presence on the guest list gave him one last chance to press his case. He arrived in Germany three days before the wedding, at the beginning of April. The next morning he went directly to Alix and formally proposed, to be met with continuing intransigence. Two hours of conversation proved fruitless. All Alix could reply to Nicholas's entreaties, as the tears rolled down her cheeks, was a quiet but emphatic, 'No, I cannot.'[2]

Nicholas, however, was determined, and he had unlikely allies among the other royal visitors. Over the course of the week almost all of them would add their persuasive powers to his. An aunt explained to the young princess how easy she had found her own conversion after marrying a Russian grand duke; so did Alix's sister Ella. Her cousin Kaiser Wilhelm II of Prussia saw political advantage in the renewal of Russo-German ties and did all he could to encourage the match. Only Alix's grandmother Queen Victoria disapproved. She liked Nicholas but could not bear the idea of losing her favourite granddaughter to Russian society and 'its total want of principle from the Grand Dukes downwards'.[3] Victoria too was in Coburg for the wedding but, perhaps crucially, she remained silent.

Alix finally capitulated on 8 April 1894, one day after her brother's wedding. There were to be no more doubts. Nicholas's joy was unconfined. He told his mother, 'the whole world is changed for me: nature, mankind, everything; and all seem to be good and lovable and happy'.[4] Only Nicholas's duties as a good Orthodox Christian dampened his celebratory mood. Although his Western relations had already celebrated Easter, for him it had yet to arrive. As he wrote in his diary a few days later, 'It is not very convenient to keep Lent abroad, and I had to refuse many things.'[5]

Orthodox Easter arrived soon enough.* At Gatchina Marie Fedorovna received her tenth annual creation from Fabergé. The 1894 *Renaissance Egg* is carved of translucently thin agate, a type of quartz. Apparently as fragile as a real egg, it is decorated almost like a cake, with diamonds, rubies and coloured enamels. One of the few Fabergé eggs designed to lie on its side,

---

* The Orthodox and Western Christian traditions calculate Easter day in different ways. In 1894 the difference in date was more than a month. So while Alix and her relations celebrated Easter on 25 March, the equivalent of 13 March in the Julian calendar, for Orthodox Christians the equivalent dates were 29 April and 17 April.

and oddly bulbous, it has the appearance of a jewelled box; it is clearly modelled on an eighteenth-century casket that Fabergé would have seen as a schoolboy in Dresden. The egg's contents, however, have long since disappeared; and in the absence of its surprise, the piece is relatively unexciting. No matter; Marie's thoughts would surely have been in Germany, where her own Easter presents to the happy couple had arrived. There were the ubiquitous eggs, of course, although no masterpieces from Fabergé, and there was Marie's own more personal present for Alix – a stunning emerald bracelet, whose recipient protested modestly, 'It is much too beautiful for me.' At the same time, and for future reference, Marie asked Nicholas which stones his fiancée liked best: sapphires or emeralds? The original of her letter preserves some of Nicholas's response – 'has none', written against 'sapphires'.[6]

Alix was not to be so deprived for long. As the younger daughter of a minor German princeling she had been far from rich, and the thrift she had practised as an unmarried princess would continue to affect her behaviour as Tsarina years later. Now, however, she was marrying into extraordinary wealth. Her formal engagement present from Nicholas was a pearl and diamond necklace, bought from Fabergé for 165,500 roubles (£16,550, £1.2 million). His parents went even further for the future daughter-in-law they now welcomed with every outward enthusiasm. They gave her a *sautoir*[*] of pearls, each carefully selected by Fabergé himself. Valued at 250,000 roubles (£25,000, £1.9 million), it was the most expensive item ever to emerge from his workshops.

THERE WAS a reason for Alexander and Marie Fedorovna's sudden acceptance of Alix as a potential wife for their son. During the previous winter the Tsar, always so strong, had found

---

[*]   A long, rope-like necklace, often with tassels.

himself prey to exhaustion. For the first time he became aware
of his own mortality. All too soon, Nicholas might be Tsar. It was
unthinkable that he should ascend the throne unmarried. If
Princess Alix was the only candidate that Nicholas would coun-
tenance, then, for all her imperfections, she would have to do.

Over the summer following Nicholas and Alix's engagement,
the truth behind Alexander's condition emerged. He had incur-
able kidney disease, and its diagnosis coincided with the
Emperor's rapid deterioration. In a vain attempt to recover,
he moved to Livadia, a favourite palace on the Black Sea coast.
As it became clear that he was dying, family members hurried
to his side, and Nicholas was given permission to send for his
fiancée. Alix arrived declaring her willingness to convert to
orthodoxy as soon as possible and in time to receive her future
father-in-law's blessing. Ten days later, on 20 October 1894,
Alexander died; he was only forty-nine. Whatever posterity
might say about his autocratic tendencies, he had achieved at
least two things which no previous tsar could claim: he had not
embroiled his country in any foreign wars, and he had remained
faithful to his wife. Alexander himself summed up his marriage,
as he lay dying: 'I have even before my death got to know an
angel.'[7]

The next morning saw a short service of consecration
witnessed only by members of the Imperial family. The new
Tsar, Nicholas II, then issued his first decree. It proclaimed
the new faith and title of the woman who would become his
wife. Princess Alix of Hesse, former Lutheran, was now the
'truly believing Grand Duchess Alexandra Fedorovna'. The
path towards marriage was clear. Nicholas favoured an immediate ceremony in Livadia. His uncles, however, persuaded
him that such an important event had to take place publicly,
in St Petersburg.

So, one week after the funeral of a father-in-law she had
hardly known, Alexandra Fedorovna put on the dress worn by
generations of Russian grand duchesses on their wedding day.

Made of silver tissue, its eight-foot train was trimmed with ermine. 'Yes, I know how heavy it is,' Marie Fedorovna is said to have commented, 'but I'm afraid that it's only one of the lesser weights which must be borne by a Russian empress.'[8]

Before the ceremony itself came the procession through the Winter Palace. Ten thousand guests filled its massive state-rooms, craning for a glimpse of the young couple. Afterwards, thousands more filled the Nevsky Prospekt, St Petersburg's main street, cheering their new Tsar and alarming his bride with the intensity of their devotion. When it was finally all over, the newly-marrieds took an early dinner and, in the words of Nicholas's diary, 'went to bed early as she had a bad headache!'.[9] The next day the Court was back in mourning, and Nicholas, struggling to come to terms with his new responsibilities, was at work. Alexandra's verdict on the whole day is perhaps only to be expected: 'The wedding seemed only a continuation of the long funeral ceremonies she had so lately attended.'[10]

CARL FABERGÉ too was feeling the effects of death in the family. In 1893 his father had died, aged seventy-nine. Gustav had of course long since retired; while the name of the company he had founded had been changed – to C. Fabergé – some time before his death. The death from lung disease of Carl's younger brother Agathon in 1895 would be far more untimely. He was only thirty-three. Born after the family's move to Dresden, Agathon had an even more European outlook than his brother; as chief designer he had played a crucial role in the growth of the business. It may just be coincidence that the firm first came to the attention of the Imperial family in 1882, the year Agathon came on board, but it is unquestionable that his designs had played a large part in its subsequent success. François Birbaum, who took over Agathon's position, later recalled how his predecessor's drawings showed him to be just as sensitive, 'if not more so' than his brother Carl; he 'sought inspiration everywhere'.[11]

Agathon Fabergé may already have been ill by the end of 1894, but even if he was still apparently healthy, his brother would have had a lot to think about. Court suppliers are always vulnerable to a change of regime. What if the new Tsar's taste differed from his father's? Four months before Nicholas's untimely accession, his sister the Grand Duchess Xenia had married their cousin the Grand Duke Alexander Mikhailovitch. Her trousseau had been meticulously prepared in a way that was impossible for that of Alexandra, married at a few weeks' notice. All the jewellery in it was made by Fabergé's great rival Bolin. He was, according to Xenia's husband, 'the best craftsman of St Petersburg'.*[12] Meanwhile, the candified and derivative 1894 *Renaissance Egg* – the last that Marie received from her husband – seemed to show Fabergé struggling for inspiration. The new Tsar might well have decided that it was time for a change.

Nicholas, however, was only twenty-six; weak-willed and anxious to please, he was woefully unprepared for his new responsibilities. Liberals dared to hope that this might mean that he would be willing to accept advice, perhaps even the counsel of a democratic body, and that the long-stalled process of reform would at last gather pace. They were to be disappointed. Nicholas knew no better than to vow that he would imitate his father in all things. On 17 January 1895 Nicholas made his now notorious address to Russia's regional assemblies, the Zemstvos. Characterizing their wish to take part in the business of government as 'senseless dreams', he went on to make his

---

* The list of the trousseau's contents is undeniably impressive. It included furs, dresses and coats for four seasons, linen, silver plate and glasses for ninety-six, and a gold toilette set of 144 articles, as well as Bolin's jewellery, comprising 'a pearl necklace consisting of five rows of pearls, a diamond necklace, a ruby necklace, an emerald necklace, and a sapphire necklace; emerald-and-ruby diadems, diamond-and-emerald bracelets and diamond breast ornaments'.

position absolutely clear: 'Let everyone know that I will retain the principles of autocracy as firmly and unbendingly as my unforgettable late father.'[13] The reformers would have to wait.

At a more private level, the Tsar's attitude gave Fabergé the luck he needed. Nicholas was in no mood to change a well-established Easter tradition. The inertia of Court protocol was on Fabergé's side too. Nicholas once complained that even to change the colour of one pair of his tennis socks required the involvement of ten different officials. In any case, his unwillingness to disturb the status quo was reinforced by his affection for his widowed mother. For the first few months of their married life the Imperial couple kept Marie company, living in Nicholas's old bachelor apartments in the Anitchkov Palace. This was partly because there were no married quarters fit for a tsar elsewhere, but it was also a sign of the bond between mother and son. 'How he looks after her, so quietly and tenderly,'[14] Alexandra wrote admiringly to her sister. Jewels were important to Marie. The new Tsar would not dream of adding to his mother's grief by cancelling a gift which had given her such pleasure.

Moreover, Nicholas was equally devoted to his wife. He closed his diary for 1894 with a reflection on the events of the year: his father's death, his subsequent accession to the throne and, most of all, his marriage to Alexandra – 'Together with this irrevocable grief the Lord has rewarded me also with a happiness which I could never have imagined. He has given me Alix.'[15] For his mother's sake, Nicholas would continue the tradition of giving a Fabergé egg each Easter. For his wife's, he would double it.

In 1895, therefore, Marie Fedorovna received her eleventh Fabergé egg, and Alexandra her first. Neither was particularly elaborate. After all, Fabergé only had a few months to plan them after Alexander's death. Marie's was the *Twelve Monogram Egg*. Made of blue enamel, it carries six sets of the initials AIII and MF, picked out in diamonds. Inside, only a velvet lining remains;

the surprise it once protected is now missing. Presumably,
like the egg itself, it was a memento of Marie's long and happy
marriage to Alexander III.

Alexandra's *Rosebud Egg* was relatively small. Its red enamel
could be said by the unkind to recall rather too vividly the
blotches of embarrassment that covered the Tsarina's face in
social situations, and the choice of yellow for the colour of the
enamelled rosebud inside the egg seems similarly ill-chosen.
Although in Germany this was regarded as the noblest colour
for a rose, Alexandra may also have been aware of the traditional use of yellow roses as a gift to mark the end of a
relationship. If so, she would hardly have worried. She was
pregnant and rejoicing in married life. In any case, she must
have been charmed by the egg's final two surprises, revealed
when the rosebud's petals were unfurled: an imperial crown and
a ruby pendant similar to those within the hen in Marie's first
egg. The parallel was surely intentional: Fabergé was looking
forward to a relationship with the new Tsarina that would be
as happy and as lucrative as it had been with her predecessor.

Meanwhile, Nicholas and Alexandra had been preparing
their own home, or rather homes. In St Petersburg they had
refurbished a suite of rooms in the Winter Palace, and it was to
her study here that Alexandra consigned that first egg. In fact,
she and Nicholas would live in this cavernous building as little
as possible – only during the 'season' between New Year and
the beginning of Lent. Tsarskoe Selo – the 'Tsar's Village'* – was
far more important to them. This was a relatively substantial
town, fifteen miles south of St Petersburg, centred on a number
of imperial residences and entertainment pavilions. The largest
and grandest building was the eighteenth-century Catherine
Palace, famous for a host of architectural extravagances includ-

---

* The name may in fact be derived from the Finnish for high point, but
'Tsar's Village' is undoubtedly how it was understood by the average
Russian.

ing the legendary Amber Room. Nicholas and Alexandra, however, chose to live in the much more modest Alexander Palace, built by Catherine the Great for her favourite grandson, the future Alexander I.

Surrounded by a park full of trees and studded with ponds, the Alexander Palace was manageable, even cosy, in a way that was impossible for more imposing buildings. It was Nicholas's birthplace; his parents had used the building as a summer palace. In his teens he and Alix had, in presumably unconscious imitation of his mother and long-dead uncle, scratched their names together on a pane of glass there. The week they spent in the Palace soon after their wedding was the closest Nicholas and Alexandra came to any sort of honeymoon.

Decorating the Alexander Palace gave Alexandra her first opportunity, at twenty-two, to indulge and develop her own taste. Her efforts met with little approval from those attending her. Much of what she chose harked back to her childhood, particularly the homes of her grandmother Queen Victoria at Osborne, Windsor and Balmoral. Furniture from Alexandra's preferred English supplier, Maple's, lent many of the rooms a homely touch. The Pallisander sitting room, named for the Brazilian rosewood used in the construction of its furniture, was a favourite retreat for Nicholas and Alexandra in their early years. Its walls were hung with pale straw-green silk, and its floor covered with a diamond-patterned carpet again imported from Britain. It was in the connecting boudoir, however, that Alexandra really gave free rein to her creativity. The room's colour was inspired by a sprig of lilac given to her by Nicholas: mauve, the ultimately fashionable hue of the Victorian era. The silk that lined the walls came from Paris and cost more than any egg from Fabergé – an extravagance that the parsimonious Alexandra would probably have abhorred if she had ever been told how much she was spending. Eventually every available surface would be covered with knick-knacks: crystal and porcelain, curious objects in enamel and nephrite, and above all photographs. The mauve boudoir would remain Alexandra's favourite room for the next twenty years, long after its Victorian style had been overtaken by twentieth-century fashions.

Nicholas and Alexandra moved into the Alexander Palace soon after their first Easter as a married couple. From that point of view, the 1895 *Twelve Monogram Egg* can be seen as their parting gift to the Dowager Empress, as they stopped sharing her roof. Perhaps that is why the 4,500-rouble bill (£450, £35,000) for the egg carries an annotation in Nicholas's hand specifying that the cost be split between his and his wife's private purses. Alexandra would surely have appreciated the opportunity to make such a gesture. When she was only six, she had lost her own mother (Queen Victoria's daughter Alice) to diphtheria. Marie's letter to Nicholas immediately after their engagement hoped that 'dearest Alix will look upon me as a loving mother who will receive her with open arms, like her own dear child'.[16] In return, Alix addressed her as 'Darling Motherdear'. Newly arrived in an alien world, fortified only by her love for Nicholas, she sought solace in the idea that she could be a daughter to the widowed Marie.

4. 'Utterly different in character, habits and outlook'

ANY HOPES ALEXANDRA had for her future relationship with her mother-in-law were to remain unfulfilled. There had been friction even while Nicholas and Alexandra spent the first few months of their married life in the Anitchkov Palace. That was perhaps understandable. The six rooms they occupied might have been ample for a bachelor prince, but for an emperor and his wife they were barely adequate. Alix had to borrow her mother-in-law's sitting room to receive guests. Meals were taken en famille, with Marie very much in charge. Even her servants and ladies-in-waiting, Alexandra found, had been chosen for her by her mother-in-law. Nor did Alexandra find it easy to forget that, for all her welcoming words after the engagement, Marie had spent years trying to persuade her son of Alexandra's unsuitability as a wife. Most crucially perhaps, neither woman liked the idea of the Emperor sharing his love for her with another.

The minor annoyances, at least, should have evaporated once the imperial couple moved to Tsarskoe Selo. The separation, however, only served to emphasize the differences between the two women. They were, according to Nicholas's younger sister Olga, 'utterly different in character, habits and outlook'.[1] While Alexandra withdrew to the country, Marie delighted in metropolitan St Petersburg; where Alexandra wanted nothing more than domesticity and the company of her beloved 'Nicky', Marie continued to be the queen of society; above all, where

Alexandra was awkward and unapproachable, her mother-in-law was confident and friendly.

None of this should be surprising. Having lost her mother at an early age, Alexandra had only a distant relationship with her father. Instead, Queen Victoria had overseen her upbringing. A duo of Englishwomen – 'Orchie', her nurse, and 'Madgie', her governess – gave the young Alix their own brand of love, based on cleanliness and order in the first case, and a progressive education in the second. Later, an elderly lady-in-waiting had stressed the importance of self-reliance and instilled a strong sense of duty in the young princess. Alexandra had naturally grown up reserved, with a moral compass that can only be described as Victorian, and shy in a way that conveyed inapproachability, so that even her aunt the Empress of Germany saw her as 'far too much convinced of her own perfection'.[2]

Then, aged twenty-two, Alexandra had followed the love of her life to St Petersburg, arriving there as the Emperor's betrothed. There had been no time to practise the Russian she had started to learn on her engagement, and her French came with a strong German accent. She was an outsider, and as she grew to understand what was going on around her, she could hardly fail to be shocked by the stories of mistresses and adultery that seemed almost commonplace in the relaxed moral atmosphere of St Petersburg. Even at the ballet she could only be reminded of her husband's previous relationship with its prima ballerina. It is no wonder that she retreated from society.

Faced with what seemed like hauteur, Alexandra's subjects responded with active antipathy. Few of the many memoirs have a kind word for her. Constantine Petrovitch Pobedonostsev had been Nicholas's tutor; as Procurator of the Holy Synod, he was an infamous supporter of the autocratic ideal and guardian of the purity of Russian orthodoxy. He should have been a friend to the Empress, who approached her new religion with the zeal of the true convert. Yet he was recorded by one socialite describing Alexandra as 'more autocratic than Peter the Great and perhaps as cruel as Ivan the Terrible. Hers is the small mind that believes it harbours a great intelligence.'[3]

The saddest aspect of this is that with people she trusted Alexandra could be fun-loving and enjoyably indiscreet. Her childhood nickname, which her husband continued using into middle age, was 'Sunny'. Her talent for caricatures – of her husband, courtiers and ministers – frequently got her into trouble. She once admitted to her maid Marfa Mouchanow that one of the real benefits of being Empress was that it enabled her to indulge her taste for expensive lingerie. Only a few friends, however, were allowed this close. As Mouchanow herself put it, with the public as a whole Alexandra firmly believed that 'it was part of her duties to keep people at a distance'.[4]

Marie's upbringing had been so different. Her memories of a happy childhood were characterized by the holidays she continued to share with her mother and father back in Denmark; and her fifteen-year apprenticeship as Tsarevna (wife to the Tsarevitch) before her husband succeeded to the throne had given her time to adapt both to Russia and to the prospect of being its Tsarina. The result was a woman who could be appropriately regal and haughty when it was warranted, but who also believed that, when Empress, her prime duty had been to charm her subjects.

Now, as mother to the Tsar, Marie could console herself with the thought that, although she had never known a Dowager Empress during her time in Russia, she had heard they were 'awful and venerable',[5] more deferred to than anybody else in the land. An ancient law meant that only the Emperor came above her in state precedence, and this son was firmly under his mother's thumb. No one could challenge Marie's right to do as she chose and spend as she wished. She retained her palaces at Gatchina and Anitchkov, the Alexandria Estate at Peterhof, given to her as an engagement present many years before, and even her own yacht – the *Polar Star*.

While Marie undoubtedly remembered and grieved for her husband, hers was not a personality to remain forever repressed. She might no longer dance the mazurka with the eagerness of her youth, but she had become a widow at forty-seven; she could hardly be expected to retire from society. Moreover, Marie's position, despite its grandeur, made her approachable in a way that she never could have been as Tsarina. Her lightness of spirit was there for all to see.

The eggs that Fabergé produced for the Dowager Empress over the next twenty years captured all of this. Many naturally memorialized her life with Alexander; they were serious, even stolid creations – appropriately grave memorials. Others, by contrast, were delightfully whimsical concoctions, often built around family portraits and containing ingenious mechanisms and automata.

The *Pansy Egg*, for example, which Nicholas gave to Marie in 1899, takes its name from the violet enamelled pansies that are its main decoration. It contains a heart-shaped easel concealing eleven painted miniature portraits of members of the Romanov family – Marie's five children, the two spouses of those who had so far married, and her four grandchildren. The egg's real charm, however, lies in the way the surprise lives up to its name: all the easel's eleven miniatures pop out simultaneously when a tiny knob is pressed. Similarly, Marie's *Cuckoo Clock Egg* from the following year is at first sight an elaborate egg-shaped table clock. Its true ingenuity only becomes apparent when a button is pressed: a grill opens on the top of the clock, and a flapping feathered bird rises up to sing a brief song before once again descending.

An earlier creation, 1898's *Pelican Egg*, is in some ways even more ingenious. Covered in engraved gold, the egg itself unfolds into eight sections, each hinged to its neighbours to form a screen of eight oval miniatures. These show another side to the Dowager Empress's character, a reminder that even after the death of her husband she remained an important

public figure. Each miniature portrays an educational institution patronized by Marie. This was only a small sample of
her charitable commitments. According to one biography, she
was patroness to twenty-seven institutes for daughters of the
nobility, seventy-seven girls' schools, one hundred and thirteen
children's homes, twenty-three hospitals and twenty-one homes
for blind children, as well as numerous old people's homes,
orphanages and sanatoria.[6] As her younger daughter Olga put
it, 'She had her finger on every educational pulse in the empire.
She would work her secretaries to shreds, but she did not spare
herself.'[7]

The egg is also a reminder that when it mattered Marie
could be both unbendingly regal and necessarily businesslike –
the forbidding woman who to her younger children was 'always
an Empress even when she entered the nurseries'.[8] Olga once
saw her in action, dismissing the director-general of all the girls'
schools in the empire. He was an incompetent, 'disliked by
everybody', but it is still hard not to feel a little sorry for him:
'She just said in her iciest voice, "Prince, I have decided that
you must go." The man was so taken aback that he stammered,
"But ... but I would never leave Your Majesty." "And I am telling
you that you are," she answered, and swept out of the room.'
Olga followed her: 'I did not dare look at the man.'[9]

These three eggs all have symbolic meanings as well.
According to Victorian tradition, pansies were a sad declaration
of love, a mixture of happiness and heartache. So we can read
the 1899 egg as something more than a celebration of Marie's
family – a memorial too of the marriage from which it had
sprung. In fact it may have reminded Marie of an even earlier
romance. She had pressed a pansy into the end pages of her
diary for 1868, a year when her young marriage to the boorish
Alexander was still not fully secure. For one biographer at least,
this flower shows her memorializing her first, unconsummated
love – Alexander's elder brother Nicholas.

Fabergé could hardly have been expected to know the

particular symbolism of the pansy to Marie, but with the other eggs it is tempting to wonder if on occasion he and the Dowager Empress were sharing their own private joke. He had now, after all, been her favourite jeweller for over fifteen years. Only a year younger than her husband, he was of her generation, with similar cultural references.

The surprise within the *Cuckoo Clock Egg* provides an example. Ornithology was not the strongest suit of those who named it; the bird that emerges from its interior is actually a cockerel; it crows more than sings. At one level, this surprise makes an obvious Easter connection with the crucifixion story, and Jesus's prediction that Peter would 'thrice deny him' before the crowing of the cock. Any nineteenth-century Russian, however, would also have been reminded of Pushkin's fairy tale *The Golden Cockerel*. In it, the ruthless Tsar Dadon, beset by enemies on all sides, is given a golden cockerel by his chief astrologer. Whenever danger nears the bird crows and turns to face its source. The kingdom is saved, and Dadon is able to enjoy a peaceable old age. In the story's denouement, however, Dadon's two sons kill each other in a quarrel over a princess of Shamakhan who 'shimmers with beauty like the dawn'. Despite the cockerel's warning that she is the source of his kingdom's peril, Dadon falls in love with the princess and bears her back to his capital. There he refuses the astrologer's request to give him the princess and kills him, but in his turn Dadon is pecked once on the head by the cockerel, and dies.

Pushkin wrote the story as a commentary on the reactionary reign of the then Tsar, Nicholas I. It is easy to transfer the satirical intent to Nicholas II, great-grandson to his namesake. A few years later Rimsky-Korsakov would do so more explicitly in his last opera, based on the same story. There must have been a hint of that in Fabergé's mind. Marie can scarcely have been expected to approve of anything that mocked the Tsar, but did she share in at least part of the joke? Perhaps she saw a link between her statuesque daughter-in-law and the beautiful but doom-laden princess from Shamakhan, who eventually vanishes as if she had never existed.

The symbolism is even clearer in the *Pelican Egg*. The bird from which it gets its name sits on its top. She is feeding her young in the nest, and the connotations are obvious. For Marie the 'little mother' epithet, used of every Tsarina, carried real weight; the educational institutions that the egg represents are evidence enough of that. There is a reason, however, for Fabergé's choice of a pelican: it has always been a symbol of maternal love. There is a popular (but false) conception that in extremis the mother pelican will feed her offspring with her own blood: maternal love can bring pain as well as pleasure. The egg may well have captured all too well Marie's feelings about the effect on her son of his increasingly odd wife.

THERE IS NO DOUBT that Fabergé was finding the new Empress a difficult client. Kept at a distance like the rest of St Petersburg society, the jeweller never developed the same rapport with the younger woman that he had with her mother-in-law. He even experienced the effect of what Pobedonostsev, Nicholas's old tutor, called Alexandra's 'small mind': the Empress's habit of giving detailed specifications for pieces with budgets that were far too limited for what she required. Fabergé's only solution would be to produce something according to his own designs and pretend he had lost the Empress's drawings.

Whatever Fabergé's personal views about Alexandra, he still had to produce an egg to be given to her each year. Like Marie's, each had to be different from any predecessor, and, like Marie's, each had to contain a surprise that would enchant the Empress. But how could he know what would do that, when Alexandra kept her feelings so carefully hidden? Marie might be charmed by whimsy, but there was no sign that the unbending Alexandra would be similarly entranced. Nor could Fabergé use an egg to highlight the Empress's public achievements, as with Marie's *Pelican Egg*. One of the bones of contention between the two empresses was that Marie had refused to give up any of her public positions to her daughter-in-law. Alexandra's one attempt to start up something on her own – a charitable project that she called Help Through Handwork – failed when the aristocratic women who originally signed up found that membership did not give them special access to her.

Following 1895's *Rosebud Egg*, Fabergé's first solution to the problem of what to make for Alexandra was to reuse an idea already seen in Marie's *Danish Palaces Egg*: images of the palaces that might evoke happy memories in its recipient. The result was the *Revolving Miniatures Egg*. Carved from transparent rock crystal, the egg's surprise inside is immediately visible: a set of six gold panels, each carrying a miniature painting on both sides. The panels are hinged on a central shaft. When an emerald at the top of the egg is pressed, a hook descends to turn a panel like the page of a book, so that as two miniatures close together, two more are revealed.

Each exquisite picture had its own memory for the young Tsarina: the German palaces where she had been brought up and later wooed by her husband, the British residences where she would go for holidays with Queen Victoria and the Russian edifices of her marriage – the Winter Palace, where she and Nicholas had married, the Anitchkov, where they began life together, and the Alexander Palace, to which they had now moved. The whole ensemble is ingenious, charming and, crucially, personal to its recipient – proof that even when lacking any real inspiration, Fabergé could still come up with a design that was bound to please.

In 1898 Alexandra received an even more gratifying Easter gift, the *Lilies of the Valley Egg*. Of all Fabergé's creations, this is one of the most beautiful. Something about it is immediately beguiling. Perhaps it is the way its pink enamel takes on a golden tinge when seen in a certain light. Perhaps it is the delicacy with which the pearls hang on its side, each a stylized lily of the valley. This was one of Alexandra's favourite flowers, and she would have recognized and appreciated too the art nouveau style in which the egg was made, a new departure for a jeweller more used to seeking inspiration from the French eighteenth century. Fabergé would presumably have known that Alexandra's brother Prince Ernie of Hesse had turned his capital at Darmstadt into one of the European centres of this new design philosophy, which sought to replace the rigidities of classicism with curves and natural forms. Alexandra herself would go on to use an art nouveau theme when redecorating in the Alexander Palace.

Most of all, Alexandra would have found the egg's surprise entrancing. When a pearl button at the side of the egg is turned, three miniatures rise and fan out from its top: a central picture of Nicholas in military uniform, with the Grand Duchesses Olga and Tatiana, Alexandra's two oldest children, on either side. These were, without doubt, the three people whom Alexandra loved most in the world. She was born to be a mother and doted on her girls – both still less than three years old – to an extent that incurred the further displeasure of St Petersburg society. Even her famously maternal grandmother Queen Victoria thought she had gone on too long with breastfeeding.

Here, surely, was a subject whose rich vein Fabergé could mine more deeply in future eggs, celebrating the family of this very domestic Empress. To most observers, however, Alexandra's daughters provided little reason for celebration. If she had one duty as Tsarina, it was to bear her husband a son. The successors of Catherine the Great had determined that a woman would never again sit on the throne of Russia; no daughter could be tsar. If one event could have made Alexandra accepted by both her husband's people and his family, it would have been the birth of a tsarevitch. Little wonder that even she, despite her joy in motherhood, had greeted the birth of Tatiana, her second daughter, with prolonged tears of frustration.

In the absence of a son, Fabergé could not continue producing eggs that celebrated dynastically unnecessary daughters, however much their parents loved them. The *Lilies of the Valley Egg* set no trend for future creations. Fabergé had to look elsewhere for inspiration. Over the next few years, therefore, almost every egg that he produced for Alexandra would eschew the personal and either be an elaborate but anonymous ornament, or concentrate on the major events of her husband's reign. There was nowhere else for him to turn.

The egg from 1897 had already established a precedent. In that year Nicholas had given Alexandra what many consider to be the greatest of all Faberge's 'public event' eggs. It commemorated their joint coronation as Emperor and Empress in 1896, and succeeded both as an example of technical brilliance and as a piece of coherent design whose colours, metalwork and surprise all recalled the ceremony.

Made of red gold, the egg is covered in gorgeous opalescent yellow enamel, itself surrounded by a golden lattice studded with black enamelled Romanov eagles.* The colour combination was intended to evoke the golden robe worn by the Tsarina during the ceremony. Inside the egg is an exact replica of Alexandra's coronation coach. This alone took fifteen months to complete and was all the work of one young jeweller, George Stein, whose twenty-three-year-old eyes were able to cope with the golden coach's extraordinary detailing. Fully articulated, decorated with red enamel and diamonds, its windows were made of rock crystal and its tyres of platinum. Even today it retains a sense of remarkable delicacy – the coach's suspension looks springy and responsive in a way that is scarcely possible.

At one level, therefore, the *Coronation Egg* is a clear demonstration of Faberge's genius – proof that the loss of his

----

* The double-headed eagle was a symbol of the Roman and then Byzantine empires. In 1469 Tsar Ivan III had married the niece of the last Byzantine emperor and adopted the symbol for himself and his successors.

brother Agathon as chief designer had been no more than a temporary setback. From the point of view of the egg's recipient, however, it is doubtful whether any design could have been less welcome. It hardly matters that to modern tastes the whole concoction may be too rich, or that the miniature coach itself is a technical achievement rather than a piece of true artistry. What is important is that by Easter 1897 the Imperial couple would surely have preferred to forget an event that should have been one of the high points of Nicholas's reign, but turned out very differently.

Even before the coronation Nicholas was confiding to his mother, 'I believe we should regard all these difficult ceremonies in Moscow as a great ordeal sent by God.'[10] After it his main emotion was simply one of relief that it was all over. As for Alexandra, that replica of her state coach can only have been an unpleasant reminder of her journey into Moscow: the huge cheers received by her mother-in-law, the rather more muted welcome for her husband and the deathly silence that greeted her, the German interloper. She was already marked by the unpopularity that would characterize her reign.

Overshadowing all the pageantry of the coronation, however, was the tragedy that had taken place a few days later on Khodynka Meadow, just outside Moscow. It was the traditional place for Muscovites to acclaim their new Tsar, but the city had expanded hugely in the thirteen years since Alexander III had been crowned. The authorities were totally unprepared for the arrival of perhaps half a million people, all hoping to enjoy free beer and receive a special commemorative cup. When a rumour spread that there were not enough cups to go around, control measures proved inadequate. The number killed in the resulting stampede can only be estimated; Nicholas's officials put it at 500, but the true figure may have been closer to 5,000.

Recriminations were quick to follow. Most blamed the Governor of Moscow, the Grand Duke Serge. He was, however, both Nicholas's uncle and Alexandra's brother-in-law, and was exonerated in the eventual enquiry; for the Tsar's disillusioned subjects this had the air of a whitewash. What many, including members of the Imperial family, found even harder to forgive was Nicholas's more immediate reaction to the tragedy. Guided once again by his domineering uncles, who closed ranks around their beleaguered brother Serge, the Tsar did not ask for the French ambassador's ball that evening to be cancelled. Instead, the court danced while the wounded died. The Emperor's subsequent hospital visits and the donations he made to the family of every victim were entirely overshadowed. The whole affair would remain a cause of resentment for the rest of Nicholas's reign.

There was another implication too: if so many people were prepared to die simply for the sake of a little alcohol and a mass-produced ornament, what did that say about the conditions in which Russia's urban poor were living? The contrast between the pageantry of Nicholas's coronation and the squalid existence endured by most of his subjects had been thrown into sharp relief.

All these considerations seem to have passed over Fabergé's head. He attended the coronation and certainly knew about the tragedy – it became a cause célèbre throughout Europe – but he passed down only one story about his attendance, one that had nothing to do with the public events. His first biographer, Henry Bainbridge, tells how Fabergé attended the ceremonies using a '4-wheeler which turned out to be past its prime. During the course of the journey the bottom fell out, but its occupant continued on foot, still inside the cab.'[11] The image is delightful; but it's clear that the jeweller was thinking about a conveyance very different from Alexandra's carriage.

What Fabergé could not have known was that for Alexandra in particular the coronation held one more unwelcome memory. According to her maid Marfa Mouchanow, the strain of the events surrounding it had caused her to suffer a miscarriage. Under any circumstances that would have been awful enough, but, even worse, Alexandra's doctor was convinced that the unborn child would have been a boy, the Tsarevitch for whom she and Nicholas so desperately yearned. Every sight of her *Coronation Egg* must surely have reminded the Empress of the agony of loss.

5. 'The warm and brilliant shop of Carl Fabergé'

WHATEVER the failings of its ruler and the autocratic system he embodied, Russia was booming. By the end of the nineteenth century it had the fastest-growing economy in Europe. Factories had sprung up around every major city; enterprises were expanding; fortunes were being made. The country's cultural life was vibrant too. In literature Turgenev and Dostoevsky were dead, but Anton Chekhov was at his peak, Maxim Gorky's career was just beginning and even Tolstoy remained active, promulgating moral theories on the renunciation of property that ensured he was persona non grata with the tsarist authorities. Composers like Glazunov, Taneiev and Rachmaninov had taken up the baton laid down by Tchaikovsky. The painter Vasili Kandinsky, the actor-director Konstantin Stanislavsky and the choreographer Sergei Diaghilev were developing the ideas that would lead to revolutions in their art forms. Even in the sciences Russia could claim breakthroughs – like Dmitri Mendeleev's formulation of the periodic table and Ivan Pavlov's discovery of the conditioned reflex.

So 1900 marked an appropriate year for Nicholas to give his wife an Easter present that was both a piece of art and a celebration of Russia's growing industrial power: the *Trans-Siberian Railway Egg*. The greatest engineering project that the country had yet undertaken, financed largely with French loans, the Trans-Siberian Railway both symbolized Russia's economic development and had done much to kick-start it. Nicholas had been involved from its inception. He had laid the foundation stone for the Vladivostok terminus on his way back from that ill-fated trip to Japan, and his appointment as president of the Trans-Siberian Railroad was one of the few official positions his father had allowed him as Tsarevitch.

Nicholas, however, was only a figurehead. The project – even his appointment as its president – had been the brainchild of Sergius Witte, the finance minister Nicholas had inherited from his father. Brilliant but supremely egotistical, Witte had worked his way up to his current position from traffic supervisor on the Southwestern District Railroad. A passionate advocate of rail transport ever since, he had had a vision of a railway that would cross the empire from east to west, one that would enable Russia to dominate not only the affairs of Asia from 'the shores of the Pacific and the heights of the Himalayas',[1] but also those of Europe.

The egg captures much of Witte's triumph. On a broad silver band around its middle is an engraved map showing the 4,000-mile route of the railway, from St Petersburg to Vladivostok, with each station between these termini marked by a precious stone. The base of the egg rests on three griffins, and it is topped by a Romanov eagle, symbolizing the Tsar's own oversight of the project. Its green enamel lid opens to reveal one of Fabergé's most elaborate surprises: a miniature clockwork model of the Trans-Siberian Express, wound with a golden key. Three sections come together to make an entire train one foot long. The platinum locomotive has diamond headlights and a ruby lantern on its tender. It pulls five gold coaches – 'mail', 'for ladies only', 'smoking', 'non-smoking' and finally a chapel, complete with miniature bells. The egg is both a delightful ensemble and a potent symbol of growing industrial power.

Jewellery-making may not have been quite the sort of industry that Witte had in mind as being stimulated by railway investment, but it provides as good an example as any of the opportunities created by Russia's economic expansion. At around the time Fabergé made the *Trans-Siberian Railway Egg* he moved his business into purpose-built premises on Bolshaya Morskaya, paying out one million roubles (£100,000, £7.4 million) for the site and the same again on construction. These were vast amounts, reflecting the scale of an enterprise which employed 350 people in these headquarters alone, with another 250 at work elsewhere in St Petersburg.

On the building's ground floor the shop and trade counter presented Fabergé's face to the world. At the top were apartments for the Fabergé family, their panelled splendour a species of luxury far removed from what we normally understand as 'living above the shop'. In between were the design studio and the workshops, the engine room of the enterprise, their bare walls and crowded workbenches a stark contrast to the rest of the building. A worker on overtime might spend sixteen hours a day here, only taking off a half day on Sunday.

By all accounts Carl Fabergé was a model employer. Even so, like every industrialist of his era, he needed – and exploited – the cheap labour of Russia's working class. Peasants had flooded into the cities, attempting to escape conditions on the land that were in many ways worse than they had been for their serf grandfathers fifty years before. Few were fortunate enough to find skilled employment at a firm like Fabergé's. They became unskilled factory hands, on wages of around one and a half roubles (20p,* £10) per week, and lived in unimaginably squalid conditions – fifteen to a room if they were lucky, on a plank bed in the factory barracks if they were not. Landlords and entrepreneurs made fortunes, but precious little of it trickled down to the poor. Russia's frantic expansion was creating a proletariat with genuine grievances. For the time being, however, only a few idealists and revolutionaries gave

---

* At the time the pound sterling was of course divided into shillings and (old) pence. For ease of comparison these have been converted into post-1971 decimal pence.

any thought to the consequences. St Petersburg in 1900 was a good place to be rich.

PARIS GREETED the twentieth century with its own celebration of the prosperity brought by international trade, the Exposition Universelle of 1900. It was a measure of Carl Fabergé's growing status that he was invited to sit on the jury judging the exposition's jewellery. The honour meant he could not take part in the competition, but he could still exhibit; naturally he wanted to show off his firm's greatest creations – its eggs. So, with the permission of Alexandra and Marie, perhaps even their encouragement, Fabergé arrived in Paris bearing a number of their favourite Easter gifts, including, at least, the *Memory of Azov*, *Lilies of the Valley* and *Pansy* eggs.

The official response was clear: 'Monsieur Fabergé's work,' according to one notice, 'reaches the limits of perfection, with jewels being transformed into real objets d'art.'[2] Later, Henry Bainbridge put the reaction of French goldsmiths more colourfully: '"Louis XIV, Louis XV, Louis XVI! Where are they now?" they said, and themselves replied: "In St Petersburg, for we now call them Fabergé."'[3] The acclaim was not universal; followers of Art Nouveau found many of the designs old-fashioned; to them the groundbreaking jewellery of the Frenchman René Lalique was unmatchable. One of Fabergé's fellow jury members, René Chanteclair, found the *Memory of Azov Egg* 'a little overdone' and criticized the design of the *Lilies of the Valley Egg*. Nevertheless, this was a crucial moment in the history of Fabergé's firm, as it achieved full international recognition. The jeweller himself was awarded the Knight's Cross of France's Légion d'Honneur and his son Eugène, who had joined the firm in 1895, was made an officer of the French Academy. Fabergé was at his peak.

Two years later, in 1902, the inhabitants of St Petersburg were accorded the same privilege as their Parisian counterparts when, according to a contemporary advertisement, an exhibition of 'Fabergé artefacts, antique miniatures and snuffboxes belonging to members of the Imperial family and private persons' was held at the 'von Dervis mansion'.⁴ The entrance fee was 'one rouble, 10 kopeks' (10p, £7), hardly a prohibitive sum but enough to keep out the riff-raff for whom this was most of their weekly wage. Interestingly, the advertisement also states that the exhibition was being held 'in aid of schools under the august patronage of Her Majesty the Empress Alexandra Fedorovna and the Imperial Ladies Patriotic Society'. Alexandra had, it seems, finally managed to carve out at least one educational role for herself.

There, in the gold drawing room of Vera von Dervis's recently renovated house on the so-called English Embankment, one of the Russian capital's smartest residential streets, pride of place was taken by two glass display cases. One was devoted to objects belonging to the Empress Alexandra, the other to those of the Empress Marie. In both of them most of the space was taken by Fabergé eggs. At least fifteen were on display. It would be the largest public gathering of the Imperial eggs for the next seventy-five years.

Until these two exhibitions Fabergé's eggs had been a well-kept secret, part of the Tsar's private life. Now, for the first time, the public became aware of what the jeweller could achieve when supported by Romanov patronage. The eggs started to acquire their status as the ultimate symbols of tsarist wealth and extravagance. By 1906, when the English nanny to Alexandra's children, Margaret Eagar, wrote her memoirs, it was natural for her to tell her readers of the Yellow Room in the Winter Palace, next to the Empress's bedroom, where 'are exhibited the famous Easter eggs which were at the Paris exhibition. These are the work of Fabergé, the most renowned goldsmith in Europe.'⁵

A visit to Fabergé's new premises became one of the highlights of any trip to the Russian capital. An English tourist, the journalist and diplomat Harold Nicolson, wrote many years later of coming from the 'wide arch which led from the square of the Winter Palace at St Petersburg' on to Bolshaya Morskaya: 'The snow in the roadway was the colour of sand; the snow which edged the deep red pediments and lintels of the Winter Palace was dazzling white. The feet of the horses in the roadway made a rapid muffled sound; the feet of the pedestrians upon the pavement flopped and slopped in snow-boots or galoshes. One thus pushed the door and entered the warm and brilliant shop of Carl Fabergé.'[6]

Through that door, the visitor found himself in a chamber lined with display cases – jewellery on one side, objects of fantasy on the other. Particularly favoured customers might get a handshake from Fabergé himself, emerging from a back room in well-cut tweeds and tailcoat. Objects would be not so much sold as unveiled; the salesmen said little; each unique creation spoke for itself, both as a perfectly executed piece of craftsmanship and as a design that was, necessarily, à la mode. As an 1899 catalogue boasted, 'Goods which have gone out of fashion will not remain in our shop: once a year they are collected and melted down.'[7]

Not everyone was impressed. Nicolson's description of the route to Fabergé's premises may be supremely evocative, but within he found an ephemeral gaudiness that only emphasized the vast gulf between rich and poor: 'These costly trinkets appeared to me as symbols of Tsarist Russia. Inside that warm and brilliant shop the silly enamelled eggs would be laid out upon a black velvet napkin; outside the rime gathered slowly on the coachman's beard.' The novelist Vladimir Nabokov too recalled his sleigh 'drifting past the show windows of Fabergé whose mineral monstrosities, jewelled troikas poised on marble ostrich eggs, and the like, highly appreciated by the imperial family, were emblems of grotesque garishness to ourselves'.[8]

Garish and costly his objects may have been, but Fabergé's fame was spreading beyond Europe. The American financier J. P. Morgan, Junior, found himself returning to his yacht anchored on the Neva with a miniature pink enamelled sedan chair, a gift for his famous father. Henry Walters, the son of a Baltimore banking and railway tycoon, had sailed in on the 505-ton *Narada*, to be met by a granddaughter of the US president and Civil War general Ulysses S. Grant, who had married a Russian nobleman and become Princess Cantacuzène. She immediately took him to Fabergé's store on Bolshaya Morskaya. When the *Narada* left, it bore an array of animals carved from hardstone and a selection of enamelled parasol handles for the Walters nieces.

Consuelo Vanderbilt, however, did better than either of her compatriots. In 1895 her social-climbing mother had forced her to marry the Duke of Marlborough (whose family fortunes, in turn, needed bolstering by the Vanderbilts' railway millions). It was a famously unhappy marriage. Consuelo probably derived scant consolation from the fact that on a trip to Russia with her husband in 1902 she had sufficient social status to be placed next to the Tsar at one Winter Palace ball, and to dance with his brother, the Grand Duke Michael, at another. She was also received into the homes of St Petersburg society, where even her wealth had not prepared her for the magnificence of the jewels on display. Like every other visitor, however, she was charmed by Marie Fedorovna. We can guess that she saw at least one Fabergé egg during her visit to the Anitchkov, the *Blue Serpent Clock Egg*, which the jeweller had made for the Dowager Empress in 1887. Consuelo returned from St Petersburg with an egg that was almost a direct copy of this original, the *Pink Serpent Clock Egg*. The colour had been changed, but not much more than that.

The Duchess's elaborate creation was not the first egg that Fabergé had made for a commoner, but for years it was thought to be the only one ever commissioned by a non-Russian.* Soon enough it was on display in the Marlboroughs' ducal residence, Blenheim Palace. Mrs Vanderbilt, at least, must have approved.

CARL FABERGÉ was now a recognized member of the international elite. He had the reputation of being prepared to travel at a moment's notice, with his passport always to hand. On one trip to Paris, in 1902, he met an Austrian actress who had married well, the Duchess Iohanna-Amalia Tsitsianova. Known more familiarly as 'Nina', she became the jeweller's close friend and travelling companion for the next fourteen years. The two may well have been lovers. In the meantime, however, Carl remained married to Augusta. She presumably turned a blind eye to the liaison; such arrangements were hardly unusual in turn-of-the-century St Petersburg.

However much Fabergé travelled, international growth from a Russian base could only be taken so far. In 1903 he decided to open a sales office in London. It was to be managed by his youngest son, Nicholas, now aged twenty, together with Charles and Arthur Bowe, whose brother Allan had been a founding partner of the Moscow branch. Three years later the British venture was ready for expansion. Henry Bainbridge, a former chemical engineer, was hired to assist Nicholas Fabergé, eventually replacing the Bowe brothers. He came over to St Petersburg for an induction into what it meant to work for Carl Fabergé. That visit and subsequent trips to Russia provided the material for what was to be the first biography of the jeweller and the only real character study of him to be drawn from personal experience.[9]

---

*   The discovery of a previously unknown Fabergé egg, given as an engagement present to Baron Edouard de Rothschild, was announced in October 2007.

Bainbridge remembered his employer as a man of 'hyper-sensibility' and kindness, who saw good in everyone but whose sense of the ridiculous could still lead to a sarcastic remark. There was no waste about his actions or his speech: 'When he worked, he worked; when he ate, he ate; and when he talked, if one word would do, he used it, and if a gesture were better still he limited himself to that.' For six weeks Fabergé took the callow Englishman under his wing, with the 'sole idea' that he 'should gain some knowledge of Russia'. Seeing Bainbridge off at the station for his return to London, Fabergé waited until the train was on the move before pulling down his new employee's head for two last words of advice: 'Be noble.'

6. 'The ancestor who appeals to me least of all'

JUST AS FABERGÉ was using the *Trans-Siberian Railway Egg* to celebrate Russia's modernization, Nicholas and Alexandra were rediscovering a love for their country's past. For Easter 1900 they had decided to revive an ancient tradition, that the Emperor and Empress should spend the Orthodox Church's most important festival in Moscow. So at the beginning of Holy Week they arrived in Russia's former capital for their first official visit since the disasters of the coronation, four years earlier. Each subsequent day was spent celebrating matins, mass or evensong in one of the countless churches within the confines of the Kremlin. A vast complex, this city within a city was first walled off in the fourteenth century, but its origins stretch back to prehistory. Onion domes and a warren-like layout give it an oriental feel that is very different from the wide streets and classical facades of St Petersburg – a reminder that Russia and its Christianity are imbued with the traditions and rituals of the East. The decisive factor in Russia's conversion to Christianity at the end of the tenth century had been the effect on its emissaries of Byzantium's great domed cathedral, Hagia Sophia, completed by the Emperor Justinian in AD 548. The churches in the Kremlin continued to reflect their ancient Byzantine inspiration, creating an atmosphere that Nicholas and Alexandra found as uplifting as had those early Russian converts 900 years before. The Tsar closed the week with a letter to his mother: 'I never knew I was able to reach such heights of religious ecstasy as this Lent has brought me to.'[1]

Later that year, while on holiday in the Crimea, Nicholas fell ill with typhoid fever. For a month he was close to death, nursed constantly by his devoted wife. Recovery brought a deepening not just of the Emperor's love for Alexandra, but also of their mutual commitment to God. Moreover, the religion that they espoused, building on their experience in Moscow that Easter, was explicitly oriental. From now on the Tsar and his wife would look to the East for comfort and inspiration, as they came to appreciate ever more the Slavic roots of the Romanov throne.

For a Westerner, the rituals of Orthodox ceremony have always held an element of the unknown. The murmured incantations, the dark churches, the icons and the pungent smell of incense all speak of a level of spirituality that seems more primitive, less rational, than the intellectualized Christianity of Augustine and Aquinas. It was perhaps inevitable that the Empress, the Lutheran who had agonized so long before she became the 'truly believing Grand Duchess Alexandra Fedorovna', should move even further towards blind devotion. There is no one so fanatical as a convert. At the root of Alexandra's behaviour, however, was her increasingly urgent need to bear a son. In June 1901 she gave birth to her fourth daughter, Anastasia, a sister to Olga, Tatiana and Maria. All were grand duchesses but none could inherit the throne. Nicholas loved his wife as much as ever, but their joint failure to secure the succession isolated them still further from their subjects. Only Alexandra's faith assured her that eventually she would give birth to a son.

This mixture of conviction and desperation was always likely to render Alexandra vulnerable to charlatans. The hypnotist and self-professed medium Philippe Vachot was already known to the French authorities by the time he developed a following in Russia. There he was taken up by the daughters of the King of Montenegro, Anastasia and Militsa. Vivacious and unconventional, these two sisters had married well for princesses from a minor Balkan state – one to Duke George of Leuchtenberg and the other to Nicholas's cousin Grand Duke Peter Nikolaevitch. They drew Alexandra into their circle in St Petersburg and introduced her to 'our friend Philippe', as both she and Nicholas came to call him. By the end of 1901 the Empress had asked the medium to help her conceive an heir, a tsarevitch.

FOR THE MOST PART, Nicholas and Alexandra kept their passion for Russia's oriental past as private as every other aspect of their life together. In February 1903, however, they publicized it in the most lavish manner imaginable, at that month's two great Winter Palace balls. Nothing conjures up the splendour and excess of tsarist Russia quite as successfully as the mention of these elaborate set pieces. They were sumptuous gatherings centred on the presence of the Tsar and Tsarina, and it almost goes without saying that Nicholas and Alexandra did not enjoy them. The Empress once told a lady-in-waiting that they made her 'long to disappear under the ground'.² Nevertheless, in a normal year even this reclusive pair had to host at least the two balls that tradition and precedent dictated.

The first, 'Court', ball had a guest list of 3,000. It always began with a polonaise – little more than a procession around the ballroom with the Tsar and Tsarina in the first two couples. Through the evening the dancing would get more informal, culminating in the mazurka, Marie Fedorovna's favourite but of little interest to the shy Alexandra. The other state occasion, the Bal des Palmiers, was a much more intimate affair, where only perhaps 500 guests sat down to dinner. Once, the palm trees specially brought in from the Tsarskoe Selo hothouses to decorate every table had been a novel idea. Now, however, they were dictated by tradition as much as every other part of the evening.

It is all the more remarkable therefore that in 1903 these two great state occasions were markedly different from their predecessors. By order of the Tsar, all the guests came dressed not in

the usual gilded uniforms appropriate to rank, whose designs
dated back to Nicholas I, but in something more ancient still –
the caftans, fur hats and jewelled headdresses of the seventeenth
century. Guests spent months preparing their outfits. Nicholas
and Alexandra ransacked the Kremlin strongrooms for theirs.
He, in a costume of raspberry, gold and silver, came as Tsar
Alexis, Russia's ruler from 1645 to 1676; and she played Alexis's
wife, Maria, wearing a dress of gold brocade trimmed with
emeralds and silver thread, and earrings so heavy she could
hardly lift her head. For a few hours the Imperial couple could
pretend to be an oriental potentate and his consort, not the
anachronistic rulers of a rapidly modernizing empire.

The spectacle was magnificent, and the statement it made
about Nicholas's preferences was rendered more powerful by
the year in which it took place. In choosing 1903 as the year
to identify himself with Alexis, 'the most gentle Tsar', the softly
spoken Nicholas was explicitly repudiating the legacy of Alexis's
famously dynamic and brutal son, Peter the Great, the six-foot,
eight-inch giant who had defeated the Swedes, killed his own son
and set the Romanovs on the path towards their present prosperity. Two hundred years before, in 1703, Peter had ordered
the foundation of St Petersburg; in 1712 it became Russia's new
capital, its window on the West. Over 100,000 men had died to
build the city on marshland by the river Neva. To some visitors
the result was magnificent – the 'Venice of the north'. To others
it was a uniform dirty red, its subsoil saturated with sewage
and its main thoroughfares little better than rutted tracks.
Whichever view one took, the city was above all a reminder of
its founder, of his zeal for modernity and of the ruthlessness with
which he pursued his vision. Yet Nicholas chose St Petersburg's
bicentenary year to remember, as if it were a golden age, what
Russia had been like before Peter's rule, when Moscow was still
its capital. As he bluntly admitted to his court marshal, Peter
'is the ancestor who appeals to me least of all'.[3]

*

By THE TIME invitations were sent out for 1903's February balls it was too late for Fabergé to change the design for that year's egg, due to be presented by Nicholas to Alexandra at Easter two months later. Still taking his cue from public events, he had naturally chosen a theme to coincide with the capital's bicentenary; the result was the *Peter the Great Egg*.

Made of *quatre-couleur* gold and white enamel, the egg opened to reveal a miniature bronze replica of St Petersburg's greatest monument to its founder: a statue of Peter on horseback by the French sculptor Etienne Falconet. Completed in 1782, the monument had taken twelve years to carve. Catherine the Great had commissioned it and had ordered the installation by the Neva of the 1,000-ton granite boulder up which Peter's horse charges. That was a feat of engineering which recalled the construction of the city; 400 men had needed two years to move the boulder into position. Fabergé's egg commemorated, none too subtly, what the autocrats who were Nicholas's predecessors had been able to achieve.

With its golden swags and scrolls studded with diamonds, the egg was also a rococo masterpiece – a suitable swansong for workmaster Mikhail Perkhin, who supervised its construction but died in a lunatic asylum later that year. This was a sad end to a great collaboration. Perkhin had been responsible for the production of twenty-eight Imperial eggs, more than half the final total. Taken together they represent their own monument to the exacting standards of craftsmanship that Perkhin expected from himself and his workmen. The nature of his death illustrates perhaps the narrowness of the gap between madness and perfectionism. Perkhin's place as senior workmaster was taken by his friend and assistant Henrik Wigström.

Nicholas had been trained from childhood to keep his feelings well hidden; Fabergé would surely not have picked up from him any ambivalence about the theme of the *Peter the Great Egg*. Nevertheless, the goldsmith must have gathered, possibly from those balls, that his Emperor's real passion lay elsewhere.

The following year, 1904, Nicholas's gift to Alexandra would be something much more explicitly oriental, a direct celebration of Moscow, the ancient capital supplanted by St Petersburg – the *Moscow Kremlin Egg*.

Enamelled white and crowned by a golden onion dome, the egg is modelled on one of the cupolas that top the Kremlin's most important place of worship, the Uspenski Cathedral. This was where Nicholas had been crowned in 1896, and where he had celebrated Easter day itself on that crucial visit in 1900. Windows in the egg's side give a view of an interior where carpets, icons and decorations are so faithfully rendered you can almost smell the incense. It is surrounded and supported by four golden towers architecturally similar to those in the Kremlin walls. Two of these contain chiming clocks and another clockwork mechanism plays the tunes of cherubim chants – traditional Easter hymns particularly admired by Nicholas in 1900. The whole ensemble has a deliberately oriental feel, reflecting how Byzantine architecture and ritual had inspired the Uspenki's builders and clergy.

The *Moscow Kremlin Egg* may well be the most ambitious of them all. At over fourteen inches high, it is certainly the most substantial, and its cost – 11,800 roubles (£1,200, £85,000) – made it the most expensive egg that Fabergé had yet made. Interestingly, it is also the least like an egg. It is as if, in his effort to produce something oriental, Fabergé found himself forced to subvert the original rules that he and Alexander had established. For all its magnificence, the *Moscow Kremlin Egg* stands alone in the sequence; it is more like an architect's model than an object of fantasy; no subsequent egg takes a similar form. Nevertheless, there must have been more than the usual air of satisfaction in the workshops as the creation was completed, safe in the knowledge that here was a subject close to the heart of the Imperial couple. The date 1904 was engraved in white enamel on a gold plate at the foot of the egg; Fabergé waited for the command to deliver it to the Tsar.

7. 'We shall have to show dirty nappies'

ON THE EVENING of 26 January 1904 Nicholas returned from the theatre to be handed a telegram: 'About midnight, Japanese destroyers made a sudden attack on the squadron anchored in the outer roadstead of Port Arthur. The battleships *Retvizan*, *Tsarevitch*, and the cruiser *Pallada* were torpedoed. The importance of the damage is being ascertained.'[1]

There had been no declaration of war, but the attack should have come as little surprise. The fortified warm-water harbour of Port Arthur, on China's northern coast, had been a potential flashpoint since at least 1895, when it was briefly occupied by Japan. At that point Russia, which had spent the previous century expanding across Asia towards the Pacific, had been strong enough to force the Japanese to withdraw. The Russians had subsequently extracted a ninety-nine-year lease over the fortress from the helpless Chinese, in whose empire Port Arthur nominally lay. Japan, however, had always regarded its withdrawal as only a temporary setback and had been unsuccessfully seeking a diplomatic compromise with Russia ever since. Nicholas's intransigence rested partly on strategic considerations – finally his empire had a port that remained free from ice throughout the year – and partly on prejudice. To him the Japanese were still the 'monkeys' in whose country he had nearly been assassinated. How dare they claim a piece of the disintegrating Chinese empire? In any case, what could they do against the might of the Russian bear? Japanese attempts at negotiation had never even got off the ground. Three days before the attack their envoy in St Petersburg had been called home.

Japan's success in the opening engagement was only a foretaste of the victories it would enjoy in what came to be known as the Russo-Japanese War. The very size of Russia's empire counted against it, as the Tsar's government attempted to oversee a conflict taking place 4,000 miles away. The much vaunted Trans-Siberian Railway remained single track and was still not completed, so supplies for the beleaguered defenders of Port Arthur had to cross Siberia's Lake Baikal by either sledge or ferry, depending on the season. Moreover, Russian tactics remained rooted in the nineteenth century, and were consistently trumped by an enemy which had successfully made the leap from feudal society to industrial power in a single generation.

The final blow came in May 1905. Russia's Baltic fleet had spent seven months sailing halfway around the world to challenge Japan's superiority in the Pacific. Finally, it arrived in the Straits of Tsushima between Japan and Korea. The Japanese fleet was waiting. In forty-five minutes of shells and torpedoes, Russian sea power was eradicated. By then, Port Arthur had already fallen. It only remained to negotiate an end to the war. The eventual settlement, overseen by President Roosevelt, was far better than Russia could have expected: a tribute to the diplomatic skills of the Russian envoy, Sergius Witte.

MEANWHILE, Russia was slipping into anarchy. The war had ruthlessly exposed the inadequacies of the autocratic system. While the liberal opposition pressed for reform from within, more radical elements demanded greater concessions, even the abdication of the Tsar. The urban proletariat created by the economic expansion of the previous two decades began to flex its political muscles. In St Petersburg a small strike in a steelworks spread until, by the beginning of 1905, the city was close to paralysis.

On Sunday 9 January matters came to a head. A delegation of workers led by Father George Gapon, a police agent but also an ideologue, had planned to march to the Winter Palace to present a petition to the Tsar. Among other requests, they were seeking a constituent assembly elected by universal suffrage, education for all and a minimum wage. Nicholas, however, was already out of the capital, staying at Tsarskoe Selo, and his government, alarmed by the prospect of civil disturbances, was determined to appear strong. Lines of troops backed by Cossacks blocked every road to Palace Square. Unaware of the Tsar's absence, the marchers pressed on, driven by weight of numbers and the conviction that he would at least hear their grievances. A cavalry charge attempted to break up the march. When that failed, a line of infantry fired two warning volleys and then a third, at close range, into the heart of the crowd. As the mob scattered in panic, leaving behind at least forty dead, Father Gapon was heard to say in disbelief, 'There is no God any longer. There is no Tsar.'

The day had yet to reach its climax. The protesters moved to St Petersburg's main thoroughfare, the Nevsky Prospekt, to make a final push towards the palace. Here soldiers first attempted to clear the crowd with whips and the flats of their sabres, and then, to the sound of a bugle, fired directly into the crowd. The shooting was indiscriminate; men on their knees were mown down; women bearing icons were riddled with bullets; children fell from the trees where they had been watching. In all, about 200 people were killed and 800 wounded.

Repression was nothing new in tsarist Russia, but this was a massacre of peaceful demonstrators in front of bourgeois promenaders on St Petersburg's main street. The world's press was there to witness it. 'Bloody Sunday' would become one of the defining events of Nicholas's reign. It destroyed the moral basis of his regime in the eyes of both the world and his people. Before, it was said, Russians had both loved and feared the Tsar in equal measure. Now there was only fear.

The immediate response to the massacre, however, was anger. That evening workers rampaged around the centre of St Petersburg, looting shops and smashing up houses, before they finally dispersed, leaderless, in the small hours of the night. Within weeks, strikes were breaking out across Russia. After twenty years of relative quiet, political assassinations gathered pace. During the summer of 1905 the failure of another harvest spread unrest through the countryside. Mobs occupied the houses of the gentry; burning manors lit up the night sky. As the army was repeatedly called in to quell disturbances, even it showed signs of revolt. In June sailors on the battleship *Potemkin* overpowered their officers; the mutiny nearly spread to the rest of the Black Sea fleet. The autocracy attempted to respond to the crisis with proposals for limited reform, but it was too little and too late.

On 20 September Moscow's printers came out on strike. Over the next few weeks they were joined by printers in other cities and then by other workers: first the railwaymen, then millions of employees in factories and shops, banks and offices, even hospitals and universities. Strikers took to the streets. Initially peaceful protests quickly turned to violence as mass demonstrations clashed with police. The lights went out at night; looting became commonplace. By the middle of October food was becoming scarce. Russia was paralysed.

It was only then that Nicholas turned to the most capable of all his ministers, Count Witte, newly ennobled after his surprisingly triumphant return from peace negotiations with the Japanese. Nicholas had never particularly liked the technocratic adviser he had inherited from his father, but such was the crisis that he suppressed his antipathy. No one doubted Witte's ability. The statesman arrived at the Winter Palace with a memorandum already written. With the country close to revolution, Nicholas must concede a reform programme – a constitution that included a guarantee of civil liberties, cabinet government and a democratically elected parliament, a Duma.

The only alternative was a repressive military dictatorship, and even that could be only a temporary solution.

Still Nicholas failed to appreciate the extent of the crisis. He was not a stupid man: there is enough evidence from the memoirs of his ministers to show that he could grasp complex problems and come up with insightful solutions. But he had taken a vow at his coronation to uphold the autocracy and pass it on, like a sacred trust, to the next generation. The commitment blinded him. He went so far as to ask his cousin, the six-foot, six-inch Grand Duke Nicholas Nikolaevitch, the Romanov with most military experience, to assume the role of dictator. His reaction finally convinced the Tsar that concessions were inevitable. Taking out a revolver, the Grand Duke threatened to shoot himself there and then unless Witte's recommendations were adopted. Two days later Nicholas signed Witte's October Manifesto. Russia was on the path to democracy.

Jubilation greeted the proclamation of the new freedoms. The general strike was called off; the liberal intelligentsia revelled in what had been achieved; publishers gleefully exploited the relaxation in censorship rules; political parties began to think about how to contest the forthcoming elections. Even Carl Fabergé, who had been careful never to ally himself with any special interest, showed his sympathies. He joined the Octobrists, a loyalist group which had adopted this name to signify its support for the new constitution and the Tsar.

The euphoria was short-lived. Polarization between left and right developed into open street warfare. For the first time Vladimir Lenin and his Bolsheviks played a part. Seeking not just the Tsar's overthrow but the destruction of the entire capitalist system, they called for an armed insurrection to establish a communist state. In December 1905, the Moscow uprising turned the former capital into one vast battleground.

The time for full revolution, however, had not yet come. Apparently re-legitimized by its constitutional concessions, Nicholas's regime embarked on a punitive campaign against its own people. Drunken Cossacks burned villages, shot supposed agitators and raped women and girls. The intention was not just to punish the resistance, but to humiliate it, to break the spirit of the Russian peasantry. As Nicholas himself put it, 'terror must be met by terror'.[2] In the six months after the publication of the October Manifesto an estimated 15,000 people were executed, at least 20,000 wounded and 45,000 deported or sent into internal exile. The government eventually re-established its authority, but the manner in which it did so was, in the words of one modern historian, 'hardly a promising start to the new parliamentary order'.[3]

IT MUST HAVE been a relatively easy decision for the Tsar to cancel his orders for Fabergé eggs, first in 1904 and then the following year. Such extravagances were all very well in times of peace but they were inappropriate for the monarch of a country at war, let alone one on the verge of revolution. As if to confirm the extent of the crisis, in Easter 1905 the threat of assassination had reached Tsarskoe Selo itself: a plot to smuggle in bombs under the vestments of members of the choir was discovered only just in time. The *Moscow Kremlin Egg* remained unwanted in Fabergé's storerooms, its future uncertain.

Fabergé was losing other customers too. Barbara and Alexander Kelch had been one of the richest couples in Russia: he was a gold magnate and industrialist; she was the daughter of wealthy Moscow merchants. Like Nicholas and Alexandra they had married in 1894 and, like Nicholas's mother Marie Fedorovna, Barbara had previously been engaged to the deceased older brother of her husband. In her case, however, she had even been married to him. The apparent insouciance with which Barbara replaced one dead brother with a live one emphasizes the extent to which her marriages were designed as unions of business interests rather than born out of love. She and Alexander spent their first four years as husband and wife in separate cities. Nevertheless, in 1898 Barbara had moved to her husband's home in St Petersburg. Perhaps that is why in the same year Alexander emulated his Tsar by giving his wife an Easter egg from Fabergé. He continued the practice for six subsequent Easters, creating a collection of eggs outshone only by the Tsarinas' own. After seven years, however, the sequence came to an end. The pressures of the war proved too much for many of the Kelches' business interests. A marriage that had begun only as a means of uniting two vast fortunes ceased to have any meaning. In 1905 the Kelches separated and Barbara moved to Paris, taking her eggs with her.

Fabergé's fortune was even more newly acquired than that of the Kelches, but it proved to be built on more solid foundations. He can hardly have anticipated war, revolution and economic collapse when he made his investment in new premises only five years before, yet he seems to have been able to weather the slowdown in demand with relative ease. More than that, he continued to be, by the standards of the time, a generous employer, paying his workers to stay at home when street disturbances made it impossible for them to come to work. He had clearly built up substantial capital over the previous twenty years as Imperial jeweller. He used it to sit out the crisis in anticipation of better times ahead.

In 1906 Fabergé's optimism proved justified: once again the Tsar was ready to purchase Easter eggs for his wife and mother. War with Japan was over. It was true that the internal situation was not yet entirely peaceful – a breakaway peasant republic less than eighty miles from Moscow was only finally suppressed in July – but Nicholas was not the sort of person to let a minor civil war disturb the rhythm of his life. When the internal crisis was at its peak the previous autumn he had spent most of his days out hunting.

So for Easter 1906 Nicholas finally gave Alexandra the *Moscow Kremlin Egg*. There is evidence that the order took Fabergé by surprise; the egg still bears the inscription of the year when it was originally intended for presentation, 1904. Surely, with time to prepare, the perfectionist within the goldsmith would have changed the plaque? Marie Fedorovna received another remarkable piece of ornithological invention: the *Swan Egg*, made of mauve enamel and containing a superbly worked clockwork swan on a flat 'lake' made of aquamarine. This could not have been rushed off in a matter of months; presumably it too had spent the last two years in Fabergé's storerooms.

The *Moscow Kremlin Egg* can hardly have evoked happy memories for its recipient. Of all the political assassinations during the troubles of the previous two years, the bloodiest had been the murder of the Grand Duke Serge, Nicholas's uncle and still Governor of Moscow. A revolutionary had thrown a bomb into his carriage just as it was leaving the safety of the Kremlin. His wife, the Grand Duchess Ella, who had heard the explosion, rushed out to find her husband literally blown to pieces. Struggling to understand the horror, she visited her husband's killer in prison, embraced asceticism and turned to God. Within a few years she would become a nun in an order she herself had founded.

Not only was Nicholas Serge's nephew; Alexandra was Ella's sister. Twenty years before, their wedding had provided the stage for Nicky and Alix's first meeting. For years before her own marriage, Serge and Ella had been Alexandra's best friends in Russia. One might think that she would scarcely have appreciated her Easter reminder of the tragic end to her sister's happiness. Yet the *Moscow Kremlin Egg* was not hidden away like an uncomfortable memento but given pride of place in Alexandra's mauve boudoir in the Alexander Palace. For all its connotations, this representation of the Uspenski Cathedral was the closest Fabergé had yet got to creating an Easter icon; that alone was enough to make it a favourite.

Even in those two years of turmoil Alexandra's faith had been strengthened immeasurably by what seemed to her to be a direct response to prayer. On 30 July 1904 she had finally given birth to a son. The war meant there had been little to rejoice at in the months before, and there would be even less in the year that followed, but the birth of an heir provided a brief moment of celebration across the Empire. The ecstatic Tsar made every army combatant a godfather to the boy, who was christened Alexis in honour of his parents' favourite predecessor.

Alexandra knew who to thank for the longed-for arrival. Her sessions with Vachot had initially led only to false hope: a phantom pregnancy that was probably the result of anaemia. But her faith in the Frenchman had not wavered, even when he commanded her to pray to an apparently non-existent saint by the name of Serafim. Luckily, research soon uncovered the story of a monk, Serafim of Sarov, an eighteenth-century holy man. He was duly canonized; the miracles attributed to him multiplied, and in July 1903 Alexandra had bathed in his holy pool. A year later Alexis was born. Others might mock Vachot, but as far as Alexandra was concerned, he had helped her conceive a son. She had done her dynastic duty.

No event since the coronation could have provided Fabergé with a better subject for an egg than the arrival of the Tsarevitch, and the jeweller had been planning a suitable commemoration since the news of the birth. Early discussion within the firm had focused on using the fact that the baby had already been appointed chief of the Russian army's infantry units. Surely that could provide a suitable theme? 'Yes,' replied Fabergé, 'but we shall have to show dirty nappies, as that is the only result of his shooting so far.'[4]

Such disrespect did not of course manifest itself in the celebratory eggs that eventually appeared – delayed until 1907 by the two-year hiatus in royal commissions. That year both Alexandra and Marie received eggs whose surprises bore Fabergé's first pictures of the young Tsarevitch. In Marie's *Love Trophies Egg* this was a miniature easel carrying a portrait of all the Imperial children, while Alexandra's *Rose Trellis Egg* held a locket containing a picture of Alexis alone, painted on ivory. Both these surprises have since been lost.

The eggs themselves are both made of highly decorated enamel. Marie's is pale blue and lies on its side, held in the air by four columns between which hang swags of pink enamelled roses. Alexandra's is pale green and covered in a latticework of diamonds and pink enamelled roses – the rose trellis that gives the egg its name. There is no questioning the quality of each egg's craftsmanship or their success as decorative pieces, but neither seems particularly inspired. They display none of the ingenuity that by then had become almost the norm. It may be that Fabergé felt that the portraits were enough: a momentous event like the birth of an heir should not be overshadowed by gadgetry or rococo exuberance. With hindsight, however, the eggs' muted nature seems all too appropriate. By 1907 Nicholas and Alexandra's joy at Alexis's birth was overlaid with a deep and fearful anxiety.

When he was only a few weeks old Alexis had started bleeding from his navel. Such a small thing should not have been cause for worry, but it took three days before the flow of blood finally stopped. As the baby grew into a toddler and started to move around, little tumbles produced bruises that obstinately refused to heal. Bumps would grow into dark swellings beneath the skin. By the time he was two, Alexis's condition was clear. He had inherited the gene for the 'royal disease' from his mother, who had in turn inherited it through her own mother from Queen Victoria. His blood would not clot; he had haemophilia.

Alexandra was all too familiar with the condition. It had killed her three-year-old brother 'Frittie' when she was a baby and her uncle Leopold when she was twelve. Her nephew Prince Henry of Prussia died at four years old, just before Alexis's birth. Triggered by a recessive gene on the X chromosome, haemophilia only ever manifested itself in men.* Women, how-

---

* For a woman to have haemophilia, both her X chromosomes would have to contain the mutation. Since each would have been inherited from one parent, this means that her father would have had to be a haemophiliac, and

ever, were carriers. This was the fatal curse that Alexandra brought into the family of the Tsar. She was still only thirty-three, but there were to be no more children. There seems to have been no reason for this except that perhaps the royal couple could not face the prospect of another haemophiliac child. Alexis was the sole chance for the continuation of Nicholas's line on the throne of Russia, but the odds were against him even surviving childhood, let alone becoming Tsar and fathering further heirs of his own.

------

her mother a carrier. Improved survival rates among male haemophiliacs mean that this is now a possibility, and there are rare cases of female haemophiliacs.

8. 'A good, religious, simple-minded Russian'

FOR MORE THAN a decade after the Tsarevitch's birth the eggs that Fabergé made for both Marie and Alexandra would almost entirely shun the colour red. There is the occasional sparkle of an understated ruby but no more eggs carved from bloodstone, and the scarlets and fuchsias in Fabergé's pallet of enamels remained unused. The absence is striking: a demonstration, some have suspected, of the jeweller's tact, as he ensured that nothing might act as an unpleasant reminder of the heir's haemophilia. If that is the case, however, and Fabergé knew that Alexis was, in the language of the time, a 'bleeder', then he was part of a very select circle. Nicholas and Alexandra feared that public knowledge of Alexis's illness would destabilize the throne. They guarded the truth about his condition extremely closely. Even Marie may not have known of her grandson's deadly inheritance.

It is surely reading too much into the eggs to assume that their colours were the result of anything more than Fabergé's remorseless search for original and pleasing themes. Nevertheless, there is no doubt that in the years following the 1905 revolution his understanding of the Imperial family increased. The eggs from three successive years, in particular, show that he was finally beginning to know how to please Alexandra, by concentrating on eggs that were personal to her rather than commemorations of her husband's reign.

From the turn of the century Nicholas and Alexandra had been spending more and more time in the Alexander Palace at Tsarskoe Selo, and by 1906 they were hardly to be seen in St Petersburg. There were no more great Winter Palace balls; their apartments there were practically unused. Ostensibly, such a move was justified by security considerations alone. Like Gatchina, Tsarskoe Selo was far enough away from the capital to be relatively immune from disturbances. Unlike Alexander and Marie's retreat from the terrorist threat twenty-five years before, however, this was no grudging displacement. Nicholas and Alexandra moved to the Alexander Palace because they wanted to. From the very beginning they had thought of it as a place where they could bring up their children and live their own lives away from the distractions of St Petersburg society. In 1902 Alexandra had overseen further extensive alterations to the palace, adding several new reception rooms, now firmly in the art nouveau style, and a large new playroom for her daughters, the four grand duchesses. By the time Alexis was born, the Alexander Palace was already not just a summer residence, but a year-round home.

So Alexandra's Easter gift in 1908 was especially appropriate. The *Alexander Palace Egg* captures a building that was both the focus of her existence and the embodiment of her taste. The egg is carved from nephrite, a type of jade whose green translucence made it one of Alexandra's favourite ornamental materials. Miniature watercolours of her five children around its circumference are each decorated with wreaths of gold, diamonds and rubies. Within the egg is the surprise, a tiny but amazingly accurate replica of the palace itself, less than three inches across. Made of gold and silver, and with a green-enamelled roof, the building is surrounded by gardens of green gold and a driveway of granulated red gold. Like every piece from Fabergé, the egg demonstrates superlative workmanship, but it is also an ensemble which – in its choice of materials and reminders of family and home – captures the personality of its recipient more successfully than any since 1898's *Lilies of the Valley Egg*.

This happy conjunction of theme and design may simply be the result of luck. In 1901 Marie Fedorovna had received a similar Easter gift based around her own summer residence – the *Gatchina Palace Egg*. Alexandra's present seven years later was hardly an exact copy of Marie's, which was made of white enamel and included no family pictures, but it took similar inspiration. It could be read as an example of the jeweller still struggling to understand his younger client and being forced to fall back on an old idea. Nevertheless, the *Alexander Palace Egg* was undoubtedly a success with its recipient. She kept it beside her in the mauve boudoir, her favourite room in the palace that the egg commemorated. From now on, every egg that Nicholas gave her would end up in the same place. By contrast, the *Gatchina Palace Egg* had been a rare instance of the jeweller failing to understand Marie Fedorovna. She had always preferred St Petersburg and the Anitchkov Palace, and she continued to do so: 'What is the use of my four hundred rooms at Gatchina? I never use more than two.'[1]

There are similar grounds for thinking that Alexandra's Easter present the following year was another redevelopment of an earlier gift to her mother-in-law. Nevertheless, it too would have called up only happy memories, as it celebrated another Royal residence, but one of an entirely different kind. Carved from a single piece of transparent rock crystal, the egg lies on its side, on a stand of lapis lazuli and rock crystal. The upper half opens out and is hollow; the lower half has been left solid, but its internal surface has been carved to resemble waves. On this sea sails another miniature replica – of the Tsar's yacht, the *Standart*.

Commissioned by Alexander III in Copenhagen at a cost of just under four million roubles (£400,000, £29 million), the *Standart* was then the largest yacht in the world. Its thirty rooms contained every conceivable luxury, including a chapel and

Carl Gustavovitch Fabergé sorting a pile of loose stones, and his wife Augusta. To Henry Bainbridge, Fabergé had the 'air of a country gentleman' or an 'immaculate gamekeeper with large pockets'.

The 'warm and brilliant' interior of the St Petersburg shop.

The floors above the shop included the design studio – shown above in a photograph
taken by Nicholas Fabergé that also shows his brothers Eugène (standing next to a seated
man) and Alexander (seated by a window) – and (*below*) the workshop overseen by
Mikhail Perkhin (bearded, standing fourth from left). The egg on the front right table
has been tentatively identified as the recently discovered *Rothschild Egg*.

The first eggs received by the two Tsarinas are each missing two of their three surprises. Tsar Alexander III hoped that Marie Fedorovna's 1885 *Hen Egg* (*above*) 'would have the desired effect on its future owner'. Alexandra's 1895 *Rosebud Egg* (*right*) has been inexpertly repaired after being damaged in a marital argument.

A little something from Fabergé became the present of choice for Europe's aristocracy.

Marie Fedorovna (seated) was petite and dark, and was outshone in beauty by her elder sister, Queen Alexandra, whose complexion remained so good, even in old age, that it was said to be enamelled.

Many of Fabergé's eggs reminded the Empress of her Danish roots, such as the 1903 *Royal Danish Egg* (*right*), which has been missing since the Revolution, and the 1890 *Danish Palaces Egg* (*below*).

Alexandra in the year of her marriage. Anna Vyrubova remembered her as a 'tall, slender, graceful woman, lovely beyond description, with a wealth of golden hair and eyes like stars, the very picture of what an Empress should be.' The 1898 *Lilies of the Valley Egg* (*right*) captured a theme close to Alexandra's heart – she adored her husband and gloried in motherhood, but her daughters could never inherit the throne.

To Kenneth Snowman, the 1897 *Coronation Egg* was Fabergé's masterpiece, but it is doubtful whether any gift held more unwelcome memories for its recipient.

Large sections of the Gatchina Palace (*left*) are now in disrepair, and the Alexander Palace (*below, left*) is mainly offices; but their heydays are captured in Marie Fedorovna's 1901 *Gatchina Palace Egg* (*opposite*) and the surprise from Alexandra's 1908 *Alexander Palace Egg* (*opposite, bottom*).

Alexandra's 1900 *Trans-Siberian Railway Egg* (*bottom, left*) commemorates an achievement that Witte hoped would enable Russia to dominate the affairs of Asia from 'the shores of the Pacific and the heights of the Himalayas'.

The *Kremlin Egg* (*below*) that Alexandra received in 1906 stands alone in the sequence of Imperial eggs. It is as if, in his efforts to reproduce an oriental theme, Fabergé had to subvert the rules he had originally established with Alexander III.

In 1913 the two Tsarinas received eggs that show Fabergé at the peak of his genius. For Geoffrey Munn, Marie Fedorovna's *Winter Egg* is 'the absolute swansong and greatest masterpiece of all the eggs'. Alexandra's *Romanov Tercentenary Egg* (*below, left*) is a fabulously opulent demonstration of the dynasty's wealth.

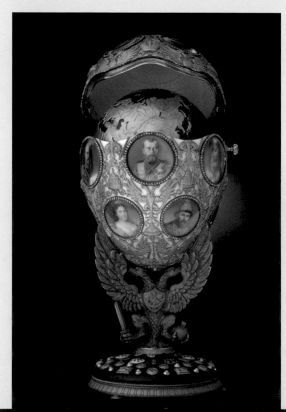

An original Fabergé photograph of what is thought to be Marie Fedorovna's 1909 *Alexander III Commemorative Egg*, missing since the Revolution.

stabling for a cow – the royal children could hardly be expected to do without fresh milk when at sea. It was the envy of heads of state from Kaiser Wilhelm of Germany to Edward VII of Great Britain. They encountered the yacht when Nicholas used it as a floating embassy – mooring close to Wilhelm's smaller one for talks in the Baltic or anchoring off Cowes to receive the British royal family during a celebrated family get-together in 1909 (the year this egg was presented). At other times the Tsar enjoyed his yacht more privately. Every summer the Imperial family and a few close friends would embark for six weeks of sailing along the Baltic coast. Released from the cares of office except when a launch arrived with fresh reports, Nicholas would lead expeditions ashore to gather mushrooms or walk in the woods. Back on board, he ceded at least nominal command to the captain, a suitably distinguished admiral who took responsibility for the Tsar's safety while at sea. The passengers mixed freely with officers specially chosen for their charm and social graces. Even Alexandra, according to a senior courtier, 'grew gay and communicative on board the *Standart*'.[2]

The inspiration for the *Standart Egg* might have come from the *Memory of Azov Egg* that Marie Fedorovna received in 1891, with its replica of the ship in which her sons were then travelling. It is more likely, however, that Fabergé and his designers decided to produce the egg as the result of an event in 1907 which made the yacht famous across the world. It occurred during that year's summer cruise. The sea was calm and the band was playing as Nicholas and Alexandra, their children and their guests were taking tea. Suddenly, a terrific shock sent the china crashing to the deck. The yacht came to a dead halt and began to list alarmingly. The *Standart* had run aground; it might start to sink at any moment. There was, however, no panic. Alexandra in particular could look back on the incident with satisfaction. Showing admirable decisiveness, she ensured that all the passengers were safely stowed in the lifeboats and gathered together valuables before she herself left the yacht.

   The eventual enquiry placed the blame on the Finnish pilot,
although there were also whispers that perhaps the crew had
been chosen with rather too much attention to its social skills
and rather too little to its seamanship. On this occasion, however, courtly incompetence had no greater consequence than a
disrupted holiday. The boat did not sink and there were no
injuries. The closest the incident came to producing a casualty
was when the Tsar only narrowly prevented the *Standart*'s
captain, Admiral Nilov, from committing suicide. It was in fact
an inconsequential drama, the perfect occasion for Fabergé to
commemorate in an egg.

ALEXANDRA was not always so energetic. Sciatica had troubled
her since her youth, and as she grew older she became less and
less active. She began suffering from other illnesses; a heart
defect was diagnosed; for months she would be confined to her
bed. She was still in her thirties and remained handsome, her
complexion 'delicately fair',[3] her figure 'as supple as a willow
wand', but her mother had died at only thirty-five, and her
son seemed likely to die at any moment. Every visitor could not
fail to notice the 'infinitely tragic eyes' that spoke of nameless
sorrow.

   Increasingly, Nicholas and Alexandra retreated from the
world. In the Alexander Palace meals provided the routine
around which days were structured. Nicholas and the girls
would meet for breakfast before each then went off to work –
he to his study and a succession of reports and meetings, they
to the schoolroom and lessons in arithmetic, geography, history,
Russian, French and English. During the day they would meet
again, at mealtimes and for an afternoon walk in the park. Tea
followed a menu of hot bread and biscuits unchanged since the
days of Catherine the Great, so rooted in tradition that Alexandra found it impossible to change. Then for an hour the younger
children would play at the feet of their parents while the older
girls occupied themselves with needlework or embroidery. After

supper, served promptly at eight, Nicholas read aloud; the children would be bathed and taken to bed; and at eleven Nicholas and Alexandra themselves would retire, sharing a bed throughout their married life, the Emperor kept awake not by the cares of his office but by his wife, crunching her English biscuits as she lay beside him reading into the night.

Only at lunchtime would the outside world intrude upon this domestic idyll, when courtiers joined the family around the table. Morning visitors to the Tsar might be favoured with an invitation they could not refuse: 'You'll stay to lunch, of course.' This gave them the chance to savour the cooking of Cubat, the palace chef imported from France, and to sample the contents of the legendary Imperial cellars. Sadly, the Tsar's concern that meals should not overrun took precedence over the desires of his palate, which were anyway rather simple. Food kept warm until it was needed hardly did justice to the skills of its renowned creator. Similarly, the finest wines were served only on special occasions (which experienced courtiers became adept at identifying); patriotism dictated that on normal days guests drank the products of Russian vines. Even so, these were sought-after invitations: a chance to see the grand duchesses and the heir at close quarters, to observe a mix of childish exuberance and Victorian table manners, and to understand that at heart Nicholas and Alexandra longed only to be with their family.

Carl Fabergé would never have attended one of these luncheons. He was after all only a tradesman, rarely mentioned in the diaries or letters of his most famous clients. Nevertheless, Easter gave him at least one good opportunity every year to observe the Imperial family. For weeks beforehand excitement mounted in his workshops as that year's eggs neared completion. In Holy Week the shop would be especially crowded, not just with customers buying their own Easter gifts, but also with sightseers hoping for a glimpse of what the Tsarinas were to receive. Finally, on Good Friday Fabergé himself would present them to the Tsar. No accident could be allowed to interfere with delivery. Until Fabergé returned from his mission, the eggs safely handed over and approved, all his craftsmen would remain at their posts.

The jeweller's annual pilgrimage to the Alexander Palace became part of a ritual that Nicholas and Alexandra had inherited and adapted from generations of previous tsars. Their own private exchange of Easter gifts and greetings was at the top of a strict hierarchy. In the course of the morning every member of the Court and staff, every servant and every guardsman would line up to accept the traditional Easter kiss on the cheek from the Emperor and to receive the hand of his wife. Afterwards each would be given an egg appropriate to his rank: for senior members of the household a jewelled or enamelled pendant, for lowlier individuals something from the imperial porcelain factory. Early in his reign Nicholas estimated that, judging by the number of eggs distributed, he had embraced 1,600 people – 'a whole regiment!'[4] – leaving his cheeks 'terribly sore'. By now the royal children could play an active role: they sat at the feet of their parents throughout the ceremony and handed over each egg.

There is a tendency now to think of the four girls en bloc: pretty clones dressed in white. This is perhaps understandable, given their closeness and their habit of using the initial letters of their names – OTMA – as a collective signature. Their parents divided the quartet into two pairs: 'big' and 'little'. Olga and Tatiana slept in one bedroom, Maria and Anastasia shared another. Sometimes all four would dress alike; often only the pairs matched. Nevertheless, their individual characters were very different: Olga, fourteen years old in 1909, was fair and tall, clever, slightly earnest and devoted to her father; Tatiana, twelve, was dark and pale, unselfish, practical and her parents' favourite; Maria, ten, was big-eyed and plump, a talented artist but ruled entirely by her younger sister Anastasia, seven, destined perhaps for great beauty, an imp of a child, witty, disinclined to work and a source of mischief.

The girls are all represented allegorically on the *Colonnade Egg* that Nicholas gave Alexandra in 1910, the third Easter present in succession to be based around a theme close to the Empress's heart. The egg itself is covered in opalescent pink enamel and is effectively an elaborate rotary clock. It is dwarfed, however, by the base, which gives the egg its name. Six green columns of bowenite, a hardstone similar to nephrite, support the egg, so that the whole structure has the look of an ancient Greek love temple. Below the columns sit four golden girls – the grand duchesses. Another figure, however, dominates the scene: a winged cupid, who kneels astride the top of the egg and looks down with condescending hauteur on the subservient females below. The import of the egg is clear: of the Tsar's five children, it was the youngest, the heir, to whom all the others must defer.

Fabergé's design reflected the reality. Nicholas and Alexandra were bringing their daughters up to be polite, deferential and self-denying. Luxury was inevitable, but there was to be no laziness, no casual disrespect and no needless extravagance. The Tsarevitch, however, was treated differently. It was not just that he was the long-awaited heir with all that implied, but that the only available treatment for his condition was to pamper him. When even a small bump might be fatal, all risks had to be minimized. A sailor from the *Standart*, Derevenko, was his constant companion, there to intervene if play became too rough and to carry him if an obstacle seemed too challenging. Even tantrums could not be allowed; Alexis might bruise himself in a childish rage. It was surely against his parents' better judgement, but in his early years Alexis was indulged.

All the precautions in the world could not prevent the occasional accident. A knock against a piece of furniture would create a bruise. As internal haemorrhaging continued the bruise would develop into a lump; eventually the swelling would grow taut beneath the skin as the blood had nowhere else to go. Then, finally, the internal bleeding would stop, but not before the young boy had been through enormous pain. Sometimes blood would get into his joints; this directly irritated the nerves and was even more excruciating; every episode could have left the Tsarevitch a permanent cripple. His mother would nurse the child, confined to bed by pain, in the same way as she looked after all her children, but she could provide no relief. One man, however, could: bearded, dishevelled and unconcerned by majesty – the son of a Siberian peasant – Gregory Yefimovitch Rasputin.

The mysterious Philippe Vachot had died in the summer of 1905, but not before prophesying that after his death there would come another, bearing his spirit. Later that year Nicholas and Alexandra met Rasputin for the first time. As with Vachot, the introduction came from the Montenegrin sisters, Militsa and Anastasia, but the peasant also came with a recommendation from Alexandra's former confessor, the Archimandrite Theophan. Here was a mystic carrying the Church's blessing, a holy man in the Orthodox tradition, a *staretz* who already had a reputation as a healer. All who met him were struck by his good humour, his evident sincerity and above all by his piercing, mesmeric eyes.

During that first meeting Rasputin talked only to the parents. On subsequent visits to Tsarskoe Selo he met the children too; he would tell them old Russian tales and lead them in prayer. To Nicholas he was a 'good, religious, simple-minded Russian'; a talk with him left the Emperor at peace, whatever the doubts or troubles that assailed him. To the children he was a friend, a bearded giant in whose presence they were instantly at ease. To Alexandra he was much more, a character whose combination of peasant simplicity and ascetic mysticism appealed strongly to her twin obsessions of deep religiosity and fervent domesticity. In Rasputin, Alexandra grew increasingly convinced, she had found the man who could heal her son and release the Romanovs from the curse she had brought into the family.

Nicholas's sister the Grand Duchess Olga witnessed Ras-

putin's powers. In 1907 the Tsarevitch had developed internal
bleeding after a fall in the gardens at Tsarskoe Selo. He was only
three years old.

> The poor child lay in such pain, dark patches under his eyes
> and his little body all distorted, and the leg terribly swollen.
> The doctors were just useless. They looked more frightened
> than any of us and they kept whispering among themselves.
> There seemed nothing they could do, and hours went by
> until they had given up all hope. It was getting late and I
> was persuaded to go to my rooms. Alicky [Alexandra] then
> sent a message to Rasputin in St Petersburg. He reached
> the palace about midnight or even later. By that time I had
> reached my apartments and early in the morning Alicky
> called me to go to Alex's room. I just could not believe my
> eyes. The little boy was not just alive – but well. He was sit-
> ting up in bed, the fever gone, the eyes clear and bright, not
> a sign of any swelling on his leg. The horror of the evening
> before became an incredibly distant nightmare. Later I
> learned from Alicky that Rasputin had not even touched the
> child but merely stood at the foot of the bed and prayed.[5]

For Alexandra there was no doubt: Rasputin had been sent
from God to help her, her husband and her son.

9. 'The little one will not die'

By 1910 CARL FABERGÉ was in his mid-sixties, with a neat white beard that gave him the appearance, to the Bolshaya Morskaya shop's younger visitors, of Father Christmas. His liaison with Nina Tsitsianova continued, but it does not seem to have affected his relationship with his children. All four sons, now grown up, were helping their father in the business. The elder two, Eugène and Agathon, managed the St Petersburg headquarters with him. Each had his own specialities, Eugène as a self-described 'public relations man', although others thought of him as a designer, and Agathon as an expert gemmologist. The third brother, Alexander, had taken over from Allan Bowe as manager of the Moscow branch. The youngest, Nicholas, continued to run the only overseas outlet, in London, with the help of Henry Bainbridge.

Perhaps Eugène was impatiently waiting for the chance to take more direct control of the business. That is one interpretation that might be placed on a letter he wrote to the Court Ministry that October. After detailing his father's many achievements, closeness to the Tsar and existing honours, Eugène concludes:

> It was only recently that I found out that the title of Supplier to the Imperial Court is not identical to the title of Jeweller to the Court. Therefore, taking into consideration all of the above and mainly the fact that C.G. Fabergé has already indeed for long been the Jeweller to the Imperial Court, having a personal relationship with their Imperial Majesties, I am honoured to address myself to Your Excel-

lency and humbly request that the title 'Jeweller to the Court' be awarded to Carl Gustavovitch Fabergé.[1]

The title was duly granted. Carrying no additional responsibilities and no benefit apart from glory, it might well be seen as the sort of honour that rounds off a career. If so, it does not seem to have encouraged thoughts of retirement in its recipient. Perhaps that was never the intention. Superficially at least the existing arrangements suited all concerned.

The firm Carl Fabergé had inherited from his own father had become a hugely successful business, one of the biggest enterprises in the whole of Russia. International sales had continued to grow ever since the Paris Exposition of 1900, and within Russia there were now sales branches in Odessa and Kiev to add to the main centres at St Petersburg and Moscow. Turnover amounted to 16,500,000 roubles (£1.7 million, £110 million); across the empire the firm was responsible for employing as many as 1,500 people.

In Russia industrial expansion had created a whole new class of customers. Entrepreneurs, rich from sugar-refining, finance or trade, proved perfect clients. They knew what they wanted and how much they were willing to spend but were otherwise quite happy to leave the details of a piece to Fabergé and his designers. The contrast with Nicholas's court – penny-pinching and with a tendency to design by committee – was marked. The annual commission for Easter eggs might have long since become automatic, but orders for other pieces from the Court had become so dependent on 'ingratiating oneself and beating a path to the doors of the office that Fabergé stopped visiting in person'.[2]

That last quote is from the memoirs of François Birbaum, Fabergé's chief designer since the death of Carl's brother Agathon in 1895. It suggests that in the decade before the First World War the firm had got to such a size that it could contemplate a reduction in Imperial orders with equanimity.

Moreover, it hints that within the company, despite a relationship that now spanned a quarter of a century and despite
humble requests for honorifics, the Imperial court was held in
something like contempt.

Naturally, Fabergé's eggs for the royal family carry no
suggestion of discontent; they were intended as amusing and
brilliant diversions, not political statements. Nevertheless, the
egg that Alexandra received in 1911 can, by its very nature, be
read as a commentary on Nicholas's reign. As its name suggests,
the theme of the *Fifteenth Anniversary Egg* is retrospection.
It looks back on the fifteen years since Nicholas's coronation,
through scenes depicted in the phenomenally detailed watercolours that cover the egg's surface.

In all, the egg carries sixteen miniatures. Seven of them are
portraits of Nicholas, Alexandra and the five children – the
Emperor handsome and bearded, his wife beginning to look
slightly matronly, the girls gazing directly at the artist, each
with a single strand of pearls around her neck, and Alexis, his
stare equally intent, dressed in the sailor suit that was the standard uniform of royal children in that era. By now Alexandra's
annual egg was carrying representations of the Imperial children more often than not; the jeweller knew what interested
the Empress. It is the nine remaining pictures that have a story
to tell: they cover topics that can be read as a chronicle of
Nicholas's achievements. Is it only hindsight that makes them
seem particularly uninspiring?

Four of the miniatures show Nicholas's participation in
events that celebrated his more illustrious predecessors: the completion of a museum in St Petersburg endowed by Alexander III
and subsequently named after him; the opening of a bridge in
Paris also named after Alexander III in recognition of his role
in creating the Franco-Russian alliance; and the inauguration
of two separate monuments to Peter the Great, one commemorating the bicentenary of his final victory over the Swedes in
1709, the other a bronze statue of him on horseback, unveiled

in Riga in 1910. Two further panels show scenes from Nicholas's coronation: the procession to the Uspenski Cathedral and the moment at which Nicholas received the crown. Even fifteen years on, memories of the subsequent tragedy at Khodynka Meadow were still fresh; references to the coronation were unavoidable on an egg like this but they can hardly have been welcome.

Finally, there are the three pictures that memorialize the supposed highlights of Nicholas's reign. The first, in chronological order, shows the Huis ten Bosch Palace in The Hague. This was the location in 1899 of a peace conference that Nicholas had co-sponsored with Queen Wilhelmina of the Netherlands, after he had written to his European counterparts lamenting competitive rearmament and calling for a forum for civilized dispute resolution that might forestall unnecessary wars. The initiative resulted in one permanent legacy – the International Court of Arbitration at The Hague that still exists today – but the 1905 war with Japan had already demonstrated the failure of its grander ambition, and the arms race that would eventually result in the First World War had, if anything, picked up pace.

The second of these three panels shows the procession that transferred the relics of the newly canonized Saint Serafim into the cathedral at Sarov in 1903. This was unquestionably an important moment for the Tsar and his wife; his diary records that he was 'enormously inspired' by the ceremony; and Alexandra credited her prayers to the newly created saint for the birth of the Tsarevitch. Nevertheless, it is hard to see the canonization itself as an event of enormous significance.

The last miniature carries a representation of Nicholas giving the speech with which he opened the first session of the Duma, in 1906. Ostensibly, the establishment of an elected parliament was the great achievement of Nicholas's reign – the beginning of a process whereby Russia would eventually become a constitutional monarchy similar to Britain or Denmark. As a loyal Octobrist, Carl Fabergé held to this view, and the panel focuses solely on the family group surrounding the Tsar. Other pictures of the occasion, however, show it in a wider perspective. It was a famously uncomfortable affair. Nicholas had summoned the Duma to the Winter Palace. On one side of its throne room the members of the Court gathered in strict hier-archy, each attired according to his rank. Opposite them, scruffily dressed in a way that suggested deliberate disrespect, were the newly elected representatives, who glared at the gilded courtiers with such 'incomprehensible hatred'[3] that Marie Fedorovna was moved to tears. The differences between the Tsar and his people had never seemed more marked.

The truth was that 1905's October Manifesto was far from a blueprint for democracy, at least as interpreted by Nicholas. He had retained all the crucial levers of power: control of the army and police, the right to dissolve the Duma and issue his own proclamations in its absence and – perhaps most crucially – the unrestricted right to appoint and dismiss ministers. Even before the Duma opened he had sacked its architect, Count Witte, replacing him as prime minister with Ivan Goremykin, a reactionary nonentity. The Duma was little more than a talking shop with limited legislative powers. It was, however, a focus for opposition to Nicholas's regime, and its deputies understood this. Within a few days of that opening ceremony they were issuing demands that, while hardly unreasonable to a modern reader, smacked of revolution to the Tsar: universal male suffrage (as opposed to a system favouring the nobility and supposedly loyal peasantry at the expense of the urban masses), the release of political prisoners and the appointment of a government answerable to the Duma rather than the crown. It was a clash that, for the time being, only Nicholas could win. The first Duma lasted for less than three months before the Tsar exercised his prerogative and ordered its dissolution.

The sixteen miniatures take up most of the surface of the egg; hidden pins secure them within a cage of green enamel that divides the egg into six longitudinal and three horizontal bands, making eighteen cells in all. The final two spaces are filled by dates picked out in diamonds – the year of Nicholas and Alexandra's marriage, 1894, and the year the egg was presented, 1911. Perhaps that was the true achievement of Nicholas's reign: a seventeen-year marriage that, despite all external pressures, remained as happy and close as ever.

There was one other unusual aspect to the egg: it was empty; it contained no surprise, at least not one in the sense that Alexandra would have come to understand the concept. Fabergé surely did not mean anything by the omission, but is it fanciful for a modern observer to draw the obvious conclusion: that for all its pomp and circumstance Nicholas's reign was hollow at its core?

However vacuous his Court, Nicholas had made at least one dynamic decision: the appointment of Peter Stolypin as prime minister. This former state governor had little experience of national government or St Petersburg society, but he combined the vision of a reformer with the tough pragmatism that Russia required after the chaos of 1905. He replaced Goremykin in July 1906, when the dissolution of the first Duma was already inevitable and while the situation across Russia remained unstable. With the reimposition of law and order as his first priority, Stolypin established field courts that could hang a man within three days of his arrest. By the end of the summer, 600 alleged revolutionaries had been sent to their death by 'Stolypin's necktie'.

Meanwhile, a second Duma proved just as obstreperous as the first. Nicholas's autocratic instinct was to abandon the whole experiment with an elected parliament: 'One has to let them do something manifestly stupid or mean and then – slap! And they are gone!'[4] Stolypin, however, persuaded the Tsar to follow a more subtle course. The second Duma followed the first into dissolution, and a new electoral law concentrated voting power in the hands of the country gentry. The resulting third Duma

was filled with Stolypin's allies. Finally, the Tsar and his prime
minister had a parliament they could work with. Russia was
as far from democracy as ever, but with the backing of both
Nicholas and the Duma Stolypin was able to embark on a
series of sweeping changes. Most notable among these were
reforms to the land system, where laws were passed for the
first time that enabled peasants to own land personally and
not as part of the commune. This, more than any other single
measure, might have finally allowed the peasantry, or at least
its more enterprising elements, to escape from the cycle of
poverty created by generations of communal mismanagement.

Inevitably, however, Stolypin found himself in conflict with
vested interests; he gradually began to lose the support of the
Tsar. In September 1911, at the opera in Kiev and in full
view of Nicholas, Stolypin was shot by a revolutionary. Before
collapsing, he was able to turn to the Tsar and make the sign of
the cross. He died six days later. Stolypin's murderer had been
allowed to enter the theatre unsearched because he was a police
double agent. There was no proper enquiry as Nicholas refused
to believe that his chief of security could be guilty of anything
more than a lapse of judgement. Alexandra was more hard-
hearted still, saying to Vladimir Kokovtsov, Stolypin's successor
as prime minister, 'One must not feel sorry for those who are
no more . . . I am sure that Stolypin died to make room for you,
and this is all for the good of Russia.'

Alexandra never did have good political judgement.
Kokovtsov had been, and remained, a highly competent finance
minister – he had overseen the recovery of Russia's exchequer
from the disasters of 1905 – but he had none of Stolypin's
imagination or charisma and was handicapped by having to
work with ministers all appointed by the Tsar. Once again the
relationship between the Duma and the crown began to founder.
With the death of Peter Stolypin, Russia's best chance of an
orderly transition to democracy also died.

Nevertheless, in the years before Stolypin's assassination

Russia had benefited from a combination of good harvests and competent government. Repression and a weariness with revolution had also played their part: the country was relatively calm. This meant that for the first time in years Nicholas and his family were able to travel through the empire, to visit the palace that had always been their favourite holiday destination, Livadia in the Crimea. Here protocol was largely forgotten: Nicholas could play tennis or go riding with his daughters while Alexandra could even drive into Yalta to shop. In 1909 Nicholas had taken the decision to replace the old villa, scene of the death of Alexander III, with a larger edifice. Two years later it was complete. So the following year, 1912, the royal family prepared to break with its usual Easter practice and spend the festival in the warm climate of the Crimea, far from Tsarskoe Selo and the Alexander Palace. 'I am only sorry for you who have to remain in this bog,' were Nicholas's parting words to the grand dukes and ministers left behind in St Petersburg.[5]

Whatever the location, Nicholas still had to give Alexandra her Easter present. Eugène Fabergé spent most of Holy Week travelling down from St Petersburg to deliver it. He would have experienced the rising spirits of every traveller as the monotony of Russia's forests, still mired in winter, gave way to the soaring peaks and rampant spring of the Black Sea coast. The Crimean peninsula itself was a piece of heaven: trees coming into blossom on every side, traditional Tartar villages hardly changed in hundreds of years and on the coast the palaces of Russia's aristocracy. The new villa at Livadia was a suitable climax – over one hundred rooms in an Italianate cliff-top confection of white limestone, all porticoes and courtyards, with sweeping vistas of sea and mountains.

The egg that Fabergé had his son deliver was, appropriately enough, a celebration of another son, Alexis. It was only two years since the *Colonnade Egg* had done something similar, but the pleasure the Tsarina took from the heir was obvious, and his importance to the dynasty could not be denied. The *Tsarevitch*

Egg made this clear. Carved from a single block of deep blue lapis lazuli, it was covered by elaborate golden cage-work containing several motifs of which the most prominent was the Romanov double-headed eagle. Within the egg was the surprise – a portrait of Alexis, naturally, framed by another Romanov eagle made of platinum and set with over 2,000 tiny diamonds.

FABERGÉ MAY NOT have known it, but the survival of Alexis was becoming something to remark on. He had reached his eighth year with no permanent injuries. Haemophilia was not in itself a death sentence; Alexandra could dare to hope that he might be one of the small minority of sufferers to survive into adulthood. Perhaps he might even, one day, inherit the throne. In the meantime, her hopes and thanks continued to rest with Rasputin.

By now many were questioning the role of the Siberian peasant and his influence on the royal couple. While Nicholas and Alexandra appreciated the mystic's essential simplicity, St Petersburg society saw an entirely different side to him. Women in particular found his sensuality as fascinating as his spirituality. Adoring disciples gathered around him and – rumours were rife – worshipped him with their bodies as much as their minds. It was inevitable that scandal would eventually touch the Imperial family. By March 1910 Nicholas's sister Xenia was recording the disquiet of one of Alexandra's aristocratic ladies-in-waiting, Sofia Tiutcheva, at Rasputin's behaviour with the young grand duchesses, especially the older pair: 'He's always there, goes into the nursery, visits Olga and Tatiana while they are getting ready for bed, sits there talking to them and caressing them.'⁶ As far as Alexandra was concerned, however, Rasputin's visits to the nursery were entirely innocent. She ignored the concerns of the well-connected Miss Tiutcheva, who instead made them known in the salons of St Petersburg.

The following year brought more damaging revelations. A letter surfaced that purported to be from the Tsarina to Rasputin: 'My soul is quiet and I relax only when you, my teacher, are sitting beside me. I kiss your hands and lean my head on your blessed shoulder. Oh how light, how light do I feel then. I only wish for one thing: to fall asleep, to fall asleep, forever on your shoulders and in your arms . . .'⁷ Questions were asked in the Duma. The gossip became more salacious: Rasputin had turned the nursery at the Alexander Palace into a harem; the Empress and all her daughters were mad for his love; the Tsar was forced to pull off the peasant's boots and wash his feet before abandoning his wife to Rasputin's lust.

The claims were absurd, but the affair refused to die. Kokovtsov found himself spending more and more of his time defending the Empress's regard for a Siberian peasant while his secret police informed him that the rumours about Rasputin's relationships with women in St Petersburg were all too true. He advised the *staretz* to leave the capital, thereby earning Alexandra's undying enmity. Rasputin protested that he never went to the palace without a summons, but soon afterwards opted for an extended sojourn in his village in Siberia, where his wife and family still lived.

THAT SAME YEAR, 1912, brought the centenary of Napoleon's invasion of Russia and subsequent retreat from Moscow. This key event in Russian history had made Nicholas's great-great-uncle Alexander I the power broker of Europe and had inspired artists from Tolstoy to Tchaikovsky. A few years before, the anniversary would have been a natural subject for Fabergé to commemorate in one of Alexandra's eggs. It is a measure of his confidence in his understanding of the Tsarina that he chose not to do so; the *Tsarevitch Egg* was much more to her liking. Instead, it was Marie Fedorovna who received that year's *Napoleonic Egg*, with its golden Romanov eagles and battle emblems, and a folding screen surprise with pictures of the Dowager Empress's regiments. That September Nicholas wrote to her from Borodino, just outside Moscow, site of the great but inconclusive battle of 1812. At the centenary celebrations there he had met a 'veteran, Sergeant-Major Voitinuik, 122 years old, who himself had fought in the battle! Just imagine, to be able to speak to a man who remembers everything, describes details of the action, indicates the place where he was wounded, etc., etc.'[8]

One of the consequences of Napoleon's eventual defeat had been the extinction of the small Polish state he had established in 1807 and the subjugation of the whole of Poland to Russian domination. It was to this part of the empire that Nicholas and his family travelled after the celebrations at Borodino. They had two destinations, both hunting lodges personal to the King of Poland, a title that devolved automatically on the Tsar of Russia.* Elk and bison roamed in the 3,000 acres of forest at Bialowieza, in the east of the country. Nicholas went riding with his daughters, despite 'constant rain', leaving Alexis to go for rows on a lake near the lodge. Then – an all too common occurrence – an accident getting into the boat left a bruise that forced the eight-year-old to spend a week in bed. By the time the family left, however, the swelling had subsided and the incident seemed to be just one more in the catalogue of minor misfortunes that punctuated the Tsarevitch's life.

---

* Nicholas's full set of titles was: Emperor and Autocrat of all the Russias; Tsar of Moscow, Kiev, Vladimir, Novgorod, Kazan, Astrakhan, Poland, Siberia, the Tauric Chersonese and Georgia; Lord of Pskov; Grand Prince of Smolensk, Lithuania, Volhynia, Podolia and Finland; Prince of Estonia, Livonia, Courland and Semigalia, Samogatia, Belostok, Karelia, Tver, Yugria, Perm, Viatka, Bulgaria and other lands; Lord and Grand Prince of Nizhnyi Novgorod and Chernigov; Ruler of Riazan, Polotsk, Rostov, Yaroslavl, Belo-Ozero, Udoria, Obdoria, Kondia, Vitebsk, Mstislavl and all the Northern Lands; Lord and Sovereign of the Iverian, Kartalinian and Karbadinian lands and of the Armenian provinces; Hereditary Lord and Suzerain of the Circassian Princes and Highland Princes and others; Lord of Turkestan; Heir to the Throne of Norway; Duke of Schleswig-Holstein, Stormarn, the Dithmarschen and Oldenburg.

The true extent of Alexis's injury only became apparent at Spala, the family's next stop. The lodge itself was little more than a dark wooden villa, more like an isolated country inn than a royal residence, but the surrounding forest was magnificent. Nicholas hunted every day, accompanied by guests from across Poland and beyond. His wife and children, on the other hand, had little to entertain them except the prospect of inspecting the day's kill each evening. So one day Alexandra and her inseparable companion, the dull but loyal Anna Vyrubova, took Alexis out for a drive. The carriage had gone a few miles, bouncing along a road little better than a sandy track, when Alexis cried out with pain in his back and stomach. Alexandra ordered an immediate return to the lodge, but the journey became what Anna Vyrubova would remember as 'an experience of horror. Every movement of the carriage, every rough place in the road, caused the child the most exquisite torture, and by the time we reached home he was almost unconscious with pain.'⁹

The internal wound from Alexis's fall at Bialowieza had not yet healed, and the journey in the carriage had exacerbated it, causing a haemorrhage in the groin. As Alexis descended into agony and his fever rose, St Petersburg's best doctors began to arrive at his bedside. They could do nothing to stop the bleeding. Gradually, blood spread across the whole lower abdomen; the swelling forced Alexis's leg to bend unnaturally, so that his knee was against his chest; the boy lost the strength even to cry.

Meanwhile, Nicholas and Alexandra continued to play the welcoming hosts to their guests; the news of the heir's illness had to be kept secret; nothing could be allowed to create uncertainty over the succession. Pierre Gilliard, tutor to the grand duchesses, recalled one evening when Maria and Anastasia put on a little entertainment:

> When the play was over I went out by the service door and found myself in the corridor opposite Aleksey Nicolaievich's room, from which a moaning sound came distinctly to my

ears. I suddenly noticed the Tsarina running up, holding her long and awkward train in her two hands. I shrank back against the wall, and she passed me without observing my presence. There was a distracted and terror-stricken look in her face. I returned to the dining room. The scene was of the most animated description. Footmen in livery were handing round refreshments on salvers. Everyone was laughing and exchanging jokes. The evening was at its height.[10]

Only the dimmest guest would not have realized there was something wrong. Over the next week rumours began to circulate in St Petersburg of an assassination attempt on the heir. When Alexis's temperature reached 105°, Nicholas was persuaded that the secrecy could no longer continue. A bulletin was issued. Russia began preparing for the death of the Tsarevitch. According to Anna Vyrubova, 'Alexei himself, in one of his rare moments of consciousness, said to his mother: "When I am dead build me a little monument of stones in the wood."'[11] The final crisis came 'on an evening after dinner when we were sitting very quietly in the Empress's boudoir, Princess Irene of Prussia, who had come to be with her sister in her trouble, appeared in the doorway very white and agitated and begged the members of the suite to retire as the child's condition was desperate. At eleven o'clock the Emperor and Empress entered the room, despair written on their faces.'[12]

It was at this point that Alexandra played her final card. Declaring that she could not believe that God had abandoned them, she asked Anna to telegraph Rasputin in Siberia. His reply came quickly: 'The little one will not die. Do not allow the doctors to bother him too much.'[13] That was the extent of the *staretz*'s involvement but it was apparently enough. Within a few days Alexis was on the mend. Although he was unable to walk for months afterwards, he eventually recovered completely.

The affair at Spala, however, had many consequences. For one, it made clear that continued secrecy about the Tsarevitch's condition was no longer viable. By November newspapers around the world were carrying the story: 'Czar's heir has bleeding disease.'[14] Whatever rumours Fabergé might have heard before, the truth was now common knowledge. Alexis would still feature on future eggs, but he would no longer provide their main theme. It could only be bad taste to celebrate the existence of an heir unlikely to outlive his father.

Then there was the response of Nicholas's immediate family to the crisis. His brother Michael, fearing that he was about to become Tsarevitch, had swiftly married his long-term lover in a small Orthodox church in Austria. Nathalie Cheremetevskaya was a commoner, twice divorced; by marrying her Michael had disqualified himself from the throne. It was a betrayal of duty which Nicholas found hard to stomach, and his immediate response was to forbid his brother to return to Russia. Left in lonely isolation, Nicholas was more dependent on Alexandra's support than ever. For her, on the other hand, the events at Spala had proved one thing. Once again Rasputin had saved her son. Let the gossips of St Petersburg say what they might; no one would now be allowed to come between her and this holy Siberian peasant. A mother's love was creating the circumstances which would eventually bring down the whole panoply of Imperial Russia, and with it the world of Fabergé. Before that, however, there was to be one last great flowering of Romanov power, and of Fabergé's genius.

10. 'An unparalleled genius'

In 1613 a specially convened assembly of Russian nobility, the *zemsky sobor*, had elected the first Romanov tsar, Nicholas's great-great-great-great-great-great-great-grandfather. Michael Romanov's claim to the throne was weak – based on little more than the fact that a great-aunt had been the first wife of Ivan the Terrible – and he was reluctant. There were, however, no other candidates, and the nobles were convinced that only the leadership of a tsar could bring an end to the Time of Troubles, the period marked by a succession of rulers and a Polish invasion that had followed Ivan's death in 1598. Their judgement had been largely vindicated by the success of the dynasty Michael began. The three-hundredth anniversary of his accession to the throne was an obvious subject for a Fabergé egg.

The *Romanov Tercentenary Egg* celebrated Michael's family on many levels. On its surface a golden pattern of double-headed eagles and Romanov crowns set off eighteen separate miniatures on white enamel. Each was a picture of a Romanov tsar – Michael and all his successors, down to Nicholas II himself. Within the egg the surprise was even more demonstrative: a rotating steel sphere divided into two halves, each a map on which the seas were made of dark blue enamel and the land masses of different coloured golds. One hemisphere showed the empire inherited by Michael Romanov in 1613, already a massive realm of 2.3 million square miles, and the other its extent in 1913 – 8.5 million square miles, unimaginably vast. On average, in each of the 300 years in which they had ruled, the Romanovs had conquered a territory more than twice the size of Wales.

The egg carried an implicit message as well. Its materials, like those used in every predecessor, were evidence of the mineral wealth within the Romanovs' vast empire: the gold, silver, diamonds, turquoise and rock crystal had all been extracted from somewhere within Russia's borders, and the sophistication of its craftsmanship showed how far Russia had progressed from the semi-barbarism that had prevailed when Michael Romanov ascended the throne.

The tercentenary of the dynasty was marked by celebrations across Russia, culminating in the grand entry of Nicholas into Moscow, riding alone sixty feet in front of his Cossack escort. To get there, he and Alexandra had journeyed round Russia's interior, sailing up the Volga to Kostroma, where Michael Romanov had received the offer of the throne, and then retracing his steps back towards Russia's former capital. At every stage of the journey the Tsar was greeted by cheering crowds; peasants waded waist-deep into rivers to get a glimpse of him; in towns workmen fell down to kiss his shadow. For the Empress, it was all evidence that the gossips in St Petersburg could be safely ignored. As she told a lady in waiting, 'We only need show ourselves, and at once their hearts are ours.'[1]

Few people outside Alexandra's immediate circle shared her confidence. Three years before, it had seemed possible that the Tsar and his parliament might work together, as Russia inched its way towards democracy. By the tercentenary year all such thoughts had been abandoned. The Duma had broken down into a number of warring factions, unable to initiate any legislation and bereft of influence, leaving the Tsar an isolated autocrat, unwilling to listen even to the Council of Ministers that he himself appointed. In the cities worker militancy was on the rise. Lenin had been in exile since the 1905 revolution, but radical communists, including his Bolshevik party, had started to take over all the larger trade unions. Between 1912 and 1914 three million workers would go out on strike. In the country-side poverty remained endemic, fostering a casual attitude to life that could all too easily descend into brutality. Stolypin's land reforms had petered out, unable to circumvent the twin obstacles of peasant indifference and a bureaucracy resistant to change. Only a gradual increase in literacy rates – to something like 40 per cent across Russia – could be counted an indicator of success. But education brought its own risks: a literate peasant could understand that there was a better way of doing things and the current regime might not have all the answers. Revolution was in the air. It seemed only a matter of time before the unfinished business of 1905 was completed.

Meanwhile, Nicholas looked on approvingly as his government resorted to populist ultra-nationalism. Pan-Slavism held that Russians should take responsibility for their fellow Slavs, wherever they lived. This inevitably soured relations with Austria-Hungary, Russia's closest western neighbour. Austria's own empire might have been on the brink of collapse, but it still regarded the Slavic states in the Balkans as lying within its sphere of influence and did not welcome Russian interference. Similarly, but within Russia's borders, the authorities pandered to age-old prejudice by sponsoring increasingly violent anti-Semitism. This tendency was highlighted by the trial of a middle-aged Jewish factory clerk, accused of the ritual murder of a young boy. The prosecution offered little evidence other than crude references to the Jewish race's supposed lust for Christian blood, and it is to the credit of the jury that the innocent clerk was eventually acquitted. The same credit cannot be given to the Tsar, who showed great personal enthusiasm for pursuing a case that he knew to be baseless.

Such crude racism might be ascribed to desperation, to a vain attempt to curry favour with the masses, but Nicholas was as blind to danger as his wife, assuring his mother that 'the people's only sorrow was that they did not see their Tsar often and close enough'.[2] Once Marie Fedorovna might have been able to contradict him, to point out his folly, but she had long since lost that kind of influence. Alexandra's devoted nursing when Nicholas almost died from typhoid in 1900 had cemented the bond between husband and wife in a way that almost inevitably excluded his mother. Soon afterwards, Marie was complaining to her daughter Xenia that Nicholas was doing all he could to avoid meeting her in private. In 1912 she had attempted to persuade Nicholas and Alexandra that Rasputin must be sent from Court, only to be rebuffed. By February 1914, when Alexandra had engineered the dismissal of Kokovtsov as prime minister (his card had been marked since suggesting to Rasputin two years before that he should leave the capital), Marie could only sympathize with the displaced statesman. As she did so, she revealed the depth of the gulf that had opened between her and the Empress: 'My daughter-in-law does not like me; she thinks that I am jealous of her power. She does not perceive that my one aspiration is to see my son happy. Yet I see that we are nearing some catastrophe and the Tsar listens to no one but flatterers, not perceiving or even suspecting what goes on all around him.'[3]

A minor but telling example of how things had altered between mother and son comes from the way the Imperial family's Easter routine changed in the years after Alexis's birth. At the beginning of Nicholas's reign it had always included a trip to Marie's palace in Gatchina on the Sunday afternoon, a chance for the Emperor to spend some time with his mother and for his children to play with their cousins. From 1908, however, Marie substituted a new routine – leaving her children and spending Easter with her sister Queen Alexandra, either in England or in the villa they had bought together, Hvidore, back in their native Denmark. Mother and son were not estranged – their letters continued to be chatty and agreeable – but they got less pleasure from each other's company.

Nevertheless, Marie continued to receive her annual Easter gifts from Fabergé. They were rarely as expensive as the eggs presented to Alexandra at the same time but they matched them in creativity, and their maker's empathy for the Dowager Empress had only deepened over the decade. For two years in a row, 1909 and 1910, he produced eggs memorializing her husband. On either side of that there had been pieces of fabulous whimsy. The *Peacock Egg* of 1908 contains its enamelled bird perched on a golden tree within a rock-crystal shell. When the peacock is lifted from its branch, wound up and placed upon a flat surface, it struts about, moving its head and spreading its tail. The *Bay Tree Egg* of 1911 is a piece of miniature topiary, whose nephrite leaves grow on a golden trunk. Pressing a jewel on the tree causes a singing bird to emerge, which moves its head, flaps its wings and opens its beak.

Beautiful and amusing though they are, both these pieces are derivative. The *Peacock Egg* was based on an enormous English clock given to Catherine the Great by her favourite, Count Potemkin. Fabergé would often have seen it in the Hermitage Museum. Similarly, the *Bay Tree Egg* drew its inspiration from a piece made in Paris in the eighteenth century. And the folding screen surprise of the *Napoleonic Egg* Marie had received in 1912 made it hardly different in overall concept from the *Danish Palaces Egg* given to her by Alexander in 1890. Nevertheless, Fabergé's designers remained capable of entirely original conceptions, as the egg Marie received in 1913 showed.

It is probably no coincidence that the idea for the egg came from one of Fabergé's few female employees. So many of the jeweller's creations, not least the Easter eggs, were made for women, it seems entirely appropriate that a woman should finally have had a role as a designer. Moreover, Alma Pihl had the kind of pedigree that counted for something in Fabergé's paternalistic world: her grandfather August Holmström had been one of Fabergé's most skilful jewellers, responsible, among other creations, for the miniature cruiser in the 1891 *Memory of Azov Egg*; and her father had headed the Moscow jewellery workshop until his death in 1897, aged only thirty-seven. Her own talent was honed under the supervision of her uncle Albert Holmström, who had succeeded his father as a senior workmaster in St Petersburg. Alma had initially been employed to draw ornaments and other precious articles for the firm's archive, then one day Uncle Albert noticed that she had also been sketching some of her own ideas for jewellery on a piece of paper. Picking it up, he found an excuse to go down to Fabergé's shop on the ground floor. On his return a little while later, he could announce, 'They've ordered them.'[4]

Alma married Nikolas Klee in 1912 but, as her daughter later remembered, she was allowed to 'continue as a designer with Holmström, since she wasn't much good in the kitchen'.[5] So Alma was at Fabergé when an order came in from Dr Emanuel Nobel, nephew of the inventor of dynamite and himself a fabulously wealthy oil magnate, for forty small pieces, preferably brooches, of a value so low they 'were not to be understood as bribes'.[6] Looking up, Alma noticed a pattern of icicles on a window pane, glistening striations of jagged beauty. The inspiration was immediate. At a dinner party given by Dr Nobel a few weeks later the ladies all received their own little icicle made from rock crystal and small diamonds.

Alma's idea had potential for more than just trinkets. In 1913 Marie's *Winter Egg* was the magnificent result. A hollow translucent shell encrusted with icicles apparently rests on a block of thawing ice. Within, viewed as if through an icy fog, hangs a basket containing flowers – wood anemones – resting on a bed of golden moss. The effect is breathtaking; it seems entirely possible that the egg is freezing to the touch. It is almost disappointing to discover that both base and shell are carved from rock crystal, one polished until it seems to melt, the other engraved on its interior to simulate ice; that the 'icicles' are careful settings of diamonds and platinum; and that the 'flowers' are carved from semi-precious stones – white quartz, green garnet and nephrite. The allegorical meaning of the egg is clear: even

in the depths of winter we can hope for spring and Easter resurrection. For many, this egg is Fabergé's masterpiece.

THE FOLLOWING WINTER, at the beginning of 1914, Marie
performed one of her more pleasant duties as grandmother to
Nicholas and Alexandra's children, when she hosted a ball at the
Anitchkov Palace for Olga and Tatiana. The two elder grand
duchesses were now eighteen and sixteen, but so far their social
life had never got beyond each summer's mild flirtations with
the officers of the *Standart*. For a brief period it had been
thought that Olga might make a suitable match for Prince Carol
of Rumania, until she made it clear that she had no intention of
leaving Russia. Now the two girls were coming out into society
as elegant young ladies. Their poise and sense of propriety only
added to their beauty, but they were ready to enjoy themselves.
They danced until four thirty in the morning, to be eventually
taken home by their doting father.

No doubt Olga and Tatiana told their younger sisters all
about the excitements of the evening. Maria, now fourteen,
would soon develop her own crush on a young officer – and tell
her father about their entirely innocent meetings in long chatty
letters. The twelve-year-old Anastasia, by contrast, was still a
little girl; her letters to Nicholas were more likely to describe
a nose-picking episode than any weightier matter. Alexis was
not yet ten, but he remained the centre of the family, worshipped
by his sisters and his parents' pride and joy.

The profiles of all five children are lined up on the surprise
inside the egg that Nicholas gave Alexandra that Easter. For her
this was a theme that could never be overdone, but it is hardly
original. It might be taken as a sign that Fabergé's creative juices
were finally beginning to run dry. The egg that contains it, however, is one of the most startlingly brilliant of them all. Once
again Alma Pihl, now twenty-five, was the designer. On this
occasion inspiration came to her at home, when she looked up
from a book to see her mother-in-law's embroidery as it caught

the light. From a distance the *Mosaic Egg* could be made from tapestry or needlepoint, but a closer look reveals that the shell is made from hundreds of precious and semi-precious stones, inset in a platinum network and arranged in flower patterns – a remarkably simple idea, beautifully executed.

For the third year in a row Alexandra received her Easter present at Livadia, by now firmly established as the Imperial family's favourite palace. Marie Fedorovna, on the other hand, had decided that year to break with her recent practice and remain at Gatchina, secure perhaps in the knowledge she would not thereby have to entertain her daughter-in-law. Separated from her sister in England, she wrote to her instead, describing that year's celebrations and her receipt of her Easter present, the *Catherine the Great Egg*:

> He [Nicholas II] wrote me a most charming letter and presented me with a most beautiful Easter egg. Fabergé brought it to me himself. It is a true chef-d'oeuvre, in pink enamel and inside a porte-chaise [sedan chair] carried by two blackamoors with Empress Catherine in it, wearing a little crown upon her head. You wind it up and then the blackamoors walk: it is an unbelievably beautiful and superb piece of work. Fabergé is the greatest genius of our time. I also told him: 'You are an unparalleled genius.'[*]

THAT JANUARY Agathon Fabergé, the jeweller's second son, had received permission from the Tsar to overhaul and re-catalogue the crown jewels. It was a long-overdue and immense task, and he set about it conscientiously, working his way up from the lesser pieces – the diadems and necklaces – to the Imperial regalia. These included the Cross and Chain of St Andrew, the orb, containing a magnificent forty-seven-carat blue sapphire, the sceptre and, finally, the Imperial crowns themselves.

---

[*] 'Vous êtes un génie incomparable,' in original letter.

By July Agathon had finished with the sceptre. Years later he would still remember how the Orlov diamond at its head had sprung satisfyingly from its setting into the palm of his hand, ready to be cleaned and weighed – one hundred and ninety-three carats of bluish-white stone. He turned his attention to the crowns. At that moment the telephone rang. His Excellency Nicholas Nikolaevitch Nowosselsk, the chief of the Cameral Department of the Cabinet of the Tsar, was on the line: 'The examination of the jewels must cease at once. All of them are to be packed in boxes and sent under guard to Moscow.'[8] The political situation across Europe was darkening. Austria was reacting with extreme belligerence to the assassination of the Archduke Ferdinand in Sarajevo a few days before. Given its pan-Slavist rhetoric, Nicholas's government could not credibly ignore a threat to Russia's fellow Slavs in Serbia. War still seemed unlikely, but if it did break out, the safety of St Petersburg could not be guaranteed. The crown jewels belonged in the security of the Kremlin, further from Russia's western border. As for the crowns, their inspection could wait for a more propitious time.

11. 'Fabergé has just brought your delightful egg'

GERMANY AND AUSTRIA declared war on Russia on 1 August 1914* and on France two days later. The day after that, Britain joined the fray. The First World War had begun. A surge in patriotism greeted Nicholas's formal announcement of hostilities. This was no distant colonial adventure like the war with Japan in 1904; Russians and their fellow Slavs were fighting for their very survival. Striking workers abandoned their demands; the Duma approved military spending plans without debate; across Russia reservists hurried from their homes. The German ambassador, for one, was confounded. He had convinced himself, and told his masters in Berlin, that Russia's industrial unrest meant it was in no position to go to war. Nicholas, meanwhile, took a solemn oath that he would 'never make peace so long as a single enemy remains on Russian soil' and appointed his cousin, the Grand Duke Nicholas Nikolaevitch, commander-in-chief of the Russian war machine. By the end of August the Tsar had publicized one more resonant decision: henceforth, his capital would not have a Germanic name but would be known as Petrograd.

The mobilization that accompanied the start of the war more than tripled the size of Russia's standing army from 1.4 to 4.5 million men. It created an enormous force with the

---

* According to the Julian calendar, still used in Russia, this date was actually 19 July, but in recounting famous First World War events I have used the generally accepted dates.

theoretical capability of delivering a decisive strike, but the logistics involved in arming it and transporting it to the theatre of battle would have taxed the most efficient modern state, let alone the bureaucratic muddle overseen by Nicholas. Russia had nothing like the artillery, ammunition or railway network of its Prussian adversaries. That final advantage provided the basis for Germany's entire strategy. It would start by ignoring Russia and focus all its efforts on the swift subjugation of France. Success in the west would then allow a transfer of resources to the east, ready to deal similarly with the Russian forces that – the Germans assumed – would only just be approaching readiness.

The Allies, however, won the race that Germany's strategy implied. The day after Berlin declared war on France, German armies crossed the Belgian border, dashing for Paris. That alone decided Britain's entry into the war: 'gallant little Belgium' could not be abandoned to the Hun. Moreover, the Belgians proved surprisingly resistant and the Russians unexpectedly efficient. Before the German advance had even passed through Belgium, Russia attacked on the eastern front, launching two armies under Generals Samsonov and Rennenkampf into Prussia, on Germany's Baltic coast. It was a foolhardy thrust which would have immediately disastrous consequences. On 30 August the defending Germans routed Samsonov's army at Tannenberg, taking 90,000 prisoners. A week later, at the Battle of the Masurian Lakes, Rennenkampf's army was also defeated. He was forced to leave the army; Samsonov had already committed suicide.

Nevertheless, the Russian offensive had been enough to throw Germany's grand strategy off balance, forcing its high command to transfer resources away from the push into France earlier than planned. At the Battle of the Marne in early September the French and British armies brought the German advance to a halt. Paris was saved, and the previously invincible Prussians were forced to retreat. Their response was to dig in. The subsequent race for the sea, as each side tried to outflank the other, created two opposing lines of fortified trenches through Belgium and France from the English Channel to the Swiss border. Germany would have no quick victory on its western front. By attacking so swiftly in the east, France's Russian allies had done what was required of them.

Russia's defeats meant that it had to withdraw from Prussia back into Poland, but further south Austria-Hungary was proving a much less formidable opponent. In a remarkably successful campaign Russian troops occupied Galicia, Austria's easternmost province, taking 130,000 prisoners. Only the Carpathian Mountains and the approach of winter prevented an advance towards Vienna. By the end of the year, as generals on both sides learned the benefits of defence, the lines had stabilized. Russia found itself defending a huge front that stretched from the Baltic to the Rumanian border. Later in 1914 Turkey joined the Austro-German alliance, adding another theatre of operations in the northern Caucasus. The stage was set for the war of attrition that would take so many lives.

THE WAR NATURALLY affected Fabergé's business. Veterans of previous crises opined that, once the first shock was past, people would be more anxious than ever to put their money into jewellery. Its value and portability made it highly desirable in times of trouble, and increased government spending meant that there was sure to be money around to pay for it. Nevertheless the immediate impact of the uncertainty and accompanying austerity was that orders almost entirely ceased. Fabergé made proposals to the War Ministry as to how his workshops might be adapted to the production of munitions, but for over a year he received no reply. It was one small example of the inefficiency being duplicated thousands of times across the empire. Once again the tsarist bureaucracy was proving itself incapable of adapting to circumstance. In the meantime Fabergé did his best to keep his workmen employed, making cheaper items out of copper and other low-value materials.

In 1915 the Russian authorities directed Fabergé to close its London branch; all available capital overseas was to be repatriated for use in the war effort. Here at least the Imperial family led the way, as Nicholas closed his overseas bank accounts and brought the money home. At the beginning of his reign his personal investments in Great Britain and the other Allied states had provided an income of up to 6,500,000 roubles (£650,000, £40 million), a significant percentage of the Tsar's total requirements, but that was not to be thought of now. He had to cut back and be seen to do so. In 1913, for example, Nicholas's personal expenses for the year had come to almost 11,000 roubles (£1,100, £72,000); by 1916 they had fallen to less than a fifth of their pre-war figure.

Even these reductions, however, represent a very relative concept of austerity. Before the war the life of a Russian peasant or unskilled worker had been pretty grim; now shortages and inflation made it even worse. Those unfortunate enough to be drafted into the army suffered most – from the combination of institutionalized incompetence and authoritarian rigidity. Everything had been planned in expectation of a short conflict: a six-week war, over well before Christmas. When it developed into attritional stalemate, Nicholas's regime was simply unable to cope. By the time Christmas finally came, conscripts were being sent to the trenches without guns, ammunition, or even shoes. Once there, they found themselves freezing, in trenches that were deep enough to flood but too shallow to provide any real protection from the German artillery, commanded by officers whose stupidity was exceeded only by the brutality they showed to their own men.

The Tsar saw little of the true situation. On his visits to the front whole regiments would be denuded of clothing and equipment so that he could be shown a battalion in good spirits. Nevertheless, it remains faintly surprising that he did not consider cancelling the following year's Easter delivery from Fabergé. To be sure, he spent less: in 1914 Fabergé's two Easter

eggs cost a total of 59,452 roubles (£5,900, £380,000) while for
the following year's two eggs Nicholas paid just 3,559 roubles
(£360, £19,000). Yet in 1904 the Russo-Japanese war had been
a good enough reason for the court to suspend its Easter order,
and this time around the fighting was on an altogether vaster
scale.

The decision to continue with the annual commission may
be just one more example of how the gulf between the Tsar and
his subjects had grown over the previous decade. With no real
conception of the living conditions endured by most Russians,
he may have considered the cutback in cost enough of a con-
cession. It may show too the extent to which Fabergé's eggs were
no longer seen as items of discretionary spending; they had
become an integral part of the Imperial family's Easter celebrations. And there may be a personal aspect to the 1915 order as
well: Alexandra, despite her German ancestry and connections,
was doing her best to contribute to the war effort. Easter gave
Nicholas the opportunity to show that he appreciated and
understood the sacrifices she was making.

The eggs the two Tsarinas received in 1915 are simple: they
carry little more decoration than an enamelled red cross on a
white background, but by doing so they highlight the main way
in which the Romanov women were helping the empire in its
time of need. Marie Fedorovna had a longstanding connection
with the Red Cross, and had been its Russian president since the
beginning of her husband's reign. Her refusal to cede the post
to her daughter-in-law on Nicholas's accession had been only
one of the many causes of bitterness between them. Eventually,
however, Alexandra had put rancour aside and sent a lady-in-
waiting to ask Marie if she might lend her own support to the
charity. The Dowager Empress had consented at once and 'with
great pleasure', telling the envoy somewhat disingenuously that
Alexandra had '"splendid ideas. But she never tells me what she
does or expects to do . . . I shall be very glad if she will only
drop her reserve."'[1]

With the outbreak of war Alexandra stepped up her commitment to the organization. By the end of 1914 she was patron of no fewer than eighty-five hospitals in the Petrograd area alone. And she went further than that. Together with her two eldest daughters and her best friend, Anna Vyrubova, Alexandra enrolled as a nurse. Within two weeks she was comforting the wounded, washing open sores and even attending amputations. The certificate she received after two months' training gave her a feeling of genuine pride. For perhaps the first time in her life she felt useful.

So Alexandra would have been pleased by the miniature portraits of herself, Olga and Tatiana dressed in their nursing uniforms, that the *Red Cross Triptych Egg* bore in addition to its red cross. Its surprise too would have appealed to her religious nature. The egg opens vertically down its middle, so that two quarters swing out on hinges that attach them to a central half, revealing a triptych of powerful painted icons. Representations of two appropriate Orthodox saints – Olga and Tatiana – flank a central panel that depicts the Harrowing of Hell. The victorious Messiah has just broken down the gates of Hades; he stands astride them and grasps Adam by his right hand. Orthodox artists had been representing the Resurrection with this image for centuries, but now it held a particular poignancy for the Tsarina. Russia, her adopted home, was going through a hell that she was witnessing daily. Her faith promised her, however, that salvation was at hand.

Aged sixty-six at the outbreak of the war, Marie was too old to enrol as a nurse, but her *Red Cross Portraits Egg* still has echoes of Alexandra's. The surprise within it is a folding screen showing pictures of the five members of the royal family by then working as Red Cross nurses: not just Alexandra and her two daughters, but also Marie's younger daughter, Olga, and her niece, the Grand Duchess Marie Pavlovna. Around the outside of the egg a quote from St John's Gospel captures the spirit in which they had all been led to volunteer: 'Greater love hath no man than this, that a man lay down his life for his comrades.'

For the first time Fabergé had produced eggs for the two Tsarinas which might be thought of as companion pieces. This was not, however, evidence that under the pressure of war the two women were finally burying their differences or coming to understand each other. Even Alexandra's activities for the Red Cross did not meet with universal approval. As an inexpert nurse, she could only do so much; surely the Empress would have been better employed in a more public role, boosting morale across whole sections of society. Alexandra, however, remained as shy and reserved as ever. Aged forty-two, she was no more capable of delivering a tub-thumping oration than she had been as a newly married Tsarina twenty years before.

A FEW WEEKS after Easter the entire Russian front collapsed under the great German spring offensive of 1915. With continuing shortages of equipment, led by generals whose tactics had hardly moved on from the cavalry charges of the nineteenth century and composed largely of untrained reservists, Nicholas's army could not respond to the massive firepower and flexible logistics of the German military machine. By July his high command had no choice but to order a general withdrawal. Territory could be sacrificed but the army must be saved.

It was at this point that Nicholas took the fateful decision to assume direct command of the army himself. He was not so vain as to assume that he had suddenly become a gifted military strategist – his chief of staff, General Michael Vasilevitch Alexeiev, would make all the key decisions – but Nicholas persuaded himself that the place for a tsar was at the front with his men. He was acting against the advice of all his ministers, who were aghast at the idea that the head of state should absent himself to army headquarters, hundreds of miles from the seat of government. 'The decision you have taken,' the Council of Ministers warned, 'threatens Russia, You, and Your dynasty with the gravest consequences.' Alexandra, however, was ecstatic.

Resenting the prestige accorded to Grand Duke Nicholas Nikolaevitch as commander-in-chief, she had convinced herself that
he was plotting to undermine her husband. Now the Emperor, at
the head of his army, could be the true, magnificent autocrat.
That autumn, as rain and mud finally brought the German
advance to a halt, he could even bask in the illusion of success.

Russia's heartland was for the time being preserved, but the
empire had received a shattering blow. Poland and the lower
Baltic states had been overrun, and the army had lost more
than half its strength – 1.4 million men killed or wounded
and 976,000 taken prisoner. Russia's greatest resource was its
supply of manpower, but it had never expected to deal with
demands on this scale. By the end of the war fifteen million men
would have been called up – 10 per cent of the empire's entire
population. Even at the beginning of 1915 the state had begun
to call on the second levy of reserves – untrained men in their
thirties who had completed their national service more than
seven years before. Fields were left untilled and businesses
denuded of their staff.

Fabergé felt the effects as badly as any employer. He pleaded
with the authorities to exempt twenty-three specific employees
from conscription – one was so vital that if he left the workshop
would have 'to be closed down'; another was 'the only experienced master in enamel technique remaining, who trained for
such work for eight years'.[2] At around the same time and with
particularly bad timing, the War Ministry finally responded to
Fabergé's suggestions from a year before and placed orders for
munitions. Nevertheless, the Moscow silver factory was converted into a manufacturer of hand grenades and casings for
artillery shells, while the workshops in St Petersburg turned out
a host of smaller items, such as syringes.

NICHOLAS'S NEW ROLE as commander-in-chief meant that he
spent much of 1916 at army headquarters in Mogilev, about
500 miles south of St Petersburg. For the first time in his

marriage he was not with Alexandra for Easter. At Mogilev, according to Sir John Hanbury-Williams, there as British attaché representing one of Russia's main allies, it was a 'perfectly beautiful'[3] morning. The Tsar presented all the members of his suite, and the diplomats attached to it, with 'china Easter eggs made by Fabergé'. This attribution, again by Hanbury-Williams, is clearly mistaken; china was one of the few materials that never featured in Fabergé's output. The error itself is an indication of the extent to which Easter eggs and Fabergé had by then become almost synonymous, at least to a casual observer.

In Petrograd, meanwhile, Carl and Eugène Fabergé, father and son, delivered Imperial eggs on Nicholas's behalf to the two Tsarinas. Both, not surprisingly, had a militaristic feel. Marie Fedorovna's egg commemorated the award to Nicholas, in October 1915, of the Cross of St George, fourth class. The classification is not as insulting as it may sound. This was almost always how the cross was initially awarded – and only on the recommendation of the army – for courage in the field of battle. Promotion to higher degrees came with further acts of bravery. Only the Emperor himself was able to grant the first two orders of St George, and Nicholas was always punctilious about not rewarding himself with honours. Even as supreme commander-in-chief of the Russian army he persisted in wearing the colonel's uniform that reflected the rank he held on his father's death. Strictly speaking, as he himself pointed out, Nicholas had not performed any act of bravery that would qualify him even for the fourth-class cross he had been awarded. He knew he was being flattered. Nevertheless, he accepted the honour with pride, recording in his diary that he 'walked around the entire day in a daze'.[4]

Marie's *Cross of St George Egg* reflects the continued austerity of wartime. It is made of silver, enamelled white and decorated with small St George crosses and a trellis of pale green leaves. On one side a white and red enamel badge of the Order of St George is suspended from a ribbon enamelled in the order's gold, red and black. When a button is pressed, the badge hinges upwards to reveal a portrait of the Tsar. On the opposite side a medal of the order, similarly fastened, hides a picture of the Tsarevitch. A week before his father he had received the medal of St George, also fourth class, for 'visiting the armies of the South West front, which were close to enemy positions'.

Alexis was spending long periods at headquarters with his father, interrupted only by a lengthy gap when another bleeding episode brought him close to death. Emperor and heir shared a room, with Nicholas frequently having to act as nurse to his invalid son. When well, Alexis continued his schooling with the two tutors who accompanied him, found occasional overawed playmates and charmed everyone around him. He might have been brought up in a way almost guaranteed to foster petulance, but despite all the odds Alexis – now eleven – was turning into 'a most happy natured attractive little fellow'.[5] The Tsarevitch's appearance with his father at a military review or hospital bedside could be guaranteed to cheer all the soldiers who saw him; while his private's uniform (he was promoted to lance corporal in May 1916) implied that he was, in some way, one of them.

The *Steel Military Egg* that Fabergé made for Alexandra in 1916 was even more explicit than her mother-in-law's *Cross of St George Egg* about Alexis's role as companion to his father. Its surprise is a miniature painting set on an easel, which shows Nicholas and his son poring over maps with a group of senior officers. A plume of smoke rises in the distance – they are close to the front. Not only does the picture show a very different scene from the careful portraits of previous eggs, but its autumnal hues depict a mood that is all too appropriate for a country that could see no end to the gloom of war. The egg itself reinforced this impression. Made of dull blackened steel and with minimal decoration, it was supported by four small artillery shells fixed in a sombre green nephrite base.

Some of the austere effect, however, was lost not long after the egg was delivered. An effort to polish off rust left the egg and shells burnished and gleaming. As a result many writers now regard it as a piece of kitsch, symbolic of the breakdown in Russian society as Fabergé, deprived of all his best craftsmen, struggled to come to terms with his annual commission. Nevertheless, there is no denying the egg's power to evoke the grimness of the times. It was as far removed from the grandeur and frivolity of its pre-war predecessors as Petrograd was from St Petersburg. It would be the last Fabergé egg that Alexandra received, but it was a worthy finale.

BOTH MARIE and Alexandra wrote to thank Nicholas for their Easter presents. The Dowager Empress's letter begins ebulliently in celebration of a recent Russian victory: 'Hurrah for Trebizond,'* and goes on: 'Christ has indeed risen! I kiss you three times and thank you with all my heart for your dear cards and lovely egg with miniatures which dear old Fabergé brought himself.'⁶ Alexandra, in her telegram after Easter, was equally enthusiastic: 'Fabergé has just brought your delightful egg for which I thank you a thousand times. The miniature group is marvellous and all the portraits are excellent.'⁷

In fact, neither letter is typical of the relationship between Nicholas and the writer. Marie Fedorovna was becoming an increasingly intermittent correspondent. She disapproved of much that her son and his wife were now doing, but she was powerless to change their course. Soon, to emphasize her separation from Nicholas and his court, she would move to Kiev, capital of the Ukraine, where her youngest daughter Olga was working as a nurse. Alexandra, by contrast, exchanged letters and telegrams with her husband at least daily. Their tone was always affectionate, even passionate; she was 'your old wify' while Nicholas was any variation of 'my own sweet beloved darling'. By Easter 1916, however, there was an added note

---

* A Turkish city on the shores of the Black Sea that Russian forces had recently occupied.

of stridency within the stream of consciousness that characterized Alexandra's correspondence, as her letters increasingly
contained advice about military strategy and requests, even
demands, for ministerial changes.

The contents of Alexandra's letters were an indication of
her new importance within government – an inevitable corollary
of the Tsar's absence. The personal nature of Nicholas's rule
was such that he had to leave behind a deputy as his eyes and
ears in the capital. That person could only be Alexandra.
Explicitly empowered by her husband, she fell into her new
role with enthusiasm, meeting ministers, receiving their reports
and watching them for signs of disloyalty. The resulting advice
was capricious – ministers fell in and out of favour almost
on a whim – but her husband rarely ignored it. In the sixteen
months before the end of 1916 Russia had four prime ministers,
five ministers of the interior, four ministers of agriculture and
three ministers of war. New appointees scarcely had time to
master their departments before being moved on; competence
was rewarded with dismissal. The empire was facing its greatest
crisis since Napoleon entered Moscow and its government was in
a state of self-induced paralysis.

If Alexandra's actions are hard to understand for us, for contemporary Russians they were harder still to forgive. Whether
her behaviour was evidence of treachery – her German roots
making themselves felt – or just inexperience, it could not be
allowed to continue. By the end of 1916 the salons of Petrograd
buzzed with rumours: Alexandra would be arrested and Nicholas
forced to abdicate in favour of his son or brother, or the Grand
Duke Nicholas Nikolaevitch, his former commander-in-chief.
Alexandra would be sent abroad or to Livadia, or into a nun-
nery. There were too many conspiracies with too little sense of
urgency for any to come to fruition. In any case, for most the
idea of plotting against the Tsar or even his wife was too awful
to contemplate. Instead, there was an easier target – Gregory
Rasputin.

The war had opened with Rasputin away from St Petersburg. During a visit to his home in Siberia he had been accosted by a woman who drove a knife into his stomach. On the same day, in Sarajevo, the Archduke Ferdinand of Austria had been assassinated, starting the chain of events that led to the declaration of war. Rasputin was rather luckier, managing to fend off further blows and crawl back to his house. His eventual full recovery only added to the supernatural aura that surrounded him. Nevertheless, in the weeks leading up to the war he had been stuck in Siberia, hardly listened to as he called for peace. By 1915, however, he was back in Petrograd. His belief in the spiritual union between the Tsar and his people had been at the core of Alexandra's insistence that her husband should assume direct command of the army. Now Rasputin's influence on the Empress was practically unlimited. By Alexandra's own frequent admission, much of the advice contained in her letters to her husband sprang from the mystical counsel of 'Our Friend'. She even persuaded Nicholas to use Rasputin's comb to bolster his confidence before meetings with ministers.

Nicholas attempted to retain some sense of proportion. A comment attributed to him at the time may be apocryphal but it probably captures something of the truth: 'I would rather put up with this man than have to endure five attacks of hysterics a day.'[8] Nevertheless, he found it hard to resist his strong-willed wife. A Siberian peasant was having a direct impact on policy and the disastrous consequences were there for all to see. As popular discontent with Rasputin's position grew, the rumours about his relationship with the Empress grew ever more lurid. Even a film showing the Emperor receiving the St George Cross had to be withdrawn from circulation. As soon as the sequence started, a voice would pipe up in the auditorium, 'Little-father Tsar is with Georgie, little-mother with Gregory.'[9] Meanwhile, Rasputin himself continued to live in modest lodgings, watched but not protected by the secret police. He was a hate object for most of Petrograd and he was vulnerable.

The plot to kill the *staretz* had an unlikely ringleader. Prince Felix Yussupov was heir to the greatest fortune in Russia. His family's Moika Palace in Petrograd was a byword for elegant ostentation. Even the Grand Duchess Olga, Nicholas's sister, had been struck as a child by its 'drawing-rooms and tables crammed with crystal bowls filled with uncut sapphires, emeralds, and opals – all used as decorations'.[10] For their twenty-fifth wedding anniversary the prince's father had given his famously beautiful wife a Fabergé egg of appropriate magnificence. Prince Felix himself had a reputation for both wildness and effeteness, which he had to work hard to overcome before being allowed to marry the Princess Irina, daughter of the Grand Duchess Xenia and niece to the Tsar. He is hard to imagine as a man of action or a revolutionary. Nevertheless, convinced that Rasputin must die, by the end of 1916 he had gathered around him others of the same view, notably a member of the Imperial family, Nicholas's cousin the Grand Duke Dmitry Pavlovitch.

On the evening of 16 December 1916 Felix brought Rasputin to his basement flat in the Moika Palace. The mystic was expecting to meet the Princess Irina and had dressed to impress in an embroidered silk blouse with new velvet breeches and boots. The smell of cheap soap hung about him. In the flat Felix explained that Irina would be coming down shortly and offered his guest cakes while he waited. Each contained enough cyanide, according to the supplier, 'to kill several men instantly'. Rasputin at first refused: 'I don't want any; they're too sweet,' but then took two. There was no effect. Felix persuaded him to drink some Madeira, laced with more poison. Again Rasputin complained of nothing more than a tickling in his throat. Then his eyes lit on Felix's guitar. 'Play something cheerful; I like listening to your singing.'

The macabre scene only ended when Felix, increasingly desperate, fled upstairs to consult with his three fellow conspirators. He returned with Dmitry's revolver. After persuading Rasputin to face a crucifix, he shot him in the heart. His companions came rushing down, confirmed that the *staretz* was dead, wrapped his body in a bearskin rug and went upstairs to plan their next step. Then Felix, filled with a sense of foreboding, went back down to the basement.

> Rasputin lay exactly where we had left him. I felt his pulse: not a beat, he was dead.
>
> Scarcely knowing what I was doing I seized the corpse by the arms and shook it violently. It leaned to one side and fell back. I was just about to go, when I suddenly noticed an almost imperceptible quivering of his left eyelid. I bent over and watched him closely; slight tremors contracted his face.
>
> All of a sudden, I saw the left eye open . . . A few seconds later his right eyelid began to quiver, then opened. I then saw both eyes – the green eyes of a viper – staring at me with an expression of diabolical hatred.[11]

Rooted to the floor, Felix watched Rasputin leap to his feet, foaming at the mouth. 'A wild roar echoed through the vaulted rooms, and his hands convulsively thrashed the air. He rushed at me, trying to get at my throat, and sank his fingers into my shoulder like steel claws. His eyes were bursting from their sockets, blood oozed from his lips. And all the time he called me by name, in a low raucous voice.'

Felix tore himself away and ran upstairs for help, with Rasputin following on hands and knees, 'roaring like a wounded animal'. It took four more shots, fired by a fellow conspirator, to bring the injured man to a halt as he staggered towards the palace's courtyard gates. Even then, Felix, an unlikely berserker, pummelled the *staretz* with a rubber club until certain that he moved no more. Finally his companions gathered up the body and carried it off to the river Neva, where they pushed it through a hole in the ice. When it was recovered three days later a post-mortem found water in the lungs: poisoned, shot and beaten, Rasputin had died by drowning.

12. 'Everything seems sad'

Inconsolable in her grief, Alexandra arranged for Rasputin to be buried in a corner of the Imperial park at Tsarskoe Selo and demanded that his murderers, who had already been identified, be brought to justice. Nicholas may have been more ambivalent: at least one witness declared that he was in 'especially high spirits'[1] when news of the *staretz*'s disappearance first came through to headquarters. On his return to Petrograd for Christmas, moreover, delegations of his relatives came to plead for clemency for the plotters, culminating in a group letter from several members of the Imperial family. Nicholas's response, however, was unequivocal: 'No one has the right to commit murder. I know that many are troubled by their consciences and that Dmitry Pavlovitch is not the only one implicated in this.'[2] It was enough to deepen still further the rift between Nicholas and the rest of his family. Nevertheless, Prince Felix and Grand Duke Dmitry suffered relatively little for their bloody crime. Nicholas limited their punishment to exile from Petrograd; even that, as events turned out, proved to be a very temporary stricture.

Rasputin's killers had hoped that, freed from the influence of the *staretz*, the Tsar might grasp the reins of political power and stabilize his government. They were not alone. While Nicholas was in Petrograd a range of friendly critics, from the British ambassador to the speaker of the Duma, attempted to persuade him that the continuation of his reign depended on him making liberal concessions and appointing a strong cabinet. Nicholas responded with a mixture of arrogance – 'Do you mean that I am to regain the confidence of my people, or that they are to regain *my* confidence?'³ – and listlessness. Vladimir Kokovtsov, his pre-war prime minister, was shocked when he visited him at the Alexander Palace for the first time in a year. There was 'the same doorman at the entrance, evidently glad to see me again; the same courier who conducted me to the reception room; the same guards at the doors; the same books and albums on the table'.⁴ The Tsar, however, had changed alarmingly: 'His face had become very thin and hollow and covered with small wrinkles. His eyes, usually of a velvety dark brown, had become quite faded, and wandered aimlessly from object to object instead of looking steadily at his interlocutor.' Nicholas was as determined as ever that the autocracy should continue, yet he seemed scarcely capable of making the most basic decisions, let alone determining the destinies of 150 million people.

Meanwhile, what remained of Nicholas's personal prestige had already been substantially weakened by his decision to take command of the army. In the summer of 1916 the Russians had broken through into Austria with an offensive that might have changed the whole course of the war. Within weeks, however, the attack had ground to a halt, stopped not by the Austrians but by turf wars within Russia's high command that Nicholas's presence at headquarters had done nothing to prevent. Later in the year Rumania had finally entered the war as Russia's ally, but the diplomatic coup had turned into military catastrophe when the Balkan state neglected its defences and was overrun by German forces. As commander-in-chief, Nicholas could hardly avoid responsibility for the disaster. Even as a figurehead, he had little to show for his eighteen months in charge. Morale had continued to plummet. Troops deserted back to their villages deep in the interior or surrendered to the enemy, reasoning that life as a prisoner of war was preferable to that of a Russian soldier.

Whether Nicholas was blind to the situation, or fatalistic in his response to it, he was clearly going to do nothing to stop the rot. It was only a matter of time before he would be deposed;

the only question was how. Would his cousins persuade him to go? Would the bureaucracy revolt against the incompetence of the government it served? Would the army lead a coup d'état? Or would a German victory finally seal his fate?

IN SUCH a febrile atmosphere even Carl Fabergé could come under suspicion. He might have spent the last thirty-five years receiving ever greater recognition from the Imperial Court, but for the authorities his foreign antecedents and friendships meant that he was essentially untrustworthy. A letter recently discovered in the Russian State Historical Archives shows him complaining of how 'Everything seems sad. From time to time I am visited by a few remaining friends in the evenings, but most of the others have either been sent abroad or banished as prisoners of war.'5 The letter is in the archives because it had been intercepted and filed by the authorities. Fabergé was not just under suspicion, he was under surveillance. Although for the time being he remained personally immune, his companion Nina Tsitsianova was not so lucky. In 1916 her Austrian nationality marked her out as a possible spy. Carl tried to vouch for her, but it was no use. In the opinion of the investigators, he 'was a long way from being an individual on whose statements the military authorities could have total confidence'. Tsitsianova was sent under police escort to Yakutsk in eastern Siberia, one of the coldest cities on earth. As for what became of her there, the records are silent.

Fabergé started to prepare for the inevitable crisis. At the end of 1916 he turned the firm he had inherited from his father into a joint stock partnership – C. Fabergé – with a fixed capital of three million roubles. Four 'partners' ended up with about 10 per cent of the company between them, a few other employees received a single share each, and Carl allotted 5 per cent of the company to each of his four sons. The rest of the shares – by far the majority of the company – remained in the hands of the patriarch himself. He might be seventy, but this was no time for him to relinquish control. In that sense the incorporation was largely cosmetic, but the coincidence of the move with the escalating crisis in Petrograd is hard to ignore. By turning the business that bore his name into a properly constituted company, Fabergé may have been hoping to preserve it from the cataclysm to come.

THE RUSSIAN REVOLUTION started on the streets of Petrograd. It was not worry about the war or desire for a more liberal government or disgust with the Tsar that brought the proletariat onto the streets: it was hunger. The war had placed huge demands on Russia's railway system; pressure on rolling stock had led to shortages of flour and fuel in the capital. Petrograd was running out of bread.

Events started to gather pace on 23 February 1917, when warmer weather encouraged the inhabitants of Petrograd to come out from their homes for the first time in weeks. Many were simply hoping to find bread wherever they could; others wanted to vent their anger. It happened to be International Women's Day, and to mark it crowds of women from all social classes converged on the centre of Petrograd, marching for their rights. They were joined by striking textile workers, protesting against the shortages. Men in nearby factories downed tools. Gradually, the demonstrations built their own momentum. Ill-trained Cossacks proved unable to keep control. The next day the strikes had spread and the mob had grown. By 25 February all Petrograd's most important factories were shut, 200,000 demonstrators were on the streets and cries of 'Down with the Tsar!' were beginning to be heard.

Even at this stage a softly, softly approach avoiding provocation might have defused the situation. There was no political leadership to the uprising; the crowds had gathered spontaneously; they would have eventually dispersed. Nicholas, however, had returned to Mogilev a few days before. With no idea of the atmosphere in his capital he had only his autocratic instincts to guide him. On the evening of 25 February he sent a cable to the chief of the Petrograd military district, ordering him to use force to 'put down the disorders by tomorrow'. Overnight, the government set up checkpoints at every major street intersection. When marchers once again appeared late the following morning, on their way towards the city centre, the troops – at first – obeyed their orders and fired at the crowd. In one incident alone over fifty demonstrators were killed.

This time, however, the tactics of 1905 would not work. War had destroyed the morale of the Petrograd garrison. Veterans had seen the results of the regime's incompetence at first hand: ammunition never delivered to front-line troops but abandoned to the enemy in the general retreat of 1915; equipment sold by corrupt quartermasters; tactical blunders of monumental stupidity. And their newly conscripted colleagues saw no reason to kill fellow peasants and factory workers. Over the course of two or three days every regiment in Petrograd mutinied. Prisoners were freed, policemen murdered and tsarist officials hunted down. The city descended into mob rule.

It was not until the evening of 27 February, when his entire government resigned, that Nicholas, still at Mogilev, finally began to understand the gravity of the situation. On the same night he set out for Petrograd, not so much to take charge of the situation as to be with his family at Tsarskoe Selo. Alexandra's most recent letters and telegrams had told him that the children were suffering from measles – Alexis had a fever of 104° – but he had no idea whether the garrisons guarding the Alexander Palace had also mutinied. Who could say what danger his family was in?

Nicholas's train home got no further than Pskov, headquarters of Russia's Northern Army; the line on from there to Petrograd was blocked by workers turned revolutionaries. Here on 2 March 1917 the Tsar heard from the president of the Duma that it was now too late for liberal concessions; only a complete change of government including his own abdication could possibly restore calm on the streets of Petrograd. Here too he read the unequivocal advice of every general, telegrammed to the Imperial train: if he attempted to remain Tsar, the best he could hope for was civil war, the worst, full-scale mutiny and a German victory. He was separated from his family and accompanied by only a few advisers. That afternoon he announced his decision: 'I have made up my mind. I have decided to abdicate from the throne in favour of my son Alexis.'

The same evening Nicholas performed one last about-turn as Tsar. Having abdicated, he would never be allowed to remain as an influence over his successor. The prospect of separation from his invalid son, who might only live a few more years, was intolerable. It was a decision that, constitutionally, he had no right to make, but no one made more than a token objection: Nicholas would renounce the throne not just for himself but for Alexis as well. His brother Michael had returned to Russia at the beginning of the war. He was now thirty-eight; the studied impetuosity of his morganatic marriage had been forgiven if not forgotten; he could be Tsar.

The Grand Duke had other ideas. Meeting a delegation from the Duma the following morning, he asked its president for a guarantee of his personal safety if he became Tsar. When no such promise could be made, Michael declined to accept the throne. The Romanov dynasty had come to an end.

Meanwhile, Nicholas had at least heard from Alexandra that she and the children were safe. He returned to Mogilev to say goodbye to the same generals who had forced him to abdicate. There he was met by Marie Fedorovna, who travelled up from Kiev for a rendezvous at the railway station. The defiance of her move from Petrograd was forgotten as mother and son attempted to come to terms with their changed situation. Although Marie had been predicting some kind of disaster since before the war, her son's abdication was still an extraordinary shock. It was the phlegmatic and unemotional Nicholas who found himself in the role of consoler.

The ex-Emperor and his mother spent three days together, dining in Marie's railway car after long afternoon drives. It was a curious and exceptional interlude, brought to an end when representatives of the Duma arrived to arrest Nicholas and take him back to Tsarskoe Selo. He left Marie's carriage and crossed the platform to his own train, from which, with the cross of St George in his buttonhole, he waved goodbye to his mother. Then her train too steamed from the station, heading in the opposite direction back towards Kiev.

NICHOLAS WAS escorted back to Tsarskoe Selo by members of Russia's self-christened Provisional Government. So named to emphasize its intention to call full elections as soon as possible, this administration had no constitutional authority and had been hastily established in a largely successful attempt to restore order to the streets of Petrograd. Its leaders were liberal politicians – mainly members of the Duma; the new prime minister, Prince Lvov, had been a provincial administrator. Drawn from the middle and upper classes, these men had little in common with the demonstrators and rioters who had brought about the collapse of the previous regime.

From the beginning, therefore, the Provisional Government's existence depended entirely on the occasional cooperation of the other institution brought to prominence by the February Revolution, the Petrograd Workers' Committee or Soviet. This ad hoc council of workers' representatives was far from democratic and functioned as little more than a chaotic talking shop. Nevertheless, it carried weight with the proletariat, including, crucially, the rank and file of the army. Without the Petrograd Soviet's support, the Provisional Government was nothing. Outside Petrograd the situation was even more confused. Central authority had collapsed, to be replaced by a myriad of local administrations each in thrall to its own soviet. Here the capital had little influence and no control.

Nevertheless, the Provisional Government did its best to

exercise what power it had. Trusting in the 'good sense, states-manship, and loyalty of the peoples of Russia', it prepared for the country to become a model modern democracy. In the weeks following the fall of the Tsar Russians were granted a host of unprecedented freedoms. All the old tsarist restrictions on religion, class, race and the press were removed. Capital punishment was abolished; women were given the vote.

In one respect, however, the Provisional Government continued the policy of its autocratic predecessor: the war with Germany could not be abandoned. For the time being orders continued to flow to munitions suppliers, including Fabergé. There was demand too for the firm's jewellery. Now more than ever was the time for Russia's moneyed classes to transfer their wealth into something portable and easily traded. Business, despite all the uncertainty, continued.

One market for Fabergé's products, however, had vanished for ever. There would be no more orders from the Tsar. Work on that year's Easter eggs was abandoned. Soon enough the detailed designs had been lost and only memories remained of Fabergé's intentions. For Alexandra, a few remaining drawings suggested that he had been thinking of a night sky theme. And the egg for Marie Fedorovna, Eugène Fabergé later recalled to Henry Bainbridge, was made of wood – birch from the forests of Karelia between Russia and Finland. There was even a suggestion that this, at least, had been finished, but with the situation in Petrograd becoming increasingly chaotic both eggs disappeared. There would be no swansong. One of the greatest series of sustained creativity in the history of craftsmanship had come to an end.

13. 'Guard it well. It is the last'

THE ABSENCE of any egg from Fabergé for Easter 1917 was just one more reminder of the change in the Imperial family's circumstances. On 9 March the ex-Tsar had returned to the Alexander Palace to be challenged at the gate as 'Nicholas Romanov'. Once there, he and his family were confined to the palace, allowed few visitors and constantly watched by soldiers whose unkempt appearance and careful disrespect emphasized only too clearly the revolution that had taken place. Even walks in the surrounding park were strictly controlled. Every child, from the twelve-year-old Alexis to the twenty-one-year-old Olga, spent much of the early spring recuperating from the measles outbreak that had been the main subject of Nicholas's last communications from Alexandra while he was still Tsar. The transformation of the palace's nursery wing into a sick bay, all hushed voices and darkened rooms, can only have added to the overall gloom. Alexandra's unconventional treatment for the disease would leave every child with the shaved head of a convict – an all too appropriate resemblance.

In some respects the life of the Imperial family seemed remarkably untroubled. Visitors found servants still gliding through the rooms as noiselessly as ever, while for the first time since his accession to the throne Nicholas had free time. He got on with his reading, spent time with his children and followed the war's continuing disasters. Even without an egg from Fabergé, the ceremonies at Easter continued pretty much as they always had done, if on a smaller scale. The diary of one of Alexandra's ladies-in-waiting records a 'Grand, beautiful day, despite all human misery. Midnight Mass and morning reception in Their Majesties' apartments. The Emperor gave the prison guards the kiss of peace, and they were touched.' Later, Nicholas and Alexandra distributed 135 china eggs left over from previous Easters. 'The Emperor gave me one with his signature and said: "Guard it well. It is the last."'[1]

Nicholas was right. He could not continue to live much longer as a deposed emperor fifteen miles from his former capital. The Provisional Government's removal of press controls meant that he and his family were fair game for every newspaper with a scurrilous rumour to peddle, from details of the 'private lives' of the grand duchesses, as recounted by their fictitious 'lovers', to descriptions of the extravagant meals that supposedly continued to issue from the Alexander Palace kitchens. Most damaging of all were the stories of how 'Citizen Romanov' and 'Alexandra the German' were betraying their country to the Prussian foe in an effort to re-establish the monarchy. In the weeks following Nicholas's abdication public hatred of the ex-Tsar grew ever more pronounced.

The strength of the hostility caused immense problems for the Provisional Government and its minister of justice, Alexander Kerensky, who had responsibility for the Imperial family. This ambitious demagogue of uncertain ability was a crucial member of the administration from its inception and would eventually become its prime minister. It took Kerensky little time to determine that the allegations of Romanov treason were false, but that did not help him decide what should be done with the family. Public opinion would not allow them to remain in Tsarskoe Selo indefinitely. There was a real danger that the Petrograd mob, pacified for a time by the abdication, would again take matters into its own hands. Exile too was becoming an increasingly remote prospect. Not only would Kerensky's supporters baulk at the idea of the former tyrant enjoying a life of leisure overseas, it was not clear that any suitable country would actually be willing to take him in. The United Kingdom was an obvious refuge, but Nicholas's cousin and friend King George V had withdrawn an earlier invitation; he could not risk inflaming revolutionary sentiments at home.

The weakness of the Provisional Government undermined the Romanovs still further. In April, as Winston Churchill later put it, the Germans 'turned upon Russia the most grisly of all weapons. They transported Lenin in a sealed truck like a plague bacillus from Switzerland into Russia.'[2] On arriving back in Petrograd after twelve years in exile, the Bolsheviks' founder immediately called for an end to the war. Russia's proletariat, he said, had enemies enough at home among the bourgeoisie; its troops should be fraternizing with their German counterparts, not fighting them.

Initially Lenin's arguments were ridiculed, but as Russia's spring offensive began to go badly wrong their attraction increased. He was a masterful politician, combining inspirational oratory with a ruthless understanding of how to mobilize the masses. His fervour and brilliance soon revitalized the Bolshevik party within Russia and particularly Petrograd. It had done little to bring about the February Revolution but by the summer felt strong enough to make a bid for power from its base of trade union support. This July uprising was not successful; Lenin fled temporarily to Finland and several of his lieutenants, including Leon Trotsky, were arrested. It was nevertheless a sign of things to come. As Kerensky, by now prime minister, warned the ex-Tsar, 'The Bolsheviks are after me and then will be after you.'[3] Nicholas and his family had to leave the vicinity of Petrograd. In a few months' time, after the elections, when the government was no longer provisional, they might be able to return or finally go into exile.

The family began preparing for a destination that it hoped might be Livadia, the scene of so many happy pre-war memories. Towards the end of July, however, Kerensky returned to the palace to give notice of their departure within a few days and to tell them to take plenty of warm clothes. The Imperial family was not heading for the balmy climate of the Crimea, but to Siberia, Russia's traditional place of internal exile for centuries where winter temperatures fall to more than fifty degrees below zero. This was not an attempt to punish the Tsar – to make him suffer as his regime had made others suffer – rather, the choice had been dictated by expedience. Livadia was a thousand miles from Petrograd, along railway tracks controlled by local soviets who barely tolerated Kerensky and would relish the chance of getting their hands on 'Citizen Romanov'. The line to Siberia, by contrast, ran through sparsely populated territory, and its capital, Tobolsk, which had been selected by Kerensky as the family's final destination, remained a provincial backwater whose population probably still had some respect and sympathy for the ex-Tsar.

Alexandra took charge of the packing. Kerensky might be sending her family to Siberia, but it would at least have the use of the governor's mansion. She did what she could to ensure that their stay there would be comfortable. Packing cases were filled with appropriate and useful items: bed linen, dishes, storage jars and books to while away the winter evenings. Then there were the family keepsakes: remembrances of Alexandra's family back in Darmstadt and of her childhood holidays in Windsor, and reminders of her own children – photographs and the drawings they had made when little. By the evening of 31 July, when the family sat waiting for the cars that would take them to the train, they were surrounded by chests, with more piled up all around the palace. They had a long wait. Kerensky had told them to be ready by midnight, but had reckoned without the obstreperousness of the local railwaymen, who were unwilling to transport the Tsar. It was not until six the following morning that the parents and children, with all their retainers, finally boarded a train, clambering up from the ground into carriages placed out of sight of the station, several hundred yards from any platform.

The days before had been filled with leave-takings. Servants were given souvenirs by their former masters. Pierre Gilliard, the children's tutor, led his charges on farewell visits to places with special memories: an artificial island on one of the lakes dotted around the palace and, more prosaically, the kitchen garden. Nicholas offered emotional, but still formal, goodbyes to the courtiers being left behind. The Grand Duke Michael was brought to the palace for a final embarrassed exchange with the brother he had refused to succeed.

For Alexandra the move was yet one more break with the past. Her closest friends had already been arrested and taken away – Anna Vyrubova had been in prison for months – now it was Alexandra's turn to quit the palace that had been her home for twenty years.

Did the former Empress consider taking any of her Fabergé eggs with her? The royal family took huge quantities of jewellery to Siberia: at least £100,000 (£4 million) in precious stones, enough to bankroll an escape attempt or to fund some sort of life abroad. But the value of the eggs had never lain in their materials; beautifully worked enamel counted for little now. They were bulky and difficult to conceal. As mementos too they compared unfavourably to simpler items such as photographs or letters. They simply were not appropriate accompaniments to a life in internal exile. When Alexandra left Tsarskoe Selo, she did not take a single one of her Easter presents with her. The eggs remained where they had always been displayed – in her mauve sitting room at the Alexander Palace and in her yellow study at the Winter Palace.

AT FIRST the Imperial captives did not find life in Tobolsk particularly harsh. The governor's mansion was redecorated for them on arrival; they occupied the entire first floor and had the use of the rest of the house and a small kitchen garden. The courtiers who still attended them lived in a house across the road. Servants lodged elsewhere in the town: no fewer than thirty had followed their masters from Tsarskoe Selo, including a barber and ten footmen.

October 1917 brought the first hint of troubles to come, when plummeting temperatures revealed the inadequacies of the mansion's heating system. Nevertheless the family kept its spirits up and the children's education continued. Pierre Gilliard had come with them on the train from Tsarskoe Selo, and was soon joined by the Tsarevitch's English tutor, Sidney Gibbes; their parents also took responsibility for some lessons. In the evening Nicholas would read aloud – Turgenev was a particular favourite – while Alexandra played bezique with a courtier. With the approach of Christmas, Gilliard and Gibbes directed members of the family in scenes from plays as entertainment for both themselves and those they could persuade to watch.

Even in isolated Tobolsk, however, news was trickling through of events in Petrograd. On 25 October Kerensky's government had fallen in an almost bloodless coup d'état. Lenin and his Bolsheviks had not only recovered from their failed attempt to take power in July, they now controlled the capital. The most symbolic moment of what came to be called the October Revolution – the storming of the Winter Palace – had resulted in the arrest of almost every minister in the Provisional Government. Only Kerensky himself was nowhere to be found; he had left Petrograd in a vain attempt to garner support among the troops stationed outside.

Lenin's timing was impeccable. The Bolsheviks would never have won more than a few seats in the full elections due at the beginning of 1918. By pre-empting the vote, Lenin had wrong-footed Petrograd's more democratically minded politicians and forestalled any attempt to establish a legitimately elected government, while taking full advantage of the disillusion created by Kerensky's vacillations. Over the next few weeks, while the Bolsheviks' opponents waited for a government with so little popular support to fail, Lenin tightened his grip on power. In Petrograd this meant breaking the resistance of the civil service, which had hardly been touched by the Provisional Government, so that its members understood they now did the bidding of the Bolsheviks. In the country, by contrast, Lenin's plan called for devolution of control to local soviets, which could then be gradually 'Bolshevized'. By February 1918 the process had reached Tobolsk.

The regime in Tobolsk was tightened. New guards arrived to replace the mostly friendly soldiers who had accompanied the family from Tsarskoe Selo. Thoroughly imbued with the revolutionary spirit, they were, according to Gilliard, 'a pack of blackguardly-looking young men' who took every opportunity to make the lives of their prisoners more unpleasant. Soon one of the family's few remaining diversions was denied to them. Nicholas and members of his suite had built a 'snow mountain' in their small courtyard to provide winter amusement to the younger children, who were becoming consumed with boredom. When he and Alexandra climbed it to wave off the guards who were being replaced, the self-appointed soldiers' committee decreed that they had exposed themselves to the risk of assassination. The snow mountain was broken up. Even the soldiers doing the work looked hangdog, 'for they felt it was a mean task'.[4]

A few days before that, on 23 February,* a telegram had arrived from the Bolshevik government: 'Nicholas Romanov and his family must be put on soldiers' rations and . . . each member of the family . . . receive 600 roubles per month drawn from the interest of their personal estate.' The ex-Tsar's ironic response was that 'since everyone is appointing committees'[5] he would create one to deal with the matter of his family's budget. Ten servants had to be dismissed; butter and coffee were taken off the menu. It was a sign of things to come.

---

* One of the Bolshevik government's early acts, which came into force in February 1918, was to bring the Russian calendar into line with the West's, skipping straight from 31 January to 14 February. All dates after this date will therefore be expressed in the new style.

The approach of Easter provided one possible pastime. With no prospect of anything from Fabergé, or even the Imperial porcelain works, the family busied themselves painting their own icons and decorating hens' eggs, although even these now had to be donated by sympathetic townspeople. Easter's message of redemption also gave Alexandra, as deeply religious as ever, a reason to hope. As she wrote to her friend Anna Vyrubova, by now out of prison, 'the King of Glory will come and will save, strengthen, and give wisdom to the people who are now deceived'.[6]

Alexandra's hopes were futile. By Easter itself, 5 May 1918, she and Nicholas, together with their third daughter Maria, now aged eighteen, were in the ominously named House of Special Purpose* in Ekaterinburg, a factory city in the Urals. An envoy had arrived in Tobolsk to take the whole family to Moscow, newly established by Lenin as his capital, where Nicholas was to be the central figure in a grand show trial. Alexis, however, had recently suffered another haemorrhage and he was too ill to travel. The family had to be separated. Alexandra had agonized over who needed her more – her husband or her sick son – but eventually chose Nicholas. He had been forced to abdicate, she reasoned, without her at his side; he could not be allowed to go to Moscow alone. The capable Maria had come to provide them both with moral support. As things turned out, however, the party never made it to Moscow. Ekaterinburg was on the railway line to the capital. The casual brutality of the Tsar's regime and the deprivations of the war had left its inhabitants with little sympathy for Nicholas and his family. Once he had fallen into the hands of the local soviet, it refused to let him go any further.

In the month that they were apart the two halves of the family managed to keep in touch through frequent letters and

---

* Not a purpose-built prison but the recently confiscated and speedily adapted house of a local merchant.

telegrams. When Alexis was well enough to be moved, although he still could not walk, he and his three sisters made the journey to Ekaterinburg, accompanied by a few remaining retainers. Nicholas and Alexandra had been searched on arrival, so the ex-Empress, following a prearranged code, warned her children in one of her letters to pack the 'medicines' carefully. Her three daughters understood her meaning. They worked for several days, removing buttons and replacing them with diamonds wrapped in cloth, or hiding rubies in bodices and corsets. In this way they preserved the majority of the jewels that Alexandra had smuggled from Tsarskoe Selo.

Reunited in Ekaterinburg on 23 May, the family, with three servants and Alexandra's loyal doctor, were treated considerably worse than before. Their new captors were self-described 'genuine revolutionaries' – determined that 'the former Tsar, his family and retainers were no longer permitted to live like Tsars'.[7] Windows were painted over, letting through only the faintest light, and the family allowed out for only short exercise periods. It was a prelude to the inevitable finale.

Only their faith and the prospect of escape buoyed the prisoners' spirits. Russia's involvement in the First World War had finally ended in March 1918, when Lenin agreed to Germany's terms at Brest-Litovsk. It was a humiliating treaty, forced on Russia by the wholesale collapse of its army as a fighting force, and the resulting peace did not last long. In the course of 1918 Russia descended into civil war. Monarchists, political moderates and patriots opposed to the peace with Germany came together in a series of anti-Bolshevik White Russian alliances. In Siberia they were joined by the Czech Legion, a small army of separatists seeking Czech independence from the Austrian empire. On the basis that 'My enemy's enemy is my friend,' the legion had been fighting on the Allied side in the First World War. Russia's withdrawal from the war had left it stranded, and the Bolsheviks had been unnecessarily antagonistic. The legion was a formidable fighting force, and as the summer wore on, it began to take city after city along the Trans-Siberian Railway. The legion was approaching Ekaterinburg. Nicholas and his family might yet be rescued.

At the end of June 1918, almost a year after their transfer to Siberia, a smuggled letter gave the captives concrete grounds for hope: 'The friends sleep no longer . . . Samara, Cheliabinsk and the whole of Siberia, eastern and western, are under the control of the Provincial National Government.' A second letter instructed the family to prepare for rescue. In the early hours of one of the days to come they would hear a whistle. That would be the signal to barricade the door to their rooms and descend by rope through their single open window. Their rescuers would be waiting below.

No signal arrived. The sentries increased their vigilance and the window was fitted with iron bars. The letters had been a hoax. Nicholas's reply to the second was received by the Cheka, the Bolshevik secret police, and filed as further evidence against him. In one respect, however, that first letter had told the truth: Ekaterinburg would not remain under Bolshevik control for much longer. Lenin could not allow the Romanovs to escape him, and the idea of putting the ex-Emperor on trial no longer held any appeal. Another solution would be required.

At half past one in the morning of 17 July 1918 Jacob Yurovsky, the newly appointed commandant of the house, woke Alexandra's doctor and told him that, as there had been shooting in the town, the family and its retainers would be safer in the basement. The eleven prisoners took some time to get ready but eventually filed down to the room assigned to them. Chairs were provided for Alexandra, Nicholas and the thirteen-year-old Alexis, still unable to stand after his accident in Tobolsk. His father used his arm and shoulder to support him. The rest of the party was told to line up around them for a photograph – ostensibly as proof that they had not been kidnapped by the Whites.

With the victims thus neatly arranged, a detachment of Red Guards entered the room. Each had been assigned his target.

Yurovsky read out the order: 'In view of the fact that your relatives in Europe are continuing to attack Soviet Russia, the Ural Executive Committee has ordered you to be shot.' Nicholas had time for a disbelieving 'What?' before a bullet hit his head. In the subsequent fusillade all the prisoners fell to the floor, but Alexandra and her daughters refused to die. It took further shots, bayonet thrusts and blows with rifle butts, delivered with an increasing frenzy, before the last girl – probably Anastasia – finally stopped moving. The reason only became clear when Yurovsky began disposing of the bodies. The corsets of three of the grand duchesses contained eighteen pounds of jewellery, enough to make them armour-plated, and around Alexandra's waist, sewn into linen, was a belt of pearls made up of several necklaces.

EIGHT DAYS LATER the White Russian army entered Ekaterinburg. At the House of Special Purpose they found Alexis's spaniel Joy but no sign of the royal family or their murderers. The basement had been thoroughly cleaned, but the bullet holes in the walls told their own story. Something had happened, but what? In Moscow, meanwhile, the Bolsheviks would admit to the execution of Nicholas but pretended that his family had been transferred 'to a place of greater safety'. It was not until six months later, with Ekaterinburg still part of a short-lived White Russian republic, that a full investigation began. Soon searchers found grisly evidence in and around the Three Brothers Mine, just outside the city: belt buckles belonging to Nicholas and Alexis, a pearl earring from a pair always worn by Alexandra, a sapphire ring worn by Nicholas that had grown too tight for him to remove, the grand duchesses' shoe buckles. The chief investigator would eventually conclude that the entire family had been massacred. The few bits of jewellery were sent by a circuitous route to the West, where they would eventually be delivered to Nicholas's sister Xenia, who had managed to escape. They can hardly have evoked happy memories for her.

Of the bodies, however, there was no sign. Their value as symbols – of Bolshevik brutality and of the old regime – had been too great. They had been destroyed or hidden so well they would never be found. There would be no pilgrimages to the tomb of Saint Nicholas Romanov the Martyr.

14. 'This is life no more'

FOR CARL FABERGÉ one consequence of 1917's October Revolution was the arrest of two of his sons. It is not clear why Alexander and Agathon were picked out by the Bolsheviks when their father and elder brother went free (the youngest son, Nicholas, was still in London), but for Alexander at least it may just have been bad luck. In contrast to Petrograd, where the Bolshevik coup passed off remarkably smoothly, Moscow was the scene of fierce street fighting. The Kremlin itself came under bombardment. As manager of Fabergé's Moscow branch, Alexander may just have been in the wrong place at the wrong time. In any case, he does not seem to have been kept in prison for long.

Agathon, however, was in more serious trouble. In 1916, aged forty, he had left his father's business, possibly as the result of a family disagreement. Setting up on his own, he established an antique shop in Petrograd. It was a curious time for a new venture of that kind, but Agathon probably knew what he was doing. He was a famous connoisseur of objets d'art. Entrepreneurs enriched by the war would have sought his advice on what to buy, and Agathon's years at Fabergé gave him unrivalled access to old-money families forced to rein in their spending and perhaps looking for opportunities to make discreet sales of desirable objects. He certainly had high-level connections. Soon after the Bolsheviks seized power, one of Nicholas II's cousins, the Grand Duke Nicholas Mikhailovitch, had entrusted Agathon with his collection of miniatures, hoping, as he wrote to a French acquaintance, 'that with a bit of luck they might be saved'.[1] The

Grand Duke was arrested soon afterwards, and so, it seems, was Agathon. Presumably he was seen as too close to his aristocratic clients. By the time he was finally released, his father, mother and brothers would all have left the country.

In retrospect, Carl Fabergé was lucky to remain free. Leon Trotsky, by now Lenin's right-hand man, had already identified him as a war profiteer, asserting that in 1915 Fabergé had boasted, despite 'the lack of bread and fuel in the capital . . . that he had never before done such flourishing business'.[2] Now his firm was a target for the victorious revolutionaries. To Bolsheviks Fabergé and his customers were little more than parasites who had lived too long on the backs of the workers. They must be made to pay, to understand that it was now their turn to be oppressed.

In February 1918 the Bolsheviks renamed themselves the Russian Communist Party. Who could object to Marx's dictum 'From each according to his abilities, to each according to his needs'? But Lenin added an extra streak of vindictiveness. The month before he had fired up a group of agitators on their way to the provinces by urging them to, 'Loot the looters.' It was a signal for what was to come. No private property was sacrosanct; anything was fair game. The owners of safe-deposit boxes were forced to hand over their keys. Impossible taxes were levied on the bourgeoisie, with hostages taken to compel payment. Even the Orthodox Church had been too much a part of the old establishment; its buildings were ransacked; all religion was suppressed.

A few weeks after Lenin's speech commissars arrived to take over Fabergé's business. Carl Gustavovitch was phlegmatic. According to Henry Bainbridge, he simply said, 'Give me ten minutes to put on my hat and cloak,' before saying a final farewell to the company he had run for almost fifty years.[3]

A 'Committee of the Employees of the Carl Fabergé Company' was put in place to manage operations, but there was increasingly little to oversee. All over Russia, wherever the

Bolsheviks, now communists, were in control, similar acts of nationalization were taking place. The new utopia required that the government control the entire economy, and the results were disastrous. As Petrograd descended into shortages far worse than any experienced in tsarist Russia, former nobles were selling their jewels simply to buy bread. Inflation spiralled out of control. Annual salaries multiplied – in the case of one Fabergé departmental manager from 400 roubles in 1916 to 3,000 roubles two years later – but they still fell far behind the cost of living. Soon even diamonds had only a limited value. The peasants who risked communist reprisals to bring potatoes into Petrograd were more interested in boots.

Famine spread, reaching even Fabergé's most senior employees: that summer François Birbaum, still chief designer, lost his wife to starvation. Craftsmen fled Petrograd. Those who had no better option headed to Russia's interior, in search of food. More fortunate individuals made their way abroad. Workmasters began returning to their homes in Finland. Finally, in November 1918, came the firm's inevitable closure. 'There we stood,' remembered one engraver, Jalmari Haikonen, 'silent, with aching hearts, looking at the empty workshop around us. It was like being at a funeral, as though we had just lost a close and dearly loved relative.'[4]

Even before the final demise of the firm that bore his name Carl Fabergé had left Petrograd. He escaped the city in September and headed west in a flight from persecution that mirrored his ancestors' journey east from France three centuries earlier. One, possibly apocryphal, story has him disguised as a member of the British legation on the last regular train to leave Russia. Another fact is more certain: whether because he was most in danger or because there was space and documentation for only one person, Fabergé fled alone. Augusta and the rest of his family remained behind.

Like so many other members of the Russian bourgeoisie, Carl Fabergé had been unprepared for the virulence of Bolshevik hatred. Many had predicted the fall of the Tsar, but few had foreseen how every other stratum of society would end up being attacked or anticipated the total collapse of the Russian econ-omy that Lenin's policies would set in train. Fabergé had few assets overseas, and the restructuring he had initiated in 1916 can hardly have anticipated nationalization. Nevertheless, there is some evidence that he succeeded in taking some money with him. One source maintains that, by the closure, three quarters of his firm's assets had been converted into hard currency and sent abroad.[5] And a letter written by one of Fabergé's co-shareholders in 1939 tells how three of them were appointed to the committee overseeing the company's liquidation. Under its terms Fabergé was due to receive goods valued at around seven million roubles. Converting this sum into a modern equiv-alent, however, is more than usually difficult. By 1918 Russia was in the grip of hyperinflation. Over the next six years the rouble would fall to one fifty millionth of its pre-war value. Even in 1918 seven million roubles cannot have bought much foreign currency. Moreover, it is unclear how much of this ever made its way to Fabergé. Certainly, he never received the final payment. The chief liquidator would later maintain that there was noth-ing left to make it – everything had been sold to pay employees' salaries. Another story tells of one of the other liquidators hiding several boxes of valuables along with the company's books and records. That would have been a real treasure trove, but the secret of the hiding place was lost with the man himself when he disappeared soon after being arrested in 1927.[*]

However much Carl Fabergé received, it was clearly only a fraction of what his business had once been worth. His first place of refuge was Riga, capital of Latvia, which declared its independence from Russia on 18 November 1918, one week

---

[*] At least some of the cache seems to have come to light in 1990, when a sig-nificant amount of Fabergé jewellery was found in a building at 13 Solyanka ulitsa in Moscow that had once been inhabited by this individual.

after the armistice that ended the First World War. At the beginning of 1919, however, Riga was attacked by the Russian communist Red Army. Fabergé fled again, to Berlin, but here too a civil war was underway. Kaiser Wilhelm II had abdicated and revolutionists were fighting constitutionalists for control of most of Germany's major cities. Fabergé moved on, eventually arriving in Wiesbaden, a spa town on the banks of the Rhine. Here, in May 1920, he celebrated his seventy-fourth birthday, surrounded, according to Henry Bainbridge, by 'fifteen of his old Petersburg friends'.[6]

By now Carl's wife and all his sons, apart from Agathon, had succeeded in escaping to the West. Augusta and Eugène had fled Petrograd together in December 1918, travelling first by train, then by sledge and finally on foot through snow-blocked woods before reaching the safety of Finland, where they parted. Eugène went on to Stockholm while his mother travelled first to London, presumably to see her youngest son, Nicholas, and then to Lausanne in Switzerland. Alexander had arrived in Paris in 1919. None of them attended the Wiesbaden reunion. This is the only evidence to suggest discord, but Augusta can hardly have been pleased by her husband's fourteen-year relationship with Nina Tsitsianova, and Agathon may not have been the only son to have fallen out with his father in the previous few years.

Whether or not Carl had alienated most of his family before he left Russia, the illness he came down with soon after those birthday celebrations meant that any argument was quickly forgotten. Augusta journeyed from Switzerland to look after him, but the old patriarch was ailing rapidly. In happier times he had joked that the only doctor in whom he had any faith at all was his favourite dry white Mosel, Bernkasteler Doktor. Now, dependent on the medical profession, he would mutter weakly and repeatedly, 'This is life no more.'[7]

Augusta took her husband back to Lausanne, where they were joined by Eugène and Alexander. Carl rallied briefly but by the end of July had taken to his bed. He died on the morning of 24 September 1920, and was cremated in Lausanne. When Augusta died in Cannes five years later, her husband's ashes were taken there to be buried beside her in the Protestant cemetery. Despite a career spent creating fantasies for Russia's Orthodox elite, the world's most famous jeweller had remained faithful to his ancestors' Huguenot beliefs.

IN THE FIFTY YEARS before his death Carl Fabergé had created the largest jewellery firm in the world and overseen the pro- duction and sale of hundreds of thousands of objects. They ranged from the humble silverware of middle-class tables to the necklaces of empresses, from comically squat animals to ethereal flower stems, from cigarette cases, umbrella handles, vases, picture frames, fans, bell pushes, paper knives and clocks to tables and bureaus, vodka bowls and crucifixes. They were carved, turned, enamelled, chased, gilded, painted, cast, blown, spun and wrought, decorated in styles from prehistoric Scythian through classical, baroque, rococo and traditional Russian to twentieth-century art nouveau, and made from hardstone, gems, base and precious metals, wood, glass, leather and cloth. Much of this vast output may be in questionable taste, and its variety is almost unimaginable, but what made Fabergé's achievement truly awe-inspiring was its one point of uniformity – the skill and unerring attention to detail with which every piece was made, expressed in a consistency whose most remarkable quality was that it could be taken for granted.

Carl Fabergé died without knowing what had become of this enormous legacy. Most of his creations had never left Russia. Now they were lost to the communists. Above all, he would never know what had become of his firm's supreme creations, the fifty Imperial Easter eggs given to Alexandra and Marie Fedorovna, in which his designers' imagination and workmasters' ingenuity had been given their fullest expression. By newly written law, the eggs were now owned by the state: a few days before the Ekaterinburg massacre a decree had formally confiscated and nationalized the property of the deposed Emperor and his family. As for the eggs' location and condition little was known.

The omens were not good. A year before Fabergé's death Alexander Polovtsov, a well-known connoisseur and one of the early Bolsheviks' more unlikely collaborators, had published a record of his experiences during the eighteen months after the fall of the Tsar, when he and a few quixotic companions had done what they could to preserve Russia's artistic treasures. The resulting book, *Les Trésors d'Art en Russie sous le Régime Bolcheviste*, gave a remarkable contemporary account of what was happening to Russia's tsarist heritage during the chaos of the Revolution.

In March 1917 Polovtsov had responded to Nicholas's abdication by quitting his job at the Foreign Ministry to do what he could to safeguard the contents of royal palaces which had suddenly lost their owners. With two colleagues he began by making an inventory of Marie Fedorovna's summer palace at Gatchina, where he found over 4,000 pictures, including several old masters. Then Polovtsov turned his attention to Pavlovsk, an exquisite palace near Tsarskoe Selo that had hardly been altered since the eighteenth century and was now home to a junior branch of the Imperial family. By October 1917 he was sharing in the general concern that as the Russian army collapsed the Germans might arrive in Petrograd within weeks. Two trains loaded with treasures from the Hermitage Museum had already left for the relative safety of the Kremlin. Polovtsov followed them to make arrangements for a similar shipment from Gatchina. So he was in Moscow when the Bolsheviks launched their coup, stuck for ten days in a house opposite the Kremlin as shots were exchanged in the street below. On his return to Petrograd he went straight to the Winter Palace, headquarters of the new regime, and sought out Anatoli Lunacharsky, the new 'commissar of enlightenment'. His opening line, 'Pavlovsk must be saved,'[8] was met with, 'I quite agree; what are you going to do about it?' Alexander Polovtsov, son of one of Alexander III's most prominent ministers, had become one of the first Bolshevik functionaries.

Polovtsov could already see the damage caused by the action that would come to symbolize the Bolshevik coup. The storming of the Winter Palace had involved very little fighting, and much of the building seemed unharmed. The private apartments of Nicholas and Alexandra, however, were a scene of devastation. Here, where the wardrobes were still full of ball gowns last used in 1903, 'the mob seemed to have been inspired above all by a spirit of vengeance'.[9] Polovtsov was in a good position to assess the damage. A few weeks earlier, he had looked round the same rooms to give his opinion on the artistic value of the huge assortment of objects they contained and to select what should be included in the delivery to the Kremlin. He had spotted 'three superb Chinese bronzes, probably of the Tang dynasty', which he added to the objects being packed. 'The rest was modern, and although sometimes of great intrinsic value, offered little artistic interest.' It had all now disappeared. It was in these apartments that Alexandra had kept many of her Fabergé eggs. They were modern, and their 'artistic interest' was questionable at best. Had they been looted with the rest of Alexandra's possessions?

At the Gatchina Palace too, home to many of Marie Fedorovna's eggs, the situation was dispiriting. Kerensky had fled here on the day the Bolsheviks seized power, ostensibly to use it as a base while attempting to rally troops loyal to the Provisional Government, although he soon fled again for a life in exile. The prime minister's pursuers had ransacked and occupied the palace. Arriving with a group of officials to assess the situation some days later, Polovtsov found sailors lounging around bayoneted pictures and sideboards stripped of ornaments. If any of Marie's eggs had remained among them, then it was hard to imagine they might have survived.

Tsarskoe Selo, on the other hand, had escaped sack, and had been renamed Dietskoe Selo (Children's Town). Polovtsov's sponsor, Lunacharsky, took over the Alexander Palace for his own project: it was to be the flagship of a new kind of communist school, where children might be taken from their parents and given a model education, untainted by religion or other bourgeois influences. The private apartments of the Tsar were preserved as a snapshot of the former lifestyle of the Imperial family, then still imprisoned in Siberia. The curators appointed by Lunacharsky did their best to keep everything in place but were frustrated by the new commandant of the palace, who was apt to give light-fingered acquaintances private tours of the apartments. It was only in March 1918, according to a colleague of Polovtsov, that the valuables in the apartments, again of 'little artistic interest',[10] were packed and sent to the Winter Palace for eventual shipment to Moscow.

As 1918 WORE ON the destructive effect of Lenin's exhortation to 'Loot the looters' became apparent. Desperate to preserve their collections for some kind of posterity, the owners of private houses turned them over to the state, hoping that they would be declared museums. In this time of famine, however, public ownership was no guarantee of immunity. Local soviets might act in the name of 'the people' at any time and confiscate assets in defiance of central government. Icons were stripped of their gold – and vases were used as chamber pots. Even the writer Maxim Gorky, Lenin's muse and confidant, was appalled: 'They rob and sell churches and museums, they sell cannons and rifles, they pilfer army warehouses, they rob the palaces of former grand dukes; everything which can be plundered is plundered, everything which can be sold is sold.'[11] Later he would reflect sadly on the proletariat's 'malicious desire to ruin objects of rare beauty . . . In the course of two revolutions and one war I observed hundreds of instances of this dark vindictive urge to smash, cripple, ridicule and defame the beautiful.'[12]

The October Revolution might have begun as an attempt to establish a new system of social justice, but it had quickly descended into a quest for vengeance and was now turning iconoclastic. In this atmosphere who knew what might have become of the tsarinas' Easter presents? There were few people in any position to care. Petrograd was becoming no place for aesthetes. The curator of Gatchina was arrested for daring to suggest that the palace treasures would be better off abroad. He was lucky to be saved by the personal intervention of Lunacharsky. In November 1918 Polovtsov, like so many others, crossed the border into Finland. *Les Trésors d'Art en Russie sous le Régime Bolcheviste* was published from the safety of Paris. As for the treasures themselves, including the Fabergé Imperial eggs, their fate remained unknown.

15. 'You will have all of it when I am gone'

WHEN MARIE FEDOROVNA left Kiev for Mogilev in February 1917, heading for what proved to be her final meeting with her son, she was seen off with full honours by the governor of Ukraine and a Cossack escort. She returned three days later to an Imperial platform barred off from the rest of the station. There was no welcoming committee; she had to get a cab home. Nevertheless, it was some time before the Dowager Empress fully realized the extent to which her son's abdication had changed her own position. All those around her, including her daughter Olga and son-in-law 'Sandro' (Grand Duke Alexander Mikhailovitch, married to Xenia), were urging flight to the Crimea. Almost surrounded by the Black Sea and over a thousand miles from Petrograd, the peninsula was still relatively calm. It would be a good place to sit out the current troubles and see what kind of government was established in Russia, once the dust following Nicholas's abdication had settled. Marie, however, prevaricated. All her other children were still in Petrograd or Tsarskoe Selo; how could she desert them? Then, one day, she arrived at Kiev's main hospital for her usual morning visit, only to have the gates shut in her face and be told by the entire staff that she was no longer welcome. It was a rude awakening for an empress used to being both liked and obeyed. The next morning she announced she was prepared to go to the Crimea.

Within a few days a train had been prepared. Guarded by a handful of loyal soldiers and accompanied by Olga and Sandro, the Dowager Empress headed south. She took what she could with her. Necessarily, this was limited to whatever she had brought to Kiev from Petrograd a little less than a year before, but it included something that would subsequently become the focus for speculation and covetousness across Europe – her jewellery box.

Over the next few months the band of Romanovs in the Crimea grew steadily. Marie's elder daughter, Xenia, arrived from Petrograd to join her husband. She brought all her children; one of them, Irina, was accompanied by her husband Felix Yussupov, the murderer of Rasputin. Various more distant cousins joined them. Within a few weeks around twenty-five members of the Imperial family had made their way south, to live on their various estates scattered around the peninsula and continuing for some months to enjoy a lifestyle little different from how it been before the fall of the Tsar.

Gradually, revolutionary fervour spread. Marie Fedorovna had taken refuge in a villa at Ai Todor, as the guest of her son-in-law, Sandro. On 26 April 1917 he was woken by a pistol at his head. The Sevastopol Soviet had sent a band of sailors with a warrant to search the house. They took particular care with the Empress's bedroom, forcing her out of bed and even, according to some accounts, prising up the floorboards. After a morning's search they left, having confiscated a few old rifles, some papers and one particularly subversive text, the family Bible Marie had brought from Denmark fifty years before. The Dowager Empress had behaved with suitable coolness through-out the experience, to the extent that she was threatened with arrest for insulting the Provisional Government. Her sangfroid is emphasized by the fact that her jewellery chest was in full view throughout the search, standing at the foot of her bed, but never, for some reason, even glanced at by the sailors.

FELIX YUSSUPOV had earned immense popular approval for his role in the murder of Rasputin. It gave him some protection as he made several trips back to Moscow and Petrograd in attempts to rescue or preserve some of his family's treasures. He returned to Ai Todor from his first expedition with two Rembrandts, cut from their frames and rolled up for easy transportation, but he left behind other bulkier objects, including his family's one Fabergé egg. To hide them, Felix oversaw the construction of a series of secret rooms, in the Moika Palace in Petrograd and in the family mansion in Moscow, where he concealed a vast collection of diamonds and other valuables.* At one point Felix found time to go to Marie's Anitchkov Palace in Petrograd, to see what he could recover for his wife's grandmother, but he was too late. The Provisional Government had already crated up the palace's valuables and taken them into storage. There would be no additions to the contents of Marie's jewellery chest. If any of her Fabergé eggs remained in the hands of their rightful owner, Marie had to have taken them with her when she moved from Petrograd to Kiev in May 1916.

Felix Yussupov's last visit to Petrograd coincided with the Bolshevik coup of October 1917, but he still managed to return to the Crimea, to be greeted at the train station by a 'big Delaunay-Belleville car . . . flying a pennant with an enormous crown on it and our coat of arms on the doors'.[1] For a few weeks more, it seemed, life for Marie and the other Romanovs could carry on as normal. Gradually, however, Lenin's doctrines began to make themselves felt. The Black Sea Fleet went over to the Bolsheviks, and waves of massacre and looting spread out from the Crimea's two major cities, Sevastopol and Yalta. The Imperial family was saved for the time being by the remoteness of its palaces and by its members' own practised charm when faced with occasional marauders, but they all knew that their

---

* The Bolsheviks eventually found five separate hiding places, concealing treasures that included more than a thousand paintings and over a hundred rare violins. There is a suggestion that some secrets remain to be discovered. See *The Lost Fortune of the Tsars* by William Clarke.

relatively untroubled existence could not last. In Felix's words, 'We were never sure, on going to bed at night, of waking up alive in the morning.'[2]

It was almost a relief, therefore, when the Sevastopol Soviet took control of the situation, decreeing that all the Romanovs on the peninsula should be interned in the Dulber Palace, belonging to the Grand Duke Peter Nikolaevitch. When he had built the palace, years before, his family had mocked him for its high walls. His reply – that one could never know what might happen in the future – was to be justified in a way he can hardly have expected. As his cousin Sandro put it, 'Thanks to this extreme vision the Sevastopol Soviet possessed a well-fortified jail in November, 1917.'[3]

Dulber had been chosen not only to keep its prisoners from escaping, but also to protect them. The Romanovs in the Crimea had become a cause of contention between the peninsula's two workers' committees – at Yalta and Sevastopol. The Yalta Soviet was all for the Romanovs' immediate execution. The family could only be thankful that they had fallen into the hands of its counterpart in Sevastopol, which chose to wait for instructions from Petrograd. They might still be shot, but not until Lenin's order came.

Even at a time like this one of Marie's greatest concerns was for the safety of her jewellery. She was helped to address it by her captors' curious regard for Russia's dynastic law. This held that any Romanov who married a commoner was barred from the succession. The law had already been effectively abandoned when Nicholas's brother Michael was offered the throne, but the Sevastopol Soviet chose to observe it, to the extent of agreeing that a number of Marie's relations were not technically Romanovs. They all escaped imprisonment. Chief among them was Marie's daughter Grand Duchess Olga, who had recently divorced her first husband and married her long-time love, his aide-de-camp Colonel Nicholas Kulikovski. She took charge of Marie's jewels, placing them in small cocoa tins which she then concealed in a crevice by the beach whenever danger seemed to threaten. The white skull of a dog marked the exact hiding place. One day Olga and her husband returned to find the skull lying out of place. Olga felt 'cold drops of perspiration' forming on her forehead, as she watched her husband 'sticking his hand in every possible hole in the rock-face. What a relief when he finally pulled a cocoa tin rattling with jewels out of one hole!'⁴

For the time being Marie's jewels remained intact. The fate of their owner, however, hung in the balance. The position of the imprisoned Romanovs reached a crisis a few days before Easter 1918. In Siberia Nicholas, Alexandra and Marie were already in the House of Special Purpose, waiting for the other children to join them. In the Crimea the Yalta Soviet was growing impatient, to the extent that it was threatening to take the Dulber Palace by force. The prisoners' increasingly sympathetic jailer rushed back to his base in Sevastopol for reinforcements; the Imperial family's lives depended on him returning before the troops from Yalta. The following morning an armoured column was spotted on the Yalta road. All seemed lost.

Salvation had come, however, from an unlikely source. The Treaty of Brest-Litovsk, one month before, had ceded huge parts of Nicholas's former empire to his German adversaries: over 30 per cent of its population and agricultural land and more than half of its industry. Under its terms Russia lost the Crimea, wrested from the Tartars by Catherine the Great over a century before. The column on the Yalta road was a German advance guard, arriving to claim its prize.

There was little love lost between Marie and her Prussian saviours, but the soldiers of Emperor Wilhelm II were not going to molest one of his cousins, whatever strain the First World War had placed on their relationship. The Empress settled into the summer palace of another cousin, the Grand Duke George Mikhailovitch, at Harax, also in the Crimea. She and her entourage remained there, living a curiously unreal rural idyll, while elsewhere in Russia every Romanov in communist hands was murdered. The first was Marie's younger son Michael, shot on 12 June with his English secretary, Brian Johnson, in the Siberian city of Perm; his refusal of the throne on the grounds of his personal safety had in the end done him little good. The murder of Nicholas and his family followed a little over a month later. The day after that all the remaining Romanovs in Siberia, including Alexandra's sister Ella, were thrown down a mine, with grenades tossed after them to complete the work. The state of their bodies, when they were eventually recovered, showed that it took them some time to die. Finally, in January 1919 four more grand dukes, who had spent months imprisoned in Petrograd, were led out and shot.

By then it was clear that Marie would soon be losing her protectors. Too late for Imperial Russia, the war had finally ended in German defeat. Under the terms of the November 1918 armistice Germany had to evacuate its troops from the Crimea. Soon the peninsula would become a battleground in Russia's civil war between communist Reds and counter-revolutionary Whites. This was no place of safety for a former empress, but another cousin was ready to look out for her welfare. Feeling guilty, perhaps, at the way he had refused sanctuary to Nicholas and his family, King George V asked that a British dreadnought, the *Marlborough*, be ordered to evacuate the Empress Marie and her family from the Crimea. On the morning of 7 April 1919 its captain called at Harax with his mission: Marie should leave Russian soil that evening.

Indomitable as ever, the seventy-one-year-old Marie at first refused to consider evacuation. Then she demanded that if she were to go, all the refugees streaming to the coast in front of the advancing Red Army should be similarly rescued. Wearily, her designated saviours acquiesced. By the next day a small British flotilla had taken on nineteen members of the former Imperial family, their retinues of maids, servants and governesses, and over a thousand other evacuees. The Empress had been forced to pack quickly and to travel relatively light, but she was, of course, accompanied onto the *Marlborough* by her jewellery chest. Most of those with her were similarly prepared for life in exile, but the speed of departure inevitably meant that some valuables were left behind. Looking through the captain's binoculars for a last view of the country to which she would never return, Marie's daughter Xenia suddenly had to ask: 'What are those little black things all along the shore? The reply, 'Madame, that is your silver,'[5] can hardly have been welcome. Xenia's servants had been so afraid they would be left behind that they had dropped the fifty-four chests and run for the boat.

THROUGHOUT the rest of her life, spent in exile, Marie was notable for two final pieces of obduracy. First there was her refusal, in the face of mounting evidence, to acknowledge the death of her eldest son. As long as any doubt remained, she could not give up hope that Nicholas and his family might one day be found alive. And then there was her equally obstinate refusal, despite the budgetary constraints of living without an income, to consider selling a single item of jewellery.

Marie began her exile in Britain, where she was reunited with her increasingly frail sister Queen Alexandra, widow of Edward VII. After a few months, however, she returned to Denmark and the unwilling hospitality of her nephew King Christian X. It was a long time since Marie had been a Danish princess, careful with her money. More than fifty years of Russian extravagance had given her habits that were now diffi-cult to abandon. Olga tells a story of the King, exasperated by the rise in his electricity bills, sending a footman to request that his aunt turn off the lights. Marie's response was typically imperious: with the footman still standing before her, she rang for her own servant and commanded him to light the palace from attic to cellar. As for Christian's suggestion that she might contribute to expenses by selling some of her jewels, that was unconscionable. It soon became clear that aunt and nephew had fundamentally incompatible characters.

George V's offer of an annual pension of £10,000 (£380,000), together with a comptroller to ensure that Marie spent it wisely, brought these clashes to an end. The Dowager Empress spent her final years at Hvidore, the Danish villa that she and her sister had bought together fifteen years before. Her jewellery chest sat under her bed, its contents frequently inspected but rarely worn. Marie, who had once appeared decked with rubies, now limited herself to a diamond brooch given to her by her husband. Her two daughters would occasionally plead with her for a keepsake. They were always unsuccessful; their mother knew how bad they were at dealing with money. Xenia was a particularly soft target for fraudsters. Marie's reply was always the same: 'You will have all of it when I am gone.'[6]

Marie died at Hvidore on 13 October 1928, aged eighty-one. Her funeral brought together the last great gathering of Romanovs in exile but was not a state occasion: even after her death King Christian was not reconciled with his aunt. Worse than that, a few days later he called on Marie's grieving daughters to ask if her jewellery was still at Hvidore. Now was his chance to seek recompense for Marie's profligacy. He was too late. King George V had been keen to protect the last vestiges of Romanov glory both from the depredations of Marie's relatives and from the rumoured interest of international jewel thieves. With Xenia's approval, the chest had already travelled by diplomatic bag to London.

Six months later, on 29 May 1929 and in the presence of Xenia, King George V and his wife, Queen Mary, the box was opened at Windsor. According to the memoirs of the King's private secretary the contents included 'ropes of the most wonderful pearls . . . all graduated, the largest being the size of a big cherry. Cabochon emeralds and large rubies and sapphires.'[7] There is no mention of any Fabergé eggs. The inventory made a week later, however, points to one possibility: Item 32 is described as a 'gold chain set rubies and diamonds with gemset Easter egg' and is valued at £350 (£14,000).

Over the next few years almost all the jewels from Marie's chest were sold, several to Queen Mary. They raised over £130,000 (£5.9 million), which was shared between Xenia and Olga. The money was not split down the middle. Xenia was the elder daughter, and she had not married a commoner, although she was by then separated from Grand Duke Sandro. She took the lion's share. Xenia also kept various items from the chest, including Item 32. That description is so brief that we cannot be certain what it was – perhaps just a small egg on a chain, not one of the Imperial eggs at all. It accompanied Xenia to Frogmore Cottage, a house on the Windsor estate that had been lent to her by King George, but once there it dropped out of sight.

There was, however, another egg, of so little value that it would never have attracted the interest of either international jewel thieves or King Christian and so was not in the chest sent to London. Instead it formed part of a small group of mementos that Olga and Xenia divided between themselves soon after their mother's death. Xenia's share included a gold and nephrite seal, a pink cornelian rabbit with diamond eyes and 1916's *Cross of St George Egg*, Nicholas's last Easter present to his mother.

So Marie had brought at least one Fabergé egg with her out of Russia. It had little intrinsic value, but it included possibly the last portraits she ever received of her eldest son and grandson. Perhaps that was why she took it when she quit Petrograd for Kiev in May 1916. She could hardly have forgotten too that she had last seen Nicholas wearing his Cross of St George as his train drew out of the station at Mogilev. With the possible exception of the elusive Item 32, however, the egg's more elaborate predecessors had apparently been left behind. Like her daughter-in-law's Easter presents they had been lost in the Revolution. For years their fate had been uncertain. By the time of Marie's death, however, it was finally beginning to become clear.

16. 'Determining their fate irrevocably in a few moments'

AGATHON FABERGÉ spent eighteen months in a communist prison while his father, mother and brothers left for the West. When he was released in 1919, aged forty-three, it was to find that his house outside Petrograd – furnished with famously exquisite taste – had been pillaged by Red Army troops. His flat in Petrograd, however, had survived and was so full of treasures as still to deserve the nickname of 'Little Hermitage' that his friends had given it in happier times. He returned there, only to be arrested again. During his second spell in prison he caught typhoid and was lucky to survive, but ended up being released after only nine months.

On this second occasion Agathon had been freed for a purpose. Whatever Polovtsov and others might have thought, Lenin's exhortation to loot had not been the trigger for a rampage of destruction; rather, it had been a command to accumulate and preserve, and it had brought in a huge haul. Little more than a year after the October Revolution, at the beginning of 1919, thirty-three warehouses around Petrograd were filled with antiques and other objets d'art. Now the communist government's attention turned to the possibility of selling them abroad. One of the men who had most worried about the proletariat's urge to destroy was also a friend of Lenin, the writer Maxim Gorky. He chaired an eighty-member 'expertise commission' charged with selecting and assessing articles suitable for export. By October 1919, after examining only eight warehouses, it had already identified 120,000 possible objects, whose value, Gorky estimated in a note to Lenin, 'at 1915 prices exceeds a thousand million'.[1] Moreover, Gorky's contacts in the Paris sale-rooms told him that prices now were five to six times what they had been in 1915. Lenin was eager to pursue the opportunity. In March 1920 he demanded 'especially urgent measures for expediting the sorting of valuables'.[2] With Russia's economy in free fall, foreign currency was desperately needed. Sentiment was no reason to spare anything except the most culturally important articles, however they might be defined.

Naturally, the confiscated valuables included a huge quantity of jewellery. It needed to be appraised, and Agathon Fabergé remained his country's pre-eminent gemmologist. Twice he refused the invitation to join the valuation commission. The third time it came in a personal letter from Trotsky delivered by two soldiers. Agathon took the hint. In August 1921 he began work in Moscow as part of a team headed by an academic geologist, Alexander Fersman, on what Agathon later described as a 'mountain of loose diamonds'.[3] Modern pieces were being broken up for their intrinsic value alone. Few items of simple jewellery from the workshops of Fabergé or any of his contemporaries would survive. Agathon therefore witnessed at first hand the destruction of a large part of his father's legacy. It would have been heartbreaking work, if everybody involved had not been so concerned with their own survival.

Those loose diamonds, however, were only part of the brief handed to the Plenipotentiary Commission for the Listing and Conservation of Valuables. On 14 January 1922 it was charged with a much more high-profile task: cataloguing the contents of the crates in the Moscow Armoury Chamber. This series of rooms in the Kremlin had long since ceased to have any military function. Once the private treasury of the tsars, it had been a museum since 1814 but for the last eight years little more than a strongroom. It contained everything sent from the Hermitage to Moscow since the beginning of the First World War.

The decision to open the Armoury's crates signified that the communists' grip on power had entered a new phase. The continued German threat to Petrograd, even after the Treaty of Brest-Litovsk, meant Lenin's government had followed the crates to Moscow in March 1918. The subsequent four years had brought unimaginable horrors. Something like ten million people had died. The Volga region's great famine of 1921 had alone killed five million. Like Alexander III's administration three decades earlier, Lenin's had been unable to deal with the disaster; its own forcible grain requisitions had probably caused the famine in the first place. To almost any observer it had seemed that the communists neither could, nor should, remain in power. And yet they had. The Whites had been defeated; insurrections had been suppressed and, with the Germans' own final defeat in the First World War, much of the land ceded at Brest-Litovsk had been reoccupied. Lenin could even take some credit for the return of a small measure of prosperity to Moscow and Petrograd. The launch in 1921 of his New Economic Policy, which allowed limited private enterprise, had sparked a mini-boom, as entrepreneurs hurried to take advantage of the opportunities it presented. Now few dared to question Lenin's authority. It was time to survey the empire his party had conquered, and where better to start than with the crown jewels themselves?

So Agathon Fabergé, one of the last people to see the Imperial regalia before they were sent into storage in 1914, was one of the first to see them unpacked eight years later. More than that, he must have witnessed the opening of the other crates in the Armoury, those sent on later from the Hermitage as the Germans threatened Petrograd in September 1917. According to Alexander Polovtsov, the shipment had required two trains; another source mentions only one train, with forty wagons.[4] Whichever version is correct, it is clear that the commission was faced with a massive task. A report written by the director of the Armoury in 1923 tells how the sorting was carried out in immensely difficult conditions, at a temperature of about minus five degrees, with the inkwells continually freezing despite our constant efforts to thaw them out on a brazier, working from morning till night at an exceptionally rapid rate, more often than not sorting in a day up to several hundred items of the most varied quality: from the very finest in the world to the most worthless, determining their fate irrevocably in a few moments.[5]

It was not long before the commission found the Imperial Easter eggs. The Provisional Government had, after all, considered Fabergé's greatest works valuable enough to be protected from the Germans, and so had saved them from the worst excesses of the Bolsheviks. The Kremlin archives still contain the hurried inventories made in 1917 that catalogued each item sent to Moscow.[6] Most of the time, but not always, the individual eggs can easily be identified from their descriptions.

With three possible exceptions, every one of the twenty eggs given to Alexandra had been saved and sent to the Kremlin. The memoirs of Count Paul Benckendorff, Nicholas's last Court marshal, published in 1927, tell how this had come about, at least for the eggs in Alexandra's mauve boudoir. As the most senior courtier left behind when the Imperial family left for Tobolsk in July 1917, Benckendorff had taken responsibility for preserving what he could of his master's fortune. So in the dying days of the Provisional Government he had agreed with one of its ministers that

the objects of value which belonged personally to the Emperor and the Empress should be collected for a few days in a room on the second floor [of the Alexander Palace] and that a little later they should be transferred to the depository of the Imperial Office in the Anitchkov Palace, whence they should be sent to Moscow if the danger of the occupation of St Petersburg by the German army continued . . . A fortnight later eight packing cases filled with objects of value were, in my presence, transferred from Tsarskoe Selo to St Petersburg, and I myself signed the receipt in the Imperial Office.[7]

Benckendorff's loyalty and conscientiousness had not in the end been of any help to the Tsar, but Fabergé-lovers at least should be grateful.

For Marie's collection, the situation was less satisfactory. An inventory dated 14 September 1917 listed no fewer than thirty-four eggs as having been confiscated from her Anitchkov Palace in Petrograd and included in an eighty-four-crate shipment to the Kremlin. Only about half of these, however, can now be positively identified as Imperial Fabergé eggs, and many of these had already been separated from their surprises, even in 1917. There may have been a few more among the other eggs in the inventory – the descriptions are simply too vague for any certainty – but most were less exciting than that, probably Easter presents to Marie from people other than the two tsars.

One way or another a significant proportion of the thirty Fabergé eggs given to Marie by her husband and son had gone missing in the chaos of 1917. One of those, of course, was the 1916 *Cross of St George Egg*, which by 1922 was already safe with Marie in Hvidore, but about ten eggs – possibly all those kept at Gatchina – had disappeared. Nevertheless, in total about forty of the fifty eggs presented to the tsarinas were available to be listed once again and delivered into the custody of Gokhran, the State Valuables' Depository.

Despite its apparently innocuous name, Gokhran was more than just a warehousing facility. Since 1920, it had been the vehicle through which the communists had sold off the valuables identified by the various expertise commissions, raising much-needed hard currency in Western markets. Not everything confiscated was for sale – the Museum Fund, a division of Lunacharsky's Commissariat of Enlightenment headed by Leon Trotsky's wife, Natalya Trotskaya, identified items of special value that deserved to be kept – but little was sacrosanct. What was the point of safeguarding Russia's heritage when the coming world revolution would ensure that, as one delegate to a museum conference in 1920 put it, 'all our things will be returned to us'?

In any case the Imperial eggs would never have fallen into the category of items considered worth preserving. Lunacharsky himself was an impressive self-educated individual able to debate the finer points of eighteenth-century poetry with Alexander Polovtsov, yet his initial assertion had been that 'no object which had belonged to a member of the Imperial family could have any historical value'.[8] And Maxim Gorky had already expressed the opinion that Fabergé products were entirely suitable for sale: they were simply 'merchandise, which, owing to suspension of production, had now become antiquarian goods'.[9]

There was even the possibility that the eggs would not be sold intact, but be broken up for their material value alone, like so much other modern jewellery. This might have been economic madness – it was only the eggs' workmanship that made them interesting – but Gokhran, despite its money-raising remit, was not an economically rational institution. Moisei Larsons, a German economist who had been employed to maximize Gokhran's revenue, describes how he found one worker carefully hammering the bindings off religious service books. He had accumulated significant amounts of silver but rendered the books themselves, which dated from the seventeenth century, practically worthless. When Larsons tried to halt the process, he found himself in a clash with a communist commissar. Was he trying to protect Church property? Didn't he know that religion was the opium of the people? Larsons wisely withdrew his objection.

It was fortunate perhaps that despite having been given as Easter presents, few of the eggs contained anything that could be characterized as religious imagery. For the time being they survived, to be occasionally put on display for the benefit of potential foreign buyers. One photograph shows twelve eggs, scattered among crowns and other pieces of regalia, on a table somewhere within Gokhran's headquarters. Posing behind are members of the commission that had helped to sort them – the men standing, the ladies seated, all dressed in their best clothes. Larsons's memoirs recall the moment: 'In June 1923 all the jewels were taken out of their boxes and cases and laid out on a big table to be photographed. In the sunlight the diamonds sparkled and gleamed with incredible brilliance . . . At that time the representatives of a French jewellery firm were in Moscow wishing to acquire diamonds, and since there was nothing ready for sale as yet, we decided to show them the crown jewels.'[10]

The early 1920s, however, were not a good time to sell jewellery, however remarkable its provenance. Precious stones had been flooding out of Russia since the early days of the Revolution. Aristocrats had bribed their way to safety with their gems and sold more on arrival in the West. Some transactions were spectacular: the Grand Duke Boris parlayed a vast quantity of emeralds and diamonds into four million francs (£80,000, £2.1 million), enough to fund a reasonably comfortable exile. Felix Yussupov was greeted in Paris by a jeweller with a bag of diamonds that he had deposited before the war. Thousands of other émigrés sold what they could simply to survive. This was the period of which they would later lament, 'We ate our jewels.' The Russian government's attempts to raise money only added to the oversupply.

Nor were there many obvious buyers for Russia's treasures. Europe was only just emerging from the maelstrom of the First World War. Germany and Austria were defeated and bankrupt; their emperors had been deposed just as finally, if less bloodily, as Nicholas had been in Russia. Although Britain, France and Italy had eventually achieved some sort of victory, they were exhausted; the spirit of a generation had been broken; their economies would take years to recover. Only the Great War's other victor, America, remained relatively prosperous, but it alone could not compensate for the drop in demand caused by the impoverishment of the Old World.

The Russian authorities did their best. Some suggested swallowing their Marxist pride and linking up with De Beers, the diamond traders, to ensure the gems were properly marketed. Trotsky thought that it might be a good idea to send 'specialists from Fabergé' abroad (presumably Agathon) 'to determine the condition of the market, after whetting their interest in the profits'.[11] No amount of manoeuvring, however, could hide the basic truth: the market for jewellery was dead. Even the Imperial crowns could not command a premium over their carat value. The newly established Diamond Fund – essentially Russia's crown jewels – was kept intact, and the eggs remained unsold.

ONE CACHE of six Fabergé eggs, however, had already made its way to the West. Naturally enough, it emerged in Paris. France was the most obvious home for refugees from the communists; there was sympathy for the citizens of its wartime ally and they felt at home there – French had been the language of aristocratic Russia for centuries. In the years after the Revolution White Russians flocked to the French capital. Among them were Jacques Zolotnitzky and his nephew Léon Grinberg, who soon established a Parisian version of the jewellery business originally founded by their family in Kiev in 1851, A La Vieille Russie.

The six eggs must have been one of the transplanted dealership's first purchases. Bought by Zolotnitzky in 1920, they had already been through so many middlemen that Grinberg was unable to establish their provenance. All he could record in his diary was that 'Judging from the exceptional richness . . . we think they were presented by the Grand Duke Alexei Alexandrovich* to the ballet dancer Mrs Ballettá.'[12]

---

* Grand Duke Alexis, or Alexei (1850–1908), was one of Nicholas II's uncles and a famously undynamic grand admiral of the Russian navy. A notorious

That particular guess was spectacularly wrong, but it was an understandable mistake to make. Over the years the erroneous assumption of a link between these six eggs and the Imperial family would be compounded, as dealers and writers assumed that some of them at least were Imperial Easter eggs – presents from the tsars to the tsarinas. One, which would come to be called the *Chanticleer Egg*, was particularly large and enamelled in a dazzling royal blue. On the hour, for it was also a clock, a cockerel would emerge from the top, crowing and flapping its wings. Another was especially impressive. Its navy-blue enamel was scalloped all over with crescents of rose-cut diamonds, giving it the appearance of a pine cone. Inside was a silver wind-up elephant – the Danish royal emblem. Both of these eggs, it came to be believed, must have once belonged to Marie Fedorovna.

In fact, none of A La Vieille Russie's eggs had Imperial provenance. All had once belonged to Barbara Kelch, once one of the richest women in Russia but a resident of France since the collapse of her marriage in 1905. For fifteen years Mrs Kelch had kept the eggs beside her in exile to remind her of the time when she and her husband could emulate the Tsar. Now, with her income from Russia eradicated by the Revolution, she had been forced to sell her collection. She lived out the rest of her life in Paris in something like poverty, but at least she was better off than her former husband, who disappeared into Stalin's labour camps in 1930.

Zolotnitzky paid just 48,000 francs (£910, £24,000) for all six eggs. A decade before, a single one of them might have cost Alexander Kelch five times that sum. It was a clear demonstration not only of the collapse in world jewellery prices, but also of the extent to which Fabergé had fallen out of fashion

---

bon viveur, he was said to have devoted his life to 'fast women and slow ships'. Mrs Ballettá was presumably among the former.

since the war. Tastes had moved on from the cluttered elegance that his products exemplified. The pre-war years had been, in retrospect, a golden age for so many things. There was no point in looking back. As one English satirist put it, with his tongue firmly in his cheek, 'Once the war was over . . . it became obvious that the democracy for which we had striven was neither so safe nor so agreeable as many people had optimistically assumed . . . and all the little Fabergé knick-knacks and Dresden shepherdesses were finally routed.'[13] In the former St Petersburg mini-eggs from Fabergé had been the Easter present of choice for Russia's moneyed classes, to be accumulated and strung together on elaborate necklaces. Now, in France, poverty-stricken Russian refugees 'kept losing'[14] them on the Paris Metro, they were of so little consequence.

There could hardly have been a worse time for Eugène and Alexander Fabergé to start a new jewellery business. They had, however, been brought up for little else. After their father's death they had joined the general flow of White Russians to Paris, and it was here that in 1921 they founded the new firm of Fabergé et Compagnie. It should not have been a hopeless venture. The two brothers could call on the services of many of their father's former employees; they had their own years of experience; and they had a name that remained famous throughout Europe. But the best that can be said of the enterprise is that it survived, mainly by doing repairs. Perhaps customers would have come if the company could have replicated the products of the old work-shops in St Petersburg, but without a critical mass of specialized craftsmen, skilled in so many different techniques, that was always going to be impossible. There would be no rebirth of the Fabergé tradition.

AGATHON FABERGÉ also suffered from the collapse in world jewellery prices. Nothing had come of Trotsky's plan to send him abroad, and he remained in Russia, a distrusted member of the former bourgeoisie. The appraisals he made of the precious stones the communists were trying to sell proved hopelessly optimistic; his rehabilitation was short-lived. In 1925 he was 'persuaded' to donate a few last items from his father's old workshops – gems, semi-precious stones and some unfinished objects – to the Museum of Geology and Mineralogy in Leningrad, run by Alexander Fersman, his former colleague on the appraisal commission. Two years later Agathon and his family finally escaped from Russia, fleeing on sleighs over the frozen Gulf of Finland with the 'guns of Kronstadt firing before and behind them'.[15] For the rest of his life, spent mainly in Helsinki, Agathon Fabergé would be most famous as a stamp collector.

17. 'Pick out gold, silver and platinum from the articles of minimal museum value'

LENIN DID NOT enjoy the fruits of his victory for long. His 'rage', as his wife, Nadezhda Krupskaya, described it, had already taken many victims, and now it would claim him. From the middle of 1921 the signs of mental exhaustion were obvious in headaches and memory lapses; a year later he suffered his first major stroke. He was only fifty-two. Paralysed down one side and for a time unable to speak, Lenin considered suicide. Nevertheless he recovered, after a fashion, and was able to observe the growing power in the Communist Party of its general secretary, Josef Stalin. He did not approve, but two further strokes, in December 1922 and the following March, robbed him of the ability to intervene. By the time he died, on 21 January 1924, Stalin's position as Lenin's eventual successor was assured.

Stalin did his best to harness the grief that greeted the announcement of the passing of his predecessor. Russia had suffered so much under Lenin, but that was forgotten in the wave of sorrow that greeted his death. For all his faults, he had been the leader of the October Revolution and the architect of the world's first communist state. There were outbreaks of mass hysteria across what would soon become known as the Soviet Union; statues of him were erected in every city: even the poorest villages sent wreaths to his funeral. Petrograd, the cradle of the Revolution but no longer the country's capital, suffered one more name change – to Leningrad, in honour of the man who had subordinated it to Moscow. Lenin himself became a physical as well as a metaphorical icon. His body was embalmed and placed on display, permanently lying in state in a mausoleum by the Kremlin wall on Moscow's Red Square.

Russia's leaders have always known the power of symbols over their people. The abdication of the Tsar and the communists' suppression of the Orthodox Church had left a void that needed to be filled. Lenin's corpse performed a necessary role. Within a few years Stalin's own personality cult would have similar power. The 'man of steel' would become Russia's all-powerful autocrat, loved and feared by its people in the same way they had once loved and feared the tsars. He would also prove to be even more ruthless than his predecessor when it came to dealing with the last remaining symbols of Nicholas's reign. Poor prices were no excuse. The crown jewels deserved no special treatment; they were designated for sale. After rejecting the idea of sending a sales team to Europe and America, Stalin's government decided instead to conduct operations from Moscow, where it marketed the jewels in a way that would be recognized by any modern public relations guru: a public display of the Diamond Fund of the USSR.

The exhibition opened on 18 December 1925. Newspaper announcements invited every member of the proletariat to come and view 'the fantastic wealth of jewellery accumulated over the centuries by the ruling dynasty of the Romanovs, which has become the property of the workers since October, 1917'.[1] An illustrated catalogue accompanied the exhibition but in a limited edition of 350 copies – this was not for the general public but a sales tool to entice foreign buyers.

Within a year the campaign had done its job. In November 1926 a London gem dealer, Norman Weisz, made the first substantial purchase when he bought nine kilograms of jewellery from the Diamond Fund. It is a measure of the new regime's attitude that the sale was assessed in terms of weight rather than individual items. Originally from Hungary, Weisz was to say the least a colourful character. In 1920, when already success-fully established in London, he had served a prison sentence for racehorse fraud.* The scandal had not kept him down for long. His 1926 purchase encompassed pieces of startling beauty, including Alexandra's nuptial crown, studded with over 1,500 diamonds. The entire collection cost him just £50,000 (£1.9 million).

Diamond Fund sales were inevitably public affairs, especially when Weisz subsequently divided his purchase into 120 lots to be sold at Christie's in London. The dispersal of the Russian government's Imperial Easter eggs, by contrast, garnered little attention, but some must have gone to the West around this time. The evidence is in two inventories from 1927, which show that in June and July of that year the Moscow Jewellers Union and the Foreign Currency Fund of the Finance Ministry returned twenty-four Imperial Easter eggs to the Kremlin Armoury. Of the roughly forty eggs which had been listed and transferred to Gokhran in 1922 these were all that remained. The rest, it has to be assumed, had already been sold abroad or at least been earmarked for that fate.

No one has yet found any records to indicate what happened to the eggs between 1922 and 1927, but the descriptions of those returned to the Armoury give at least some indication. It seems that the intervening five years had not been kind to Fabergé's masterpieces: there were chips in enamel, and stones were missing from their settings. The 1906 *Moscow Kremlin Egg* is described as 'badly damaged' with broken domes and a dented cupola, and the artillery shells supporting Alexandra's final Easter gift had gone rusty. Whoever had custody of the eggs

---

* A previously successful horse was disguised by being painted a different colour and then entered under a false name for a novice race, which it duly won. Weisz's bets netted him at least £3,000 (£80,000).

in the mid-1920s had not been particularly careful with their treasures.

Almost all of the eggs that the Armoury passed to Gokhran in 1922 but did not receive back in 1927 would eventually emerge in the West, but it is impossible either to retrace the route by which all of them got there or to identify the agency responsible for the sales. Some may have been sold by the Finance Ministry or Moscow Jewellers Union before they returned their remaining unsold eggs to the Armoury. Most, however, were probably marketed by yet another part of the Soviet bureaucracy – the Antikvariat, a department of the Trade Ministry specially set up to sell works of art and antiques.

As for the eggs' purchasers, a number of dealers acquired one or two each, probably through Soviet officials in Paris and Berlin. A Parisian business associate of Norman Weisz, Michel Norman, is thought to have bought two of Marie Fedorovna's early eggs – the 1887 *Blue Serpent Clock Egg* and the 1892 *Diamond Trellis Egg* (already by then missing its wind-up elephant surprise). Some years later he probably acquired Alexandra's 1914 *Mosaic Egg* as well. Even with three eggs, however, Norman was put in the shade by a British rival. Emanuel Snowman, head of the London branch of a small jewellery firm, Wartski, was not only prepared to deal with the Soviets but to go to Russia to do so.

Wartski's unlikely origins lay in the Welsh seaside resort of Bangor. Morris Wartski had fled to north Wales from Poland and tsarist persecution of his Jewish faith in the middle of the nineteenth century. There he began as a pedlar, selling haberdashery and small wares, including the occasional watch or cheap item of jewellery, around the farms on the island of Anglesey. One hot day he was given a lift to his next stop by a gentleman driving a dog cart. They conversed about the Bible – Wartski had a detailed knowledge of scripture – and when they reached their destination Wartski's companion asked what he would do with his education if given the opportunity. The pedlar's reply, that he would much rather be a shopkeeper than an itinerant salesman, elicited an unexpected response. The cart's driver wrote a message on a visiting card, gave it to Wartski and told him that the man named in his message would give him a shop. Wartski's interlocutor turned out to be the Marquess of Anglesey, great-grandson of Wellington's second in command at Waterloo, an aristocratic eccentric who was doing his best to work his way through the family fortune. He kept his word. Wartski was set up in Bangor, later moving to another Welsh resort town, Llandudno, the 'Naples of Wales', and the Marquess became a regular customer.

Wartski prospered, but it was his son-in-law Emanuel Snowman who made the crucial move when he opened the firm's London office 'in the teeth of a certain amount of opposition'[2] in 1911. And it was Snowman who at some point in the second half of the 1920s made the decision to go to Moscow. It is impossible to be more precise about the date. Snowman did not keep records of his trips to Russia, although family reminiscences suggest that he only went there on two occasions. Such stories as he later told tended to revolve around the problems raised by the clash of cultures, as capitalist and communist attempted to do business. One series of newspaper articles towards the end of 1927 mentions a deal concluded near Paris in which Snowman is said to have paid the Soviet government £100,000 (£4 million) for eighty pieces of jewellery, which he brought back to London in a Gladstone bag. Most likely he also travelled to Russia around this time.

However he did it, by 1930 Snowman had bought no fewer than nine Imperial eggs, more than half of all those transferred to Gokhran in 1922 but not returned to the Armoury in 1927. Moreover, their quality suggests that he may have had something like the pick of them all: the 1895 *Rosebud*, 1898 *Lilies of the Valley* and 1897 *Coronation* eggs, several of Marie Fedorovna's ornithological triumphs – the 1900 *Cuckoo Clock*, 1906 *Swan*, 1908 *Peacock* and 1911 *Bay Tree* eggs – the 1910

Colonnade Egg, with its classical exaltation of the Tsarevitch, and the remarkable 1913 *Winter Egg*. Each was a masterpiece of conception and craftsmanship, yet Snowman paid only a few hundred pounds – the equivalent of perhaps ten to twenty thousand pounds today – apiece. The nine eggs undoubtedly represented a sizeable investment, but they cost Snowman little more than the value of their materials. The long hours of painstaking craftsmanship that each egg embodied apparently counted for nothing. But they had been preserved. They accompanied Snowman back to Britain – to his house in Hampstead, where he enjoyed arranging them on mantelpieces and book-shelves, to Wartski's headquarters, still in Llandudno, and eventually to the London branch for sale.

ONE OTHER NAME stands out in the list of people who appeared with Fabergé eggs around this time: Alexander Polovtsov. Like so many other émigrés he had wound up in Paris, where he set up his own small antique shop selling Russian artefacts. Polovtsov was in no position to return to Leningrad or Moscow for buying trips; as a refugee from the communists he would have immediately been arrested. Nevertheless, by the end of the 1920s he had somehow come into possession of two eggs: the *Gatchina Palace Egg*, presented to Marie Fedorovna in 1901, and Alexandra's *Rose Trellis Egg*, which had celebrated the birth of the Tsarevitch so belatedly in 1907, two years after his birth.

What is most interesting is that neither of Polovtsov's two eggs appears explicitly in the Kremlin's two inventories, either the one made in 1917 when the Armoury received roughly forty eggs, or that from 1922 when it delivered them on to Gokhran. They seem to have been among the ten or so that never made it as far as the Kremlin. This makes it possible that Polovtsov acquired the two eggs before the inventories were made, perhaps even while he was self-appointed curator of the royal palaces, and that they left Russia with him when he crossed the border into Finland at the end of 1918. His justification would have been that the eggs were better off safe abroad than destroyed at home, but the suggestion that he might have stolen them – the evidence is too weak to call it an allegation – casts a different light on the apparent altruism of his attempts to preserve the Imperial family's treasures after Nicholas's abdication.

The eventual purchaser of Polovtsov's two eggs was also someone we have met before. The railway and banking tycoon Henry Walters had visited Fabergé's shop in St Petersburg in its pre-1905 heyday, dragged there by the American-born Princess Cantacuzène. At that time Easter eggs had not been for sale and Walters had returned to his yacht with nothing more exciting than parasol handles and carved animals. He had, however, already seen some of Fabergé's eggs, at the Paris Exposition in 1900. It seems appropriate that, thirty years later, he once again saw these supreme examples of the jeweller's art in the French capital, and that this time they were available. He wasted no time, adding the eggs to a collection of Russian objects that already ranged from tapestries and miniatures to autographed letters of Catherine the Great.

Whenever and however Polovtsov had acquired his two eggs, he did not manage to sell them to Walters until 1930. Like every other dealer, including Wartski, he had found it difficult to dispose of his treasures. Fashion continued to set its face against Fabergé, and legal obstacles complicated sales. In Paris the shop A La Vieille Russie was not able to display the six Kelch eggs it had bought in 1920 because they did not conform to French regulations on the hallmarks required to show their precious metal content. More serious still was the doubt which overshadowed all the Russian government's sales of treasures in the 1920s – it was at least questionable whether it owned these objects in the first place. The communists had after all come into possession of them in a way that practically amounted to theft. It was only to be expected that the moment confiscated articles reached the West, the Russian émigrés who had once been their owners – or their heirs – would attempt to recover them.

At least two court cases resulted. In 1928 Prince Yussupov and others sued a Berlin auction house for ownership of items it had bought from the Russians, and in London a year later Princess Paley, whose husband, the Grand Duke Paul Alexandrovitch, had been murdered by the communists in 1919, brought a similar case against Norman Weisz when he tried to sell treasures from her marital home. Neither suit was successful. No one doubted that the aristocrats had once owned these objects or that they had been forced to flee Russia in terrible circumstances. Nevertheless, the communist regime now had diplomatic recognition, at least in Europe; the laws of Russia decreed who owned these objects, and by these laws, originally urged on Lenin by Maxim Gorky, the property of refugees had passed to the state. It might be contrary to natural justice, but the eggs, and every other artefact abandoned by owners who had fled to the West, were the Soviets' to sell or keep as they chose.

IN RUSSIA, meanwhile, the twenty-four Imperial eggs returned to the Kremlin Armoury in 1927 were given inventory numbers and received back into storage. This might have suggested that they would be kept, but the respite did not last. In 1928 Stalin launched his first Five Year Plan, a return to centralized control after the relative liberalization of Lenin's New Economic Policy. The dash for industrialization needed the fuel of foreign currency, and the success of the recent court cases pointed the way. Once again attention turned to the treasures in the Armoury. One year after the launch of the plan a letter from the Commissariat of Enlightenment instructed its staff 'to pick out gold, silver and platinum from the articles of minimal museum value and give them for the urgent needs of the Republic'.[3] When the Armoury seemed to be dragging its heels, an 'emergency brigade' of experts from the Antikvariat was sent in. By 30 April it had identified twelve more eggs as 'fit for export trade'.

There is no obvious rationale for the selection of the twelve deemed suitable for export. Many of those picked to be sold had features that were personal to the recipients, like Marie's 1890 *Danish Palaces Egg* and Alexandra's 1896 *Revolving Miniatures Egg*, with their representations of the two empresses' childhood homes, or the 1893 *Caucasus Egg*, memorializing the dying Grand Duke George, or the 1898 *Pelican Egg*, commemorating Marie's role as an educational patron. It is natural to imagine that Russia's new regime saw no need to retain them. Others, however, were relatively anonymous: the translucent jewelled casket that was the 1894 *Renaissance Egg*, the 1903 *Peter the Great Egg* and the 1912 *Napoleonic Egg*. And their materials ranged from the almost plain enamel of the two 1915 *Red Cross* eggs to the diamonds studding the 1912 *Tsarevitch Egg*, the leaves carved from nephrite on the 1899 *Pansy Egg*, and the elaborate pink cameos on the *Catherine the Great Egg*, about which Marie wrote to her sister in 1914.

The Antikvariat did not have to justify its decisions. Resistance by Armoury staff was met with a chilling reminder that directors of museums would bear 'personal responsibility'[4] for any delay. On 21 June 1930 the twelve eggs were handed over to be sold abroad. In one raid the Armoury had lost half of its remaining eggs.

Three years later the Antikvariat descended on the Armoury again. Five more eggs were selected for sale. The museum's director, S.I. Monakhtin, fought another rearguard action, writing to the Ministry of Education, in his best communist-speak, that removal of the eggs from the collection 'would have the effect of destroying it as a historical and artistic complex and this will make it impossible to set up a Marxist-Leninist exhibition'.[5] This was foolhardy. Stalin's purges were now in full swing. In 1931 twenty-four officials at the Hermitage had been arrested for their opposition to the sale of state treasures and put on trial as 'counter-revolutionary wreckers'.[6] Monakhtin might well have shared their fate. Nevertheless, and despite an initial rebuff, his arguments seem to have worked. Only two of the five eggs selected by the Antikvariat were sold: Alma Pihl's final masterpiece, the embroidery-inspired 1914 *Mosaic Egg*, and the *Flower Basket Egg*, a delicate concoction that Nicholas had given to Alexandra in 1901. The remaining three were returned to the Armoury.

The era of sales from the Kremlin was over, but it was too late to preserve more than the rump of what had been an extraordinary collection. Of the fifty Imperial eggs given by Alexander and Nicholas to their two tsarinas, around forty had been discovered in the Armoury in 1922, but of these only ten remained. The others had gone to the West.

18. 'I know that May was passionately fond of fine jewellery'

'I FOUND MYSELF amidst a whirl of Kings and Queens, Millionaires and Maharajahs. Fabergé objects were then passing through my fingers as fast as shoals of glistening herrings pass through the sea, and all I had to do was to look immaculate and say nothing.'[1] This was how Henry Bainbridge remembered his time at Fabergé's London branch in the halcyon days before the First World War. In 1904 he had been recovering from lead poisoning, brought on by his previous career as a chemical engineer, when a chance meeting brought an introduction to Arthur Bowe. Since the year before, Bowe had been Fabergé's London representative, operating from a room in a hotel. Now the firm was looking to expand. Bainbridge impressed both Bowe and, when he subsequently visited St Petersburg, Carl Fabergé himself. Within a short time he was appointed joint manager of the newly opened London branch, assisting the youngest Fabergé son, Nicholas. The results of that chance meeting would dominate the rest of Bainbridge's life.

Just as in Russia, British affection for Fabergé's work had been driven by demand from the top. Queen Alexandra, the wife of Edward VII, had learnt to love the jeweller's work from her sister Marie Fedorovna, and her views were soon shared by the rest of the royal family. The London shop had been set up specifically to satisfy their demand. Goods would be sent to King

Edward on approval, for him to keep what he wanted and return the rest. Once, Bainbridge recalls in his memoirs, 'he took nothing, and we all scratched our heads at 48 Dover Street where Fabergé was then established in London, in fact we came close to collapse. Fabergé had shot his bolt and the sooner we shut up shop the better, so we began to think.'[2] It was only a few weeks later, when a friend of the King came down to Dover Street, that the situation brightened. The King had refused to accept a present from him – a print of a racehorse – with the words, 'Go to Fabergé's, they have a hippopotamus cigar lighter in nephrite. If you wish to give me something, give me that.'

A little something from Fabergé became the natural gift for both King and Queen. Followers of the current generation of the royal family are apt to recall that in Edward's later years his favourite companion was Alice Keppel, great-grandmother of Camilla, now Duchess of Cornwall. She gave the King a cigarette case from Fabergé, enamelled blue and encircled by a diamond-studded snake swallowing its own tail, a symbol of eternity. She also had the idea for Edward's most famous commission from the Russian jeweller – a birthday present for his wife of a set of carved stone animals, each one a faithful representation of a favourite at the Queen's farm at Sandringham in Norfolk.

Queen Alexandra herself became almost an habitué of the Dover Street shop. On one occasion she brought her family with her: not just her daughter, Princess Victoria, but also the King of Denmark, the King and Queen of Norway and the King of Greece. Bainbridge remembers the occasion in his memoir of Fabergé with a curious mix of awe and affected nonchalance. At one meeting Alexandra told Bainbridge that if Mr Fabergé were ever to come to London, then he should be brought to see her. The opportunity arose in 1908, when Carl came to visit his only overseas branch. He was horrified, however, by the prospect of an audience with his royal patroness: he had nothing to wear; he could hardly arrive unannounced. Bainbridge's protestations of the Queen's eagerness were in vain. Fabergé asked when the next train left for Paris and within half an hour was gone. Genial and dynamic he may have been, but there was clearly a streak of shyness in Fabergé as well.

With the London branch taking responsibility for all Fabergé's international trade, from Europe to Thailand, its sales increased. By 1911 it was doing well enough to move premises, to 173 New Bond Street, the heart of London's jewellery district. Here a double-headed Romanov eagle on the shopfront advertised the firm's origins, while a uniformed doorman ensured that only suitable customers were admitted. Within were showrooms on the ground and first floors, where portraits of Nicholas and Alexandra looked down benignly on both stock and customers.

A year later, however, the situation darkened. Worried about being undercut, a group of British jewellers took Fabergé to court. It insisted, and the law agreed, that the firm could not continue selling items without a British assay mark to confirm their precious metal content. Since every item stamped with a mark then had to be returned to Russia for finishing, the effect was to destroy the economics of Fabergé's London operation. The First World War hastened its demise. The Russian government's demand for repatriation of assets in 1915 meant that Bainbridge lost his job that October, but Nicholas Fabergé and another manager kept things going after a fashion. It was only in February 1917 that they were finally forced to abandon the business. Nicholas remained in London with his wife, Marion. In 1920 he met Dorise Cladish at a Chelsea Arts Ball. His only son, Theo, was the result of that liaison. Nicholas, however, returned to Marion and eventually left London for Paris, where he died in 1939.

ANOTHER JEWELLERY firm, Lacloche Frères, bought the closing stock of Fabergé's London branch – about 200 items. It took them five years to realize their investment, such was the war's effect on tastes and fortunes. Nevertheless, for fifteen years London had been the entrepôt for all Fabergé's sales outside Russia. Inevitably, it had built up a substantial local clientele – enough to mean that in the 1920s the greatest concentration of Fabergé aficionados outside Russia was undoubtedly to be found in Britain. They included a good smattering of eccentrics. One – a Mr Blair of Llandudno – would only acquire a new item if the lunar conditions were right. Kenneth Snowman, Emanuel's son, would remember being summoned to Violet van der Elst's London house in the middle of the night to view a Fabergé collection guarded by 'two Great Danes'.* Morris Wartski's patron the Marquess of Anglesey must have been the only person ever to wear a Fabergé shirt; he had designed it himself to wear specifically when playing ping-pong. He swore that it improved his game, although that may simply have been the effect on his opponents of the emeralds with which it was liberally studded.

The royal family, however, remained at the core of Britain's appreciation for Fabergé. Edward VII had died in 1910, aged only sixty-eight, the bronchitis that killed him a sad commentary on all the Fabergé cigar lighters and cigarette cases he had

---

* Probably Alsatians – Mrs van der Elst had already been both prosecuted and sued for failing to keep them under control. This fascinating character funded an enviable lifestyle with the fortune she had made from Doge Cream, a cosmetic supposedly based on an old Venetian recipe. She owned a castle in Lincolnshire, a mansion in Sussex and a town house in London's Holland Park, where she would spend her evenings attempting to commune with the soul of her second husband, the deceased Mr van der Elst, whose ashes occupied a prized position among the antiques and Persian rugs. Her jewellery collection was valued at over £250,000 (£9.5 million), and was complemented by her furs – sables that had belonged to 'Russia's last Tsarina'. By the time of her death, in 1966, her estate was valued at only £15,000 (£190,000). The Fabergé – and all her other treasures, including her husband's ashes – had long since been sold to pay for, among other things, an ultimately successful campaign for the abolition of the death penalty.

received over the previous decades. Alexandra returned several pieces from his Fabergé collection to their original donors, including, perhaps unsurprisingly, Alice Keppel's cigarette case.* She largely retreated from London society, to the house at Sandringham that had been built for Edward fifty years before. Here she remained surrounded by Fabergé, displayed in specially built cases. Even before her death in 1925, however, the mantle of Fabergé patronage had passed to the next generation – to her unmarried daughter Princess Victoria, who would inherit much of her collection, to her son George V and, above all, to his wife, Queen Mary.

The grandmother of Britain's present queen has not been well served by history. We see her, regal and unbending, in the group portraits taken towards the end of her life, looking every inch the matriarch of the family, the sad survivor of not just her husband, King George V, but also her son George VI, and we remember stories of her acquisitive nature. Owners of private houses were said to dread a visit; they would prepare by hiding whatever they had that was valuable or beautiful, for they knew that if Queen Mary saw an object, she might well admire it with open covetousness, dropping heavy hints until the treasure was offered to her. She would take it away with her there and then.

Queen Mary's relations knew of this aspect to her character. The Grand Duchess Olga, Marie Fedorovna's daughter and therefore a cousin of George V, died believing (falsely) that the Queen was responsible for her receiving only a fraction of what she had expected from the sale of her mother's jewels. Her suspicions were aroused when many of Marie's most attractive pieces later appeared in Queen Mary's collection. As Olga later told her biographer, 'I have tried not to think about it too much,

---

* On Queen Alexandra's death, Mrs Keppel in turn returned the cigarette case to the royal family – closing the circle of ownership in a way that recalls the case's own snake motif. The case remains in the Royal Collection.

and certainly I've never talked to anyone, except my husband.
I know that May* was passionately fond of fine jewellery.'[3]

In fact Mary had paid the going rate for her cousin's jewels
– the Grand Duchess, cut out of discussions because of her
commoner husband, had simply been misinformed as to their
value. Mary's passion for fine jewellery was, however, very
real. It dated back to a childhood that was by royal standards
relatively deprived. Although she was a great-granddaughter
of George III through her mother, her father, the first Duke of
Teck, was the product of a morganatic marriage. This meant
that Princess May was ineligible for the standard career path of
minor royalty in the nineteenth century – marriage to a German
princeling. Brought up in the modest surroundings of the White
Lodge in Richmond, a London suburb, she had few expecta-
tions. Only the happy combination of dynastic need and Queen
Victoria's approval had led to her achieving the ultimate prize
for one of her birth, engagement to the eventual heir to the
British throne, the son of the Prince of Wales. Like another distant cousin, the Empress Alexandra, she valued her jewels as
insurance against the possible day when her luck might turn.

The marriage of another Russian empress, however, provided a much more direct parallel for the young May. For that
first engagement was not to her ultimate husband, George V, but
to his elder brother 'Eddy'. The sensible, well-brought-up May
had been identified as a perfect steadying influence for Edward's
charming but dissolute heir, and the news that they were to be
married had been greeted with joy throughout the Prince's
future kingdom. Less than two months later, however, in
January 1891, he was dead, killed by influenza. In the words
of her biographer, the 'desolate figure of Princess May' became
'the symbol and the centre of the nation's grief'.[4] It was not long,

---

* Queen Mary only took that name on her husband's accession to the throne.
She was baptized Victoria Mary and always known as May (the month of her
birth) to her family.

however, before the example of Eddy's aunt, the Empress Marie
Fedorovna, was remembered. She had married the younger
brother of her first fiancé; perhaps the 'desolate' Princess might
do the same? Accordingly, on 3 May 1893, George, Duke of
York, proposed and was accepted.

To add to the parallels between Queen Mary and the two
tsarinas, there were equally remarkable similarities between
George and his cousin Nicholas. They looked sufficiently alike
for a courtier at the Duke of York's wedding to mistake the
bridegroom for the then Tsarevitch, and more than twenty years
later for the servants of the Grand Duchess Xenia, on arriving
in England as refugees from the Bolsheviks, to abase themselves
before the King in the belief that their Tsar had miraculously
come back to life. More important were the similarities in the
two men's characters: the preference for country pursuits, the
tendency to follow the opinion of others, the adherence, in case
of doubt, to the status quo. It had been Nicholas's misfortune,
and his cousin's luck, that what was desirable for the constitutional monarch of a stable kingdom proved to be ultimately fatal
character flaws for a Russian autocrat.

In short, Queen Mary and her husband were ideally suited
by birth, wealth and inclination to be Fabergé lovers. Moreover,
the dispersal of the Kremlin's egg collection meant that Britain's
King and Queen were in a position to fill the one obvious gap in
the royal Fabergé collection built up by Edward and Alexandra.
So, according to her own handwritten notes, in 1931 the Queen
acquired her first Fabergé egg: the *Colonnade Egg* presented
to Alexandra in 1910, which portrays Alexis as a cupid atop a
love temple around which four allegorical figures represent his
sisters. Wartski had sold the egg in 1929 for £500 (£20,000),
but there is no record of how it came to Queen Mary. Her note
simply states that she gave it to her husband, King George V.

It is possible to question the tastefulness of the gift: not so
much the egg itself, which is far more jewel-like and attractive
than its faintly ponderous appearance in photographs might

suggest, but more the way the piece must have reminded the King of the dead Romanov children, to whom he had once refused British sanctuary. Presumably, however, both King and Queen appreciated the egg's more obvious attractions. Here was a beautifully made object that was both ornament and memento from the workshops of their family's favourite craftsman. Over the next five years they would go on to acquire several more eggs, by Fabergé and other Russian makers. Among them was one of Fabergé's masterpieces: the 1914 *Mosaic Egg*, the pointillist marvel designed by Alma Pihl that was Nicholas's last Easter gift to Alexandra before the First World War. The Queen catalogued the collection with care; in time she would come to be recognized by fellow connoisseurs like Henry Bainbridge as Britain's greatest Fabergé enthusiast.

It remained a relatively inexpensive enthusiasm. Bought by the King and Queen from a London jeweller in 1934, the 1914 *Mosaic Egg* cost no more than the 1910 *Colonnade Egg* had five years before – £500 (£20,000). This was an object that when new had cost the Tsar something like 30,000 roubles, the equivalent in 1914 of roughly £3,000, six times its cost twenty years later. Other pieces of Fabergé sold for even less. Also in 1934, Christie's had auctioned the 1885 *Hen Egg*, the gift from Alexander III to Marie Fedorovna that had begun the whole series. It fetched just £85 (£4,000), and that was one of the highest prices in a sale which only confirmed how far Fabergé's star had fallen. As *The Times* reported with some prescience, 'A century hence the work of Carl Fabergé, goldsmith to the Russian Imperial Court, will probably be realizing high prices in the auction room but yesterday a collection of objets d'art made by him . . . failed to realize more than £1,367.'[5]

Nevertheless, fuelled by royal patronage, British interest in Fabergé's works was beginning to increase. In 1935 his products would form the centrepiece of the Exhibition of Russian Art held for over a month in a private house in Belgravia, one of London's smartest residential areas. The usual suspects were all

involved: Alexander Polovtsov was on the organizing committee; Henry Bainbridge helped to set up the Fabergé section;
and the venue itself was lent for the purpose by Madame Koch
de Gooreynd, whose husband had been Bainbridge's first customer almost thirty years before. The organizers put together
a display that included no fewer than eight Imperial eggs.
One, lent by 'Her Imperial Highness the Grand Duchess Xenia
of Russia', was the 1916 *Cross of St George Egg* that she had
inherited from her mother, while the remaining seven had all
been among those Emanuel Snowman had bought from the
Antikvariat in the 1920s. Thousands queued to pay the entrance
fee of 12Hp (£5.80), with the proceeds going, appropriately
enough, to the Russian Red Cross. Queen Mary, who had lent
the 1910 *Colonnade Egg* and several other pieces, visited twice,
after hours to avoid the crowds.

ON 14 JANUARY 1936, having been largely bedridden for some
weeks, King George V was well enough to spend the morning at
Sandringham helping his wife arrange the collection of Fabergé
that he had just inherited from his sister Princess Victoria. It was
pleasing to be putting items back in the glass cases in which
Queen Alexandra had originally displayed them. The following
day the King was back in his bed. He died less than a week later,
on 20 January. Like his father he had been killed by his lungs;
his own heavy smoking can hardly have helped.

Fabergé had always been a joint enthusiasm for the King and
Queen. Without her husband by her side, Queen Mary would
acquire no more Imperial eggs. She was moreover the only long-
term collector for the jeweller's masterpieces that Emanuel
Snowman had yet identified in the UK. When she stopped buying
it only emphasized the message conveyed by the poor prices in
the saleroom. The UK alone was not a big enough market for
Fabergé. There was only one country whose citizens had both
the wealth and the taste to pay sums close to what the eggs had
cost in pre-revolutionary Russia, and that was America.

19. 'Department stores – try the department stores'

SOME TIME in the spring of 1931 Harry and Victor Hammer finally persuaded their brother Armand to return to New York. L'Ermitage, the business they had set up to sell Russian artefacts to wealthy Americans, was not doing well. In the words of Harry's telegram, 'How can we be expected to sell Fabergé eggs and Tsarist treasures when stockbrokers are jumping out of windows and former chairmen of corporations are selling apples on street corners?'[1]

Armand Hammer was a man of many faces whose reputation has sunk precipitously in the decades since his death, but he was also a man of many parts. He may be most famous as the octogenarian head of Occidental Oil who seemed to spend the 1980s hobnobbing with whichever world leader was prepared to meet him, but sixty years earlier he had spent a decade in Russia, emerging in 1930 with a fabulous collection of prerevolutionary memorabilia. His 1987 autobiography, *Hammer: Witness to History*, gives his version of how this came about. It deserves scepticism. Writing for Ronald Reagan's America, and in a vain attempt to put himself forward for a Nobel Peace Prize, Hammer makes little mention of his upbringing as the son of a well-known American communist, and paints the rest of his life in a way that few would now agree with. Nevertheless, it is hard not to get carried along by his chutzpah, as we learn how he became the man who kick-started America's love affair with Fabergé.

The book dates Hammer's first experience of Russia to 1921, when he arrived as a newly qualified doctor (he never practised) anxious to help the famine refugees then 'streaming to the Volga towns',[2] and bringing with him a fully equipped field hospital as evidence of his good intentions. Handicapped by his inability to speak Russian, Hammer was left to cool his heels in Moscow until he joined, almost by chance, a government-run tour of the region surrounding the Urals. Here in a fit of enthusiasm he promised to arrange a grain shipment from the US in exchange for Russian furs and other commodities. The promise got him noticed by Vladimir Lenin himself, at just the time when the New Economic Policy was being launched. Armand Hammer would be its first foreign concessionaire. More than sixty years later the tycoon would still trade on the prestige of being the 'man that met Lenin'.

Hammer negotiated concessions that gave him the right to exploit an asbestos mine in the Urals and to import various industrial goods, including Ford tractors. Lenin's death in 1924, however, changed the political climate, and Hammer was forced to hand his initial operations over to the state. His autobiography makes light of the setback: he soon started a pencil factory in their place. Meanwhile, Hammer had called for assistance from members of his family back in the US. His younger brother Victor came over first, learning shorthand and typing en route, and setting himself up for a lifetime as Armand's secretary and bag carrier. Eventually Hammer's parents also came out to join them.

Whatever the privations suffered by ordinary Russians in 1920s Moscow, the Hammer family lived in a manner that was positively pre-revolutionary in its magnificence. They occupied the Brown House, a thirty-room mansion that before the First World War had been the headquarters of a European entrepreneur. The surroundings must have been inspiring. Soon, Victor in particular had developed a passion for tsarist relics. As he later put it, 'I didn't know the first thing about collectibles, but

I loved to go shopping and a lot of the things I bought turned out to be pretty valuable.'[3]

Armand quickly followed his brother's example. He describes sniffing out objects as soon as rumours of their existence began to circulate. The brothers' only rivals in the hunt, the French and German ambassadors, would rush to government-owned commission stores only to be disappointed by the tag, 'Sold to Mr Hammer'. When the usual channels had nothing to offer, Victor would apparently go 'foraging in the basements of the Winter Palace in Leningrad'.[4] He also spent two years cultivating a 'former governess in the imperial household'[5] with the eventual reward – produced from under a mattress – of an album of 'intimate, unpublished photographs' of Alexandra and the children.

The brothers bought fine porcelain plates from a stall selling junk in the Moscow flea market. At one hotel they came across a 'complete banquet setting of dishes which had been made for Tsar Nicholas I'.[6] Persuading the manager to part with the delicate porcelain was easy: the dishwashers were already complaining that it was too fragile. Soon, the Hammers' collection ranged from Orthodox vestments shot with gold to icons bought 'in dozens', and the Brown House, always opulent, had the atmosphere of a private museum. When an American art dealer, Emery Sakho, came for dinner in June 1928 he toured the house in wonder, 'demanding "What did you pay for this?" and exclaiming "My God" in disbelief every time we told him'.[7]

Sakho suggested exporting Russian artefacts to America and was soon in partnership with the Hammer brothers. So when in 1929 the Soviet government decided to nationalize Armand Hammer's pencil factory, he knew what he had to negotiate in return: a licence to export all the objects that he and his brother had acquired over the previous decade, a collection which by that time 'had expanded to fill several warehouses'.[8] It was later that year, according to Hammer, that 'Victor heard from the Soviet agency Antikvariat, which had been established to sell off treasures, that a number of Fabergé eggs could be bought if the price were right. Seven or eight of them were on offer at first, for an average price of about $50,000 [£10,000, £430,000] each. I had no hesitation in purchasing every one we were offered and, eventually, we were able to acquire fifteen.'[9]

With the nationalization of his business, Armand Hammer had no reason to stay in Russia. He moved to Paris, where by his own account he began to live the life of a successful one-man merchant banker. Harry and Victor accompanied the family's Russian treasures to New York. They were going to set up their own gallery there, L'Ermitage, selling a huge variety of objects in association with Emery Sakho. When Sakho was forced to sell up by the Wall Street Crash of 1929, the Hammers found themselves operating on their own in a market they knew little about. Worse than that, the Crash had drastically reduced the number of potential purchasers for what the brothers had to sell. So Harry sent that telegram. They needed their brother's help.

Armand left his wife and young son in Paris, and returned to the land of his birth. He found that L'Ermitage was indeed losing money in what he later described as 'alarming amounts'.[10] Morris Gest, an impresario with the right contacts among the wealthy, had replaced Emery Sakho as the Hammers' partner and had made some sales, but had diverted all the proceeds into new Broadway productions. Meanwhile, the warehouse fees for storing L'Ermitage's stock were mounting, and the Hammers faced a $30,000 (£6,600, £300,000) tax bill from their previous activities running an import/export agency.

'Listen,' Armand said to his brothers, 'not everybody can have lost their money in the Crash. There will always be people who will like the idea of owning something which belonged to royalty and having it in their home.'[11] The only problem was how to reach them. Armand credited a dress manufacturer, Samuel Hoffmann, with the idea that saved his family's fortune: 'Department stores – try the department stores.'[12]

It was a piece of inspiration. Every city in America had at least one of these monuments to commerce. Over the last fifty years, they had established themselves as the place for America's urban middle classes to shop. Moreover, they had become glittering destinations in their own right – major landmarks that could both awe and entertain prospective customers. The Hammers' collection of exotica was both a retail opportunity and a potential tourist attraction. Surely any retailer would recognize what Hammer was offering?

Armand wrote to a swathe of stores across America, offering 40 per cent of the proceeds, ordered price tags bearing the Romanovs' double-eagle crest and prepared for business. For months he had no reply. Perhaps he had mistaken his market? Why should Russian trinkets be of any interest to people struggling to keep their jobs in the depth of the Great Depression? But then, finally, a telegram arrived from Scruggs-Vandervoort-Barney in America's heartland, St Louis, Missouri: 'Come immediately.'

'Right away, Victor and I went to Sixth Avenue, where a theatrical company was selling its trunks in a liquidation sale.'[13] The Hammers bought every one and sent them up to the warehouse for packing with as many of their Russian relics as would fit. On the train from New York to St Louis a friendly conductor let the two brothers take the trunks as their personal baggage, paying no haulage costs. Hammer does not say so explicitly, but he and his brothers clearly had very little money to play with. Everything rested on the success of their trip to the Midwest.

Perhaps it was inevitable that Hammer would triumph. His autobiography certainly gives the impression of a life without failure. That in itself is indicative of one skill that can be traced back to his time in St Louis: the art of media manipulation. Hammer arrived there in the middle of winter, January 1932, to demand an interview with its two daily newspapers. They were naturally reluctant to give free publicity to a commercial enterprise, but Hammer's decade in Russia gave him a good story to tell. Both the *Post-Dispatch* and the *Globe-Democrat* carried it prominently the next day. And the highlights of both stories were the photographs of the 'fabulous Fabergé eggs' that would be the centrepiece of Scruggs-Vandervoort-Barney's display.

Two eggs were featured in these initial stories: the *Danish Palaces Egg*, given to Marie Fedorovna in 1890, which represents the first full flowering of Fabergé's genius; and Alexandra's *Tsarevitch Egg* from 1912, the last joyful celebration of the heir before his haemophilia became generally known. Both were masterpieces with explicit royal connections. As Armand Hammer would later comment, 'I suppose it is one of the minor paradoxes of the century that they should have ended up in the hands of a young man from the Bronx.'[14]

Hammer's story of his years in Russia was a terrific, even inspiring, tale and enough of it was true for the rest to be convincing. It had the desired effect on the people of St Louis. According to Hammer, the opening day of the sale at Scruggs-Vandervoort-Barney attracted 5,000 visitors and sales in the first week were over $100,000 (£20,000, £1 million). The exhibition was extended; fresh supplies were shipped from the L'Ermitage warehouse in New York. Hammer had been right: middle America could not get enough of anything connected to Russia's doomed royal family.

As news of his success spread, stores who had failed to reply to Hammer's original enquiry were quick to register their interest. The first was Marshall Field and Company in Chicago, founded in 1865 to 'Give the Lady what she wants' and by now the proud occupier of an entire city block – the largest department store in the world. One of their executives suggested that Hammer write a fuller account of his years in Russia; *The Quest of the Romanoff Treasure* appeared within months, with a text that would be repeated almost verbatim in Hammer's autobiography fifty years later.

Over the next year, until January 1933, the brothers' road show criss-crossed America, from Chicago to Los Angeles, then Cleveland, Pittsburgh and Washington DC; altogether they visited fifteen different cities, sometimes returning for repeat bookings and covering over 13,000 miles. At each stop Hammer followed the same basic formula: his story guaranteed substantial coverage in the local newspapers; the department store locations and imaginative pricing usually did the rest. In the larger cities Victor Hammer might also give lectures on the Romanovs, lending a pseudo-intellectual gloss to his brother's anecdotes. Meanwhile Armand developed additional public relations techniques: local society beauties would be photographed in 'tsarist robes' or unnecessary but eye-catching armed escorts would meet the exhibition when it arrived at a new location. The best publicity of all came when some aristocratic émigré arrived at a sale and announced melodramatically that it was his family's treasures, lost in the Revolution and now stolen by the communists, that were being put on display.

Rarely if ever can there have been any substance to such claims. While there was some truth in Hammer's story, much of it was little more than fantasy. Far from being the personal relics of tsars and grand dukes, most of what the brothers had to sell was distinctly bourgeois: the debris of Russia's pre-war hotels and monasteries, or the desperate disposals of families that had once been middle class but were now rapidly joining the proletariat. This was hardly 'Romanoff Treasure'.

Moreover, little of the exhibited stock was owned by the Hammer brothers. Victor at least had always been happy to admit that the contents of the Brown House belonged to the Soviet government. It had been put there to impress Western visitors, encouraging them to follow the brothers' example and trade with the communist state. A government commissar made regular inspections to take an inventory and ensure the Hammers didn't steal anything. In any case, Armand Hammer did not make much money from his years in Russia and could never have afforded to buy all the articles he later pretended to own. There is not even any evidence that Emery Sakho, the American art dealer Hammer maintained first gave him the idea for L'Ermitage, ever actually existed.

So, without Sakho, where did the inspiration for the Hammer brothers' sally into the market for pre-revolutionary memorabilia first spring from? The most likely answer comes from reading between the lines of Armand's autobiography. By the time it came out in the 1980s Hammer had to explain the vast amount of stock sold as sales continued into the 1930s. Even he could no longer pretend that he was still selling the objects with which he and his brother had furnished the Brown House. So the memoir tells how Victor made several trips back across the Atlantic to meet representatives of the Antikvariat and replenish supplies. Hammer even boasts of how occasional problems were solved through his friendship with Anastas Mikoyan, the Antikvariat's head, who would survive Stalin's purges to become Khrushchev's deputy.

Far from being an independent dealer, L'Ermitage was in fact little more than a front for the Soviet government. From the very beginning of its operations it took stock on consignment, kept only a small commission on each sale and remitted the balance to Moscow. The department store sales were the route through which the Antikvariat tapped into the world's richest market and offloaded the vast quantities of articles 'looted from the looters' a decade before. In the words of one American art critic, Armand Hammer was 'Stalin's U.S. field representative'.[15]

The two Fabergé eggs exhibited by Hammer, however, were different. For a start, their authenticity as Tsarist relics is unchallengeable. Hammer really was selling eggs that Nicholas II and Alexander III had given to their wives for Easter. In addition, recently opened Soviet archives show that he genuinely owned them. He had bought them from the Antikvariat in the Soviets' last major sale of Fabergé eggs, in the second half of 1930. Hammer's friendship with Anastas Mikoyan had clearly given him the inside track. Of the twelve eggs removed from the Armoury by the emergency brigade, he and his brother ended up buying ten – not just the 1890 *Danish Palaces* and 1912 *Tsarevitch* eggs, but other masterpieces like the 1893 *Caucasus Egg*, with its poignant pictures of the dying Grand Duke George, and the 1898 *Pelican Egg*, celebrating Marie Fedorovna's role as an educational patron.*

In 1927 most of these eggs had been formally appraised by the Kremlin's experts. Their materials had been analysed and valued, incremented by a percentage presumably intended to take account of labour, and then multiplied by four to arrive at a 'minimum price'. The resulting figures ranged from 1,632 roubles (£160, £6,700) for the *Red Cross Portraits Egg*, presented to Marie Fedorovna in 1915, to a little under 20,000 roubles for Alexandra's 1896 *Revolving Miniatures Egg*. These bore little relation to the prices Hammer actually paid: 8,000 roubles for the 1912 *Tsarevitch Egg*, down to 500 roubles for that *Red Cross Egg*. At first sight he seems to have done well: he was able to buy almost every egg available, and there can be little doubt that he thought he was getting a bargain.

Naturally Hammer was not about to admit to his future customers how well he had done in his negotiations with the Antikvariat. So in the *The Quest of the Romanoff Treasure* he declared that the *Danish Palaces* and *Tsarevitch* eggs each cost him 100,000 'gold roubles' (£10,000, £430,000) – more than twenty times their actual cost. It is a spectacular lie, but understandable under the circumstances. More interesting is the fact

---

* These revelations clearly contradict at least two parts of Hammer's story: that he bought fifteen eggs, and that he did so in 1929. Neither discrepancy need be particularly damning, given the fifty-year gap between Hammer's purchase and his memoir. One could argue, however, that he misdated the purchase by a year in order to make it seem that he had left the Soviet Union earlier than was actually the case, in particular, before the stock market crash that supposedly wiped out the apparently fictitious Emery Sakho.

that these are the only two eggs that Hammer mentions in *The Quest of the Romanoff Treasure*. One might have thought that he would be more boastful about his purchases. Here he was, 'a young man from the Bronx', and he owned ten of the most spectacular ornaments ever made. The first lie, however, explains the second. Hammer wanted to sell his eggs for a price that was many multiples of what he had paid for them. He could only do that by emphasizing their scarcity – admitting to the existence of all the other eggs he had in storage would hardly have helped him do that.

It takes nerve to play this sort of long game. By the beginning of 1933 the travelling exhibition had sold off huge amounts of pre-revolutionary memorabilia all over America and was ready to finish with a final spectacular show at Lord and Taylor's department store in New York. From the point of view of Hammer's Soviet backers the whole exercise had been a huge success. It was failing, however, in one crucial area, much more vital to Armand Hammer's personal fortune. The press attention that Hammer so assiduously cultivated tells the story. The *New York Times* from 2 January has a piece headlined JEWELRY OF CZAR ON VIEW THIS WEEK with a teaser below: 'Gift Easter Eggs Encrusted With Gems Among Pieces Bought in Russia by Dr Hammer'. As the article makes clear, the same two Fabergé eggs with which the exhibition had set out twelve months before remained its leading attractions. Hammer had not sold either of them. Their price tags had been too great for the wallets of middle America.

The truth is that Hammer's inexperience had betrayed him. He may have thought that his Soviet connections had got him a good deal, but he paid far more for his eggs than Emanuel Snowman had parted with for often superior examples. Now, to make a profit on his investment, Hammer had to persuade Americans that these deeply unfashionable trinkets from a discredited dynasty were once again desirable objets d'art. The irony is that by doing so he had to forget his own communist sympathies and upbringing in two respects: by portraying the vanished world of the Romanovs as a golden age, and by appealing to the tastes of the only people who could afford to reimburse him for his outlay – America's capitalist elite.

20. 'Old civilisations put to the sword'

Dear Mrs Taylor,

> *As to your enquiry about the Fabergé pink Easter Egg, in 1931 I became 21 and therefore of age to inherit the Trust Funds made by our Grandfather and later Mother. Already I was very interested in art and frequented the galleries. I was fascinated by the newly opened Hammer Gallery on 57th Street. That was when I bought the Egg . . . You must know the story of Armand Hammer and how he was able to bring so much of the Russian Imperial treasure to New York.*
>
> *Wishing you a successful summer at Hillwood,*
> *With sincere regards,*
>
> *Eleanor Close Barzin*

THAT LETTER, written in 1983, gives the fullest account available of how the Hammer brothers made their first sale of a Fabergé egg. Some of the details may be questionable – the Hammer Galleries only moved to 57th Street around 1950 and, according to Armand Hammer at least, they were still trading as L'Ermitage in 1931 – but the timing of the purchase itself seems incontrovertible; Mrs Barzin would hardly have mistaken the date of her twenty-first birthday. The Hammers had sold one egg before they even started their tour of department stores.

The 'Fabergé pink Easter Egg' that Mrs Barzin had bought is nowadays known as the 1914 *Catherine the Great Egg*, the last one Marie received before the First World War. This was the egg whose surprise – the enamelled sedan chair containing the Empress Catherine – had led Marie to describe Fabergé as 'an unparalleled genius'. That surprise, however, had gone missing in the revolution. So it is all the more remarkable that Eleanor had ended up paying $12,500 (£2,750, £120,000) for the egg. This might have been less than the asking price of $18,500, but it was still a tidy sum for an object that had cost Hammer only 8,000 roubles (£800, £34,000) the year before. Moreover, it was the first transaction since the Revolution in which an egg had been sold for a price that was at least comparable with what Fabergé had charged for it, back in 1914.

Hammer must have hoped for many more such sales, but he had been concentrating on his department store tour. This had at least eased his immediate concerns about cash flow, even after remitting most of the proceeds back to Moscow. So in 1933 he could afford to start thinking in earnest about how he might dispose of his remaining investment in Fabergé eggs. The sale to Eleanor Barzin pointed the way. She had the kind of inherited wealth that gave her both confidence in her own taste and the wherewithal to indulge it. It was among people like her, surely, that Hammer would find his best customers. The sale to Eleanor, however, was a one-off. She retains the distinction of being the first buyer of a Fabergé egg on American soil, but she did not hold onto the *Catherine the Great Egg* for long. Instead she gave it to her mother, the woman whose trust fund had enabled her to make the purchase: Marjorie Merriweather Post.

One biography of this archetypal heiress calls her an 'American Empress';[1] it is easy to see why. Few other women after the First World War can have lived in a style so reminiscent of tsarist magnificence. The suicide of Marjorie's father in 1914 had left his only child with a majority shareholding in the Postum Cereal Company, maker of Grape Nuts, Post Toasties and Postum, a popular coffee substitute. Under the management of Marjorie's second husband what was already a sizeable business had expanded hugely, using the soaring stock prices of the 1920s to fund the acquisition of brands like Jell-O, Maxwell House and Birds Eye.

As the largest shareholder in what was now called General Foods, Marjorie could fund almost any indulgence she chose, including a choice of residences that a tsar would not have sniffed at. She spent summers in her own massive complex in the Adirondacks and her winters at a house in Palm Beach that had taken 600 men three years to build. In between, she split her time between homes in Manhattan and Long Island. Occasionally, she would visit her shooting lodge in South Carolina or sail on her yacht. Even Marjorie's charitable commitments seem reminiscent of the Romanovs: during the First World War she had funded a Red Cross hospital in France. Fifteen years later she responded to the Great Depression by putting her jewels in a strongbox; the insurance premiums saved were enough to fund a canteen for New York's unemployed.

It was in Palm Beach that Marjorie really came into her own. As the undisputed queen of its society she played host to visiting celebrities including in 1925 the Grand Duchess Xenia, sister to the murdered Tsar. Among Marjorie's friends in the resort were Prince Serge Obolensky, a refugee from the Bolsheviks who had married Alice Astor in 1924, and Consuelo Vanderbilt Balsan, who as Duchess of Marlborough (before her divorce and remarriage) had in 1902 been one of the few non-Russians to commission her own egg from Fabergé, the *Pink Serpent Clock Egg*. Such acquaintances fostered Marjorie's awareness of the Russian jeweller. She had the kind of taste to appreciate his flamboyance too: the original architect of her Palm Beach residence had previously been the set designer for the Ziegfeld Follies.* Marjorie had bought her first piece of Fabergé in 1927, a box made of amethyst, quartz and ruby that

---

* A series of elaborate theatrical productions, inspired by the Paris Folies-Bergère, which ran on Broadway from 1907 to 1931.

had once belonged to Prince Yussupov. Everything marked her out as a natural customer for Armand Hammer.

So it was in direct pursuit of Marjorie Post and her set that in January 1934 Hammer Galleries opened for the winter in Palm Beach. It would return there every year, employing 'Prince Mikhail Gounduroff',[2] apparently an exiled White Russian, to lend a 'princely tone' to proceedings as he welcomed visitors to the premises. By then Hammer's operation had a permanent New York showroom as well. He was not quite ready to go it alone – the outlet was a joint venture with Lord and Taylor, the department store host of that last New York exhibition – but he could still be happy with the location: the Waldorf Astoria Hotel on New York's Park Avenue.

MARJORIE MERRIWEATHER POST would become one of America's greatest collectors of Russian objects. In 1935 President Roosevelt appointed her third husband, Joseph Davies, as his ambassador to Moscow. Sent with a brief to build bridges to the communist state, Davies was only too happy to accept at face value the show trials then underway at which Stalin was using trumped-up charges to eliminate all opposition. His hosts reciprocated by doing all they could to help him and his wife indulge their mania for collecting. Storerooms were opened up at the Hermitage and special evenings arranged at the commission shops that Armand Hammer had found so fruitful a decade before. One of these shops, Marjorie found on a trip to Leningrad, was the old Fabergé building itself. She wrote excitedly of crawling on her hands and knees through rooms full of 'masses of icons stacked together . . . paintings . . . books and everything one could think of'. None of the jeweller's works were on display, but that did not dampen her enthusiasm. Here, as in every other place, she bought.

Eventually Marjorie Post would buy a Fabergé egg: the 1895 *Twelve Monogram Egg*, Nicholas II's first Easter present to Marie Fedorovna after the death of his father. That purchase, however, was in 1949, from 'Mrs Berchielli', an Italian woman who had acquired the egg some years before. Despite being courted so assiduously by Armand Hammer, and for all her evident love of Fabergé, Marjorie Merriweather Post never bought an egg from Hammer Galleries. Instead, Armand Hammer's best customer would be another woman from a very different background. Ironically enough, given Hammer's efforts to move upmarket, she would be someone who had first come across the eggs during his department store sales.

Lillian Thomas Pratt began her working life as a stenographer at the Puget Sound Flowing Mill in Tacoma on America's west coast. John Lee Pratt, whom she married around 1917, was her employer before he became her second husband, but he had equally humble origins – a father who had been a Confederate soldier in the American Civil War and returned from the final surrender at Appomattox with little more than the horse he was riding. Pratt had arrived in Tacoma, according to a Seattle newspaper, as a '$100-a-month engineer'.[3] His subsequent career had taken him, however, to General Motors at a crucial time in that company's growth. He would become one of its key executives, praised by one GM president as 'the best businessman I have ever known'. Subsequent generations should be especially grateful to him for his work in the 1920s, turning around the company's refrigerator division when most were inclined to abandon the manufacture of this troublesome new-fangled product.

By 1931 the businessman and his wife were ready to live a more refined life. They bought Chatham Manor, an eighteenth-century house in Fredericksburg, Virginia that had once played host to presidents, and set about restoring it to Georgian splendour, filling its rooms with period American furniture and pictures. Despite the Depression, they were clearly in a position to spend and so met Hammer's first prerequisite for potential customers.

The leap from Americana to Fabergé was a substantial one. Mrs Pratt made it in 1933, at Lord and Taylor's. She had a charge account at the store and so had received advance notice of Hammer's exhibition there. On 25 January she made her first purchase – a silver-gilt fork with a mother-of-pearl handle said to come from 'the Winter Palace collection in St Petersburg'. Judging from the accuracy of the provenance Hammer gave to most of what he sold, this was undoubtedly spurious, but it was enough to hook Mrs Pratt. The idea of Imperial Russian objects in a house with a presidential past was irresistible. She made several further visits and purchases, and continued to do so when Hammer Galleries moved to its own premises.

By all accounts Mrs Pratt was not impressive to look at. One story has it that on her first visit to the Hammers' boutique a salesman mistook her for the cleaning woman. He must have soon been disabused of his mistake, for on 31 October 1933 she bought her first Fabergé egg, the *Red Cross Portraits Egg*, given to Marie Fedorovna in 1915, and acquired by Armand Hammer from the Antikvariat in 1930.

None of Hammer Galleries' financial records have survived, whether for entirely innocent reasons or because Armand Hammer later wanted to conceal the full extent of his Soviet connections, so we do not know what Lillian Pratt paid for that first egg. Presumably her outlay was relatively modest, reflecting the simplicity of an egg produced during the years of wartime austerity. But she was only gearing up. By May the following year she had bought the 1912 *Tsarevitch Egg*, which *The Quest of the Romanoff Treasure* had fictitiously valued at '100,000 gold roubles'. Two or three years later the 1898 *Pelican Egg* joined her collection. Nor did Mrs Pratt neglect other Fabergé creations: as a keen gardener, she had a particular predilection for his flower stems. The story goes that she bought so much as to stretch even her substantial financial resources. Her husband's only recourse was to threaten to sue Hammer Galleries if they continued to increase his wife's credit.

*

In 1936 ARMAND and Victor Hammer were ready to go independent. They broke the link with Lord and Taylor, moving the
New York shop to its own premises on Fifth Avenue. Appearances in publications as diverse as the *Social Spectator*, the *New
Yorker* and *Time* followed. With headlines like HAMMER ICONS
and THE INNOCENTS ABROAD, the articles did little to challenge
Hammer's version of his time in Russia in *The Quest of the
Romanoff Treasure* and much to publicize whichever egg he was
admitting to owning at the time. Nor did Hammer neglect the
presentational aspect of his sales. Every object, no matter how
insignificant, was sold in a Fabergé-style fitted case with a
parchment certificate asserting its Romanov provenance.

When he had to, Armand Hammer would pay for his publicity. In 1937 he brought Henry Bainbridge over from England
for a lecture tour on Fabergé. Eggs that were proving hard to
shift might be advertised in the pages of the *Connoisseur* magazine, priced at anything from $20,000 (£4,000, £180,000)
to $50,000 (£10,000, £440,000) and enticing readers with suit-
ably grandiose claims: that Marie Fedorovna's 1912 *Napoleonic
Egg* 'took over eight years to complete', or that the 1896 *Revolving Miniatures Egg* was 'Fabergé's proudest achievement'.

In 1940 Hammer went one step further when he founded
his own magazine, *Compleat Collector*. It was an unashamed
vehicle for advertising masquerading as editorial, of which
Hammer boasts gleefully in his autobiography. Edited by
'Braset Marteau' ('arm and hammer' in French) and with frequent contributions from 'Dnamra Remmah' (Armand Hammer
backwards),* it is not surprising that this magazine did its best
to plug Fabergé.

While *Compleat Collector* might be characterized as just a
bit of fun, at least by those who did not buy objects on the

---

* At least, so Hammer claims in his autobiography. In my own reading of
Compleat Collector I have found numerous references to Braset Marteau but
none to Dnamra Remmah.

strength of its recommendations, some of Hammer's other actions were undeniably criminal. One of the curious coincidences about the years he spent in Russia in the 1920s, long before he even thought of becoming an antique dealer, is that his trading business there was headquartered in the building that had once housed Fabergé's Moscow workshops. The Special Concessions Committee controlled by the Cheka (the forerunner of the KGB) had placed him there, charging $12 per month (₤2.70, £100) for the four-storey edifice. Perhaps that was how, by the time he came to America, Hammer had also come to possess a set of apparently genuine Fabergé signature stamps. He lost little time in putting them to use, passing off cheap French reproductions as the real thing. Even as late as 1954 he proudly showed his then mistress, Bettye Murphy, how it was the work of minutes to apply the marks. The best bit, he told her, was to allow collectors who fancied themselves as experts on Fabergé to discover the 'signature' for themselves, and then to act suitably surprised if they pointed the marks out to him.

So far so reprehensible, but what Fabergé aficionados find hardest to forgive is Hammer's role in the registration of their hero's name as a label for cheap aftershave. The Spanish Civil War had forced a friend of his, Samuel Rubin, to close down his company, an importer of soap and olive oil called the Spanish Trading Corporation. In 1937 Rubin established its replacement, a manufacturer of toiletries. As he cast about for a name, Hammer suggested 'Fabergé', a brand redolent of imperial luxury and exacting standards. Rubin liked the idea and the Fabergé cosmetics company was born. Eugène and Alexander Fabergé, still running Fabergé et Compagnie in Paris, only became aware of this unlikely rival for their name some years later. Unable to afford American lawyers to fight their case, in 1951 they accepted Rubin's offer of $25,000 (£9,000, £190,000) for the rights to their family's name.

*

AMID ALL THIS activity, Hammer was still slowly offloading the eggs he had bought from the Antikvariat. By 1940 he owned no more than three of the ten he had originally acquired in 1930. Most of their purchasers had been, and would continue to be, women. That might be a comment on the eggs themselves: originally made for Empresses, their style and decoration appealed to feminine sensibilities. Or it might be a comment on Hammer himself: there is a subtext to his memoirs that he thought of himself as someone particularly well-equipped to sell to women.

The biggest exception to this rule is worth highlighting. In 1934, as Armand Hammer later remembered, 'Harry Clifton' walked into the Fifth Avenue shop. 'His arms were sticking out of the coat sleeves of his dishevelled suit, [he] wore no tie and [his] wild hair looked as if a porcupine had run through it.'[4] A quick credit check revealed that, despite appearances, Mr Clifton was after all a suitable purchaser of 'Romanoff Treasure'. His full name – Henry Talbot de Vere Clifton – gives a better indication of his antecedents: an ancient family in the north-east of England. The rents from land around Blackpool gave him one of his country's largest incomes, and his efforts to spend it would make him one of Hammer's most important customers.

In 1937 Harry married Lillian Griswold, great-niece of a president of Harvard University. Griswold was Lillian's first married name; the rapidity of her divorce and subsequent remarriage to Harry had scandalized Bostonian society. Undaunted, the newly-weds celebrated their marriage later that year with the purchase from Armand Hammer of the 1894 *Renaissance Egg*, the oddly bulbous and empty casket-egg that had been Alexander III's last Easter present to his wife before his death. Back in England, the Cliftons bought another of Fabergé's creations, probably through Wartski: the 1895 *Rosebud Egg*, the first received by Alexandra Fedorovna and one of the nine eggs that Emanuel Snowman had bought from the Antikvariat in the 1920s.

Despite these purchases, it is hard to characterize Harry Clifton as a Fabergé aficionado, keen to participate in exhibitions or to preserve his treasures for future generations. An inopportune visit to him by Henry Bainbridge once apparently ended with Fabergé's former salesman being kicked down the stairs. There were soon stories that the 1895 *Rosebud Egg* had sustained serious damage from being used as a missile in a marital argument. Unsurprisingly perhaps the Cliftons divorced in 1943.

Henry Talbot de Vere Clifton was, however, rather more than an eccentric landowner. He also fancied himself as a poet. His own works are hard to track down these days and once found not worth the trouble,* but Clifton is known to have contributed to the creation of one of twentieth-century poetry's minor masterpieces. In 1935 he had given the great Irish poet W. B. Yeats a seventieth-birthday present, a Chinese lapis lazuli carving. It inspired a poem, 'Lapis Lazuli', dedicated to 'Harry Clifton', which appeared three years later in *New Poems*, Yeats's last collection.

The poem achieved its place in the Yeats canon as a late masterwork because it showed readers how art might be a way of finding tranquillity in a world of chaos. It has another theme, however, of special resonance for Fabergé collectors. In the opening stanzas Yeats suggested that through objects like his Chinese carving we can still remember 'Old civilisations put to the sword'. The year the poem appeared – 1938 – made this a timely reminder. In Europe, barely twenty years after the 'war to end all wars' had ended, another great clash of ideologies was about to begin. The Second World War would sharpen the focus on Fabergé's eggs as windows onto the life of the tsars in pre-revolutionary Russia, onto a world that had been 'put to the sword' only twenty years before but already seemed impossibly distant.

---

* Clifton published three collections of poetry with Duckworth between 1932 and 1942 (see Bibliography). It is hard not to agree with the critic Roy Foster that he almost certainly paid for their publication.

21. 'Turn of the century trinkets'

LENINGRAD WAS a prime target for the German tank divisions as they raced through the Soviet Union in the summer of 1941. On 8 September they completed its encirclement, cutting off access to all supplies except those that could be transported, under constant gunfire, across a lake to the east of the city. The blockade that followed would not be lifted for two and a half years and would kill over a million civilians, mostly through starvation. As a symbol of Russian endurance and suffering, the 900-day siege of Leningrad has few equals.

The royal palaces outside the city were occupied by German forces. All were shelled and looted. Such was the speed of the initial German advance that curators had time to save only the most precious objects. For the previous fifteen years the Alexander Palace had been run by its communist controllers as a museum of Romanov rule, a reminder to all of the profligacy and poor taste of the ancien régime. For the duration of the siege it became a hospital for SS officers. Marie Fedorovna's old home at Gatchina, which had also been a museum in the 1930s, became a veterinary centre. By the time the Red Army reoccupied the two palaces in early 1944 little was left to remind visitors of their former status.

Gatchina had been particularly badly damaged. After Germany's final defeat in 1945 the Russian government closed the palace for a prolonged period of restoration. The outer fabric of the Alexander Palace, by contrast, was relatively intact, although its interior had been gutted. Plans to re-establish a museum there, however, were abandoned. In its pre-war incarnation the building had become a shrine more than a propaganda tool. The photographs of the children, the books and the toys, all had inevitably made the Romanovs seem more human, more like victims, than the authorities had ever intended. That could not be allowed to continue. The palace was presented to the Russian navy for its private use. A quarter of a century after Nicholas and his family had been murdered in Ekaterinburg, the most concrete reminders of their existence had been effaced.

The Romanovs themselves were not so easily forgotten. So much that related to them had been destroyed, from their palaces to their bodies, that whatever was allowed to survive inevitably increased in importance. In a gradual process the Imperial Easter eggs began to acquire the significance they now enjoy. They were, after all, personal both to the tsarinas who had received them and to the tsars who had commissioned them. Each contained a memory of the Romanov family or a great public event, or simply of the happy vulgarity that flourished in pre-revolutionary St Petersburg, at least among those with the money to enjoy it. The eggs also demonstrated the level of craftsmanship and wealth that Russia's last two tsars were able to command. They had become, almost by default, the most tangible surviving memorials to the last generations of the Romanovs.

The Armoury's remaining eggs included some of the most magnificent examples of the entire sequence, from the 1900 *Trans-Siberian Railway Egg*, celebrating the supreme engineering achievement of Nicholas's reign, to the elaborately mystical 1906 *Moscow Kremlin Egg*. There were more personal mementos too, like the *Alexander Palace Egg* from 1908 and the *Standart Egg* from the following year. In the 1930s some had occasionally been put on display, but with very little fanfare, reflecting the secular state's discomfort not only with the eggs' Imperial provenance but also with their implicit religious message.

During the Second World War even Moscow could not be

considered secure. The Kremlin's eggs, along with the Armoury's other treasures, were sent to Sverdlovsk on the other side of the Urals, far from Hitler's reach. Was it with deliberate irony that the authorities decided on Sverdlovsk as a place of safety for the Imperial memorabilia? Renamed in honour of Lenin's secretary Yakov Sverdlov, who had in 1918 overseen Moscow's involvement in the murder of the Romanovs, Sverdlovsk had until 1920 gone by another name – Ekaterinburg.

By February 1945, with Soviet forces approaching Berlin, it was clear that any threat to Moscow had long since passed. The contents of the Armoury were returned to the Kremlin, and that April the museum once again opened to visitors. The Fabergé eggs, however, were treated as dismissively as ever. When Henry Bainbridge wrote the first biography of his former employer, *Peter Carl Fabergé: His Life and Work*, in 1949 he did not even know if the Kremlin eggs had survived the hostilities.

Publication of the biography was an indication that in Britain at least interest in Carl Fabergé had continued to grow. An exhibition at Wartski, still Europe's premier dealer in Fabergé, helped the book's publicity campaign. Only five Imperial eggs were on display, but the exhibition could boast some interesting visitors. Chief among them was Eugène Fabergé, now seventy-five. In the absence of the firm's documents, lost in the Revolution, his and his brothers' memories had formed the basis for much of what Bainbridge had to say. More colourful perhaps was Prince Felix Yussupov, Rasputin's murderer, whose appearance on the eve of the opening day as 'an immaculately tailored wraith'[1] caught the attention of Kenneth Snowman, Emanuel's son. The Prince's words of patrician encouragement were duly noted: 'My old friend Carl Gustavovitch would have rejoiced to see his wares so diligently set out.' It is perhaps querulous to note that Felix Yussupov was almost fifty years younger than the jeweller with whom he claimed such friendship.

Bainbridge's book is idiosyncratic, full of charming recollections and first-hand experience, and as much an autobiography

of Bainbridge as a biography of its ostensible subject.* Four
years later Kenneth Snowman, who had taken over from his
father as chairman of Wartski, produced a very different work.
The Art of Carl Fabergé was researched in depth and beautifully illustrated. It was intended to be, as its author put it, 'a
sober evaluation of [Fabergé's] achievement' and was published
'as a guide for collectors and connoisseurs on the one hand, and
on the other as an act of justice to one of the finest goldsmiths
and jewellers of all times'.[2]

A foreword by Eugène Fabergé set the tone for the rest of
the book. In it he remembered 'the mounting excitement
which spread imperceptibly throughout the St Petersburg workshop as each year the Easter eggs for presentation to the two
Tsarinas gradually took shape and neared completion'. Eugène
was therefore 'particularly gratified to turn the pages of an
illustrated catalogue' of the Imperial Easter eggs, which was at
the core of the book. In this catalogue Snowman summarized
everything then known about these remarkable objects.

Considering how little information Snowman had to go on,
it is remarkable how much of his catalogue he got right. Nevertheless, it is the mistakes in it that are more interesting to the
modern reader. They remind us of the extent to which Snowman and his fellow dealers were operating in the dark, as they
tried to establish the history behind each of the jewelled eggs to
have emerged from Russia since the Revolution and to determine how many more Imperial eggs remained to be found. So
it is only to be expected that the catalogue linked many eggs
with the wrong year or the wrong recipient, entirely changing
their place in the story of the Romanovs. Similarly, Snowman
had been told by Eugène that the sequence started in 1884

---

* It also fails to mention Nicholas Fabergé, except in passing, despite the
fact that he and Bainbridge had been colleagues for more than a decade.
It is clear that at some point, probably when Bainbridge left the business
in 1915, the two men had fallen out.

rather than 1885, and he was unaware that no eggs were presented in 1904 and 1905, so he thought he was looking for a
total of fifty-five eggs, rather than the fifty actually presented to
the tsarinas.

It was the errors that Snowman made in classifying eggs as
'Imperial' that would have the most far-reaching repercussions.
Of the fifty-five he believed he was looking for, Snowman knew
of the existence of forty-six, of which he placed eleven in the
Kremlin and thirty-five in Europe or America. We now know,
however, that five of these thirty-five eggs were not in fact Imperial; they had not been presented by the tsars to the tsarinas.
Three were among the six Kelch eggs that A La Vieille Russie
had bought in Paris in 1920; the two others were at best gifts
to Marie Fedorovna from someone other than the Tsar. When
the true status of these eggs eventually emerged after the fall of
communism, several collections would have to be re-evaluated.

These problems were all in the future. In the meantime the
book was published by the appropriately named Faber and
Faber, the kind of firm where a bad review was grounds for a
major internal enquiry and where T. S. Eliot, the father of poetic
modernism, still worked as an editor. That it was prepared to
welcome a book about Russia's master jeweller was, surely, an
indication of how his creations were finally being valued by the
academic establishment.

Fifty years on, however, Faber's former sales director
remembers some disquiet at the decision to publish a book on
what was then seen as a vulgar subject: '[It] was presumably
intended to boost Wartski's sales. Kenneth was not the only
individual to use the cachet of the Faber name to further his
own interests.' That might seem a strange verdict on a book
which remains frequently quoted and which was for thirty
years, through several editions and reprints, the most authori-
tative work on Fabergé available. But at one level it is probably
true. The book's production was heavily subsidized by Wartski
and the owners of the objects featured in its pages. As the price

of Fabergé rose, driven in part by the interest that this book generated, their investment would be repaid many times over.

THE LUKEWARM attitude to Fabergé displayed by Snowman's publishers was matched on the other side of the Atlantic. Lillian Pratt had died in 1947, leaving her vast Fabergé collection, which by then included five Imperial eggs, to the Virginia Museum of Fine Art in Richmond. These days officials at the museum are defensive in response to any suggestion that their predecessors did not properly appreciate the bequest, which is now one of their biggest draws. Lillian Pratt was after all one of the institution's trustees. Nevertheless, they do not deny that the collection was transported to the museum in cardboard boxes in the back of its director's station wagon, a casual approach it is hard to imagine being used for valued works of art.

If the Virginia art establishment was relatively indifferent to Fabergé, its equivalent in New York displayed something close to disdain. From the late 1940s Jack and Belle Linsky had taken over from Lillian Pratt as America's chief purchasers of Fabergé's work. This was quite something for a couple who as children had been among the poorer subjects of the Tsar. Belle was born in Kiev, and Jack had emigrated from northern Russia with the rest of his family in 1904. The Swingline stapler had been their route to fortune; it boasted a piece of design that was as innovative as anything produced by Fabergé, the 'open-channel' mechanism that meant it could be loaded with new staples without being taken apart. Jack was the salesman who had ensured the Swingline was ubiquitous across America, and Belle had overseen the offices and factory.

By the late 1950s the Linskys had assembled a Fabergé collection that Belle described, possibly even correctly, as the second greatest in the world 'next to the English Queen's'.[3] It included two Imperial Easter eggs, the 1893 *Caucasus Egg* and the following year's *Renaissance Egg*, sold on by Harry and

Lillian Clifton after the break-up of their marriage. The collection was displayed in a Fifth Avenue apartment that was more
a museum than a home, to the extent that rooms were roped off
from visitors. Here the Linskys made no secret of their vision:
the inclusion of Fabergé in their own galleries at the Metropolitan Museum of Art in New York as a magnificent demonstration
of the heights that their native country's craftsmanship had
achieved. But then they had a visit from the museum's director,
James Rorimer. Scorning the collection as 'turn of the century
trinkets',[4] he told them firmly to collect more serious things.

Suitably cowed, the Linskys sold their collection soon afterwards. Another collector, however, was ready to take on at least
some of it. An heiress, so perhaps more in the mould of Marjorie
Post than Lillian Pratt or Belle Linsky, Matilda Geddings Gray
owed her wealth to oil. It enabled her to maintain one of the
finest Creole houses in New Orleans' French quarter, two other
houses elsewhere in Louisiana, of which one came with its own
plantation, a colonial *finca* in Guatemala, a townhouse in New
York and a rue Royale apartment in Paris.

Matilda had first encountered Fabergé's work in 1933, as
part of a display of Russian art which the Hammers had put
on in Chicago to coincide with the city's 'Century of Progress'
exhibition. Armand's brother Victor proved a particularly adept
salesman, appealing to the aesthetic sensibilities of a woman
who had trained as both a potter and a sculptor. She would
continue to be a customer of the Hammer Galleries for nearly
thirty years, buying cigarette cases, boxes, opera glasses, flower
fantasies and of course eggs. First came Marie Fedorovna's
1899 *Pansy Egg*, with its complex eleven-miniature surprise
and vague hint at unrequited love, but Matilda did not buy it
for herself. Instead, she gave the egg to her niece and namesake
Matilda Gray Stream for her first wedding anniversary.

There is no record of what the *Pansy Egg* cost Matilda, but
it must have been a five-figure sum. The insouciance with which
she passed the egg on remains a reminder of the difference

between the truly rich and the merely well off. If she regretted the gesture later, there was an easy solution. In the course of the 1950s Matilda bought three more Fabergé eggs. All had originally belonged to Marie Fedorovna, and all had been brought to America by Armand Hammer. First, in 1951, Matilda acquired the 1912 *Napoleonic Egg*, presented to Marie Fedorovna almost forty years before as a centenary celebration of Russia's victory in the Napoleonic Wars. Two years later she added the 1890 *Danish Palaces Egg* to her collection, long after it had first been shown to America in Hammer's department store sales. Finally, in 1959, she completed her trio with the 1893 *Caucasus Egg*, after it emerged from the break-up of the Linskys' collection. Matilda Geddings Gray, with the confidence of inherited wealth and a secure position in Louisiana society, clearly did not mind what the director of the Metropolitan Museum of Art thought.

THE CATALOGUE published by Kenneth Snowman in his 1953 book listed thirty-five eggs as having come to the West since the Revolution. He thought he knew the whereabouts of all except three: the 1895 *Rosebud Egg*, last heard of being thrown by Harry Clifton at his wife, the 1907 *Love Trophies Egg*, which was known to have gone to the United States in the 1930s but had since disappeared into a private collection, and Marie Fedorovna's 1906 *Swan Egg*, which Kenneth's father had originally brought out of Russia but had since vanished. In 1954, however, the third mystery had been solved. Snowman was in Cairo attending a special Sotheby's sale, 'The Palace Collections of Egypt'. Three eggs were up for auction. Two had similar designs to the first *Hen Egg*, which Alexander III had given to Marie Fedorovna in 1885. One of these was the first Fabergé egg given to Barbara Kelch by her husband; the other was probably not even a piece of Fabergé, although that does not seem to have stopped Armand Hammer from marketing it as the 1885 *Hen Egg* itself. The third was the *Swan Egg*.

King Farouk of Egypt had bought all three eggs at Hammer's

New York shop at the beginning of the Second World War. The
1906 *Swan Egg* alone had been advertised at $25,000 (£5,600,
£240,000), so Farouk's total outlay must have been considerable. The profligacy was typical. Farouk had succeeded to the
Egyptian throne in 1936 aged only sixteen, a slim and apparently charming young man. Within a few years, however,
debauched living ensured that he lost his youthful figure
beneath rolls of fat, and he acquired a reputation for corrup-
tion that saw him labelled the 'Thief of Cairo'. Armand Hammer
was only too happy to help him spend his country's wealth
and advertised Hammer Galleries in the pages of *Compleat
Collector* as trading 'By Appointment to His Majesty the King
of Egypt'. He explained in his autobiography how he became
Farouk's unofficial agent in New York, receiving increasingly
outlandish demands. Two of the King's missives are particularly striking: 'Buy me a Bakelite Factory' and 'Send me Lana
Turner.' Hammer was able, he said, to comply with only the first
request.

   In 1951 Farouk had prophesied his own doom: 'There will
soon be only five kings left: the Kings of England, Diamonds,
Hearts, Spades and Clubs.' He was deposed two years later in a
bloodless military coup. The auction in Cairo of the vast and
eclectic range of objects he had acquired in the seventeen years
he had ruled took place in 1954. The Fabergé pieces on sale,
however, were overshadowed by Farouk's collection of pornog-
raphy, said to be one of the most remarkable ever accumulated.
The 1906 *Swan Egg* ended up joining the 1908 *Peacock Egg*
and the 1911 *Bay Tree Egg* in the collection of Dr Maurice
Sandoz, a Swiss writer and composer who derived his fortune
from the Sandoz chemicals company. Farouk, meanwhile, had
fled Egypt for Italy and Monaco, spending the last years of his
life as flamboyantly as his more limited resources, and increasing girth, would permit. He died of a heart attack soon after a
heavy meal, aged only forty-five.

*

Two royal couples in fancy dress. Nicholas and Alexandra as Alexis and Maria at the Winter Palace ball of 1903 (*above*, *left*): for a few hours, they could pretend to be an oriental potentate and his wife, not the anachronistic rulers of a rapidly modernizing empire; George V and Queen Mary (*above*, *right*): first cousins, George and Nicholas were sufficiently alike for courtiers to confuse one with the other.

The Tsarevitch Alexis (*right*) photographed when his haemophilia was already diagnosed, but not yet common knowledge. He was adored by his four sisters, Olga, Tatiana, Maria and Anastasia – collectively known as 'OTMA' – photographed (*below*) in September 1906 in the summer palace at Peterhof.

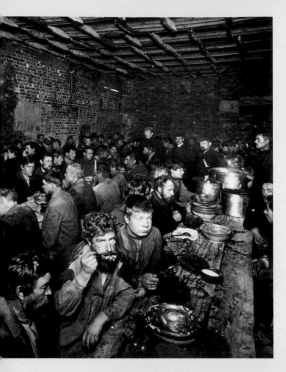

A soup kitchen for the unemployed in pre-war St Petersburg contrasts with the Ball of Coloured Wigs, held in a private house in 1914. Within months, rich and poor alike would be caught up in the maelstrom of the First World War.

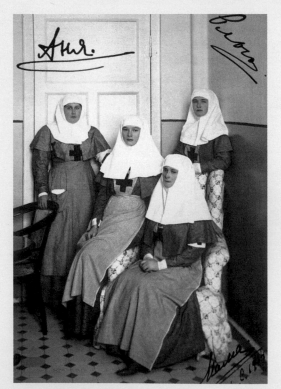

Alexandra with her elder daughters, Olga and Tatiana, and her friend Anna Vyrubova, in Red Cross uniforms. The contribution that Romanov women were making as nurses would inspire the eggs received by both empresses in 1915. In a nod to austerity, both were relatively plain, as were the last two eggs they received in 1916, shown opposite. Marie Fedorovna's *St George Cross Egg* (*top*) travelled with her into exile. Alexandra's *Steel Military Egg* was originally blackened – appropriate for a country at war. After being polished, however, it struck Kenneth Snowman as 'a banal example of kitsch'.

Gregory Efimovitch Rasputin – to Nicholas he was a 'good, religious, simple-minded Russian'; to Alexandra (in mourning after his murder) he was the only man who could manage her son's haemophilia; to their subjects he was an evil genius, the power behind the throne, as shown in this contemporary caricature by N. Ivanov.

The first stirrings of revolution on the streets of Petrograd in February 1917. The equestrian statue of Alexander III was the basis for the egg Marie Fedorovna received in 1910. It was also a popular symbol of tyranny. After the crowds had dispersed, police found the statue's nickname – 'Hippopotamus' – engraved in large letters on the plinth.

As the Bolsheviks tightened their grip, former members of the bourgeoisie were reduced to selling what they could on the streets of Petrograd simply to survive.

With Nicholas's abdication in March 1917 work on that year's Easter eggs was halted. Soon only memories – and this sketch design – remained.

Nicholas and Alexis in exile in Tobolsk. They enjoyed the mundane activity of sawing wood, and needed the fuel to heat the governor's mansion.

The basement of the House of Special Purpose, where the Imperial family was massacred, photographed soon after Ekaterinburg was occupied by White Russian forces. The Bolsheviks had done their best to clean the blood stains, but the bullet holes in the walls were not so easily hidden.

A display of the Russian crown jewels at Gokhran's headquarters in the summer of 1923. Twelve Imperial Easter Eggs are on the table. From left: the 1911 *Bay Tree Egg*, in front of the 1906 *Kremlin Egg*; the 1913 *Romanov Tercentenary Egg*, which is partially obscured by the 1896 *Revolving Miniatures Egg*, which is behind the 1916 *Steel Military Egg* (already polished); the 1908 *Peacock Egg*; the 1913 *Winter Egg*, in front of the 1898 *Pelican Egg*; the 1900 *Trans-Siberian Railway Egg*; the 1909 *Standart Egg* (between two open boxes); the 1911 *Fifteenth Anniversary Egg* (lying on its side, towards back); the 1914 *Mosaic Egg* (lying on its side, towards front).

A cross placed by the Russian Orthodox Church marks the location where the bodies of most of the massacred Romanovs were found – originally in 1970, although the discovery was only announced in 1991.

Armand Hammer photographed in June 1922 on a return visit to New York after his first year in Russia. He had already met Lenin and begun making the friends who would eventually enable him to acquire at least ten Fabergé eggs.

Malcolm Forbes holding his favourite piece of Fabergé, the 1911 *Fifteenth Anniversary Egg*, and his four sons, Timothy, Robert, Christopher and Steve, pose with the twelve eggs with which they believed their father had won the 'egg race' with the Kremlin.

WITH SALESMEN like Armand Hammer and collectors like King Farouk, it seems hardly surprising that museum directors still thought of Fabergé as not entirely serious. The jeweller would only be accepted by the art establishment when his friends and supporters became slightly more respectable. From that point of view, it is probably fortunate that Armand Hammer was already moving on, devoting himself to the career at Occidental Oil in which he would make his real fortune. His brother Victor would continue to run Hammer Galleries, but as the supply of arte-facts from the Soviet Union dried up, the business increasingly concentrated on Western art from the nineteenth and twentieth centuries. More to the point, the 1960s would see the emergence of a Fabergé collector whose enthusiasm for the Easter eggs was such that he almost single-handedly drove forward the rise in price that has led to them becoming some of the most valuable objects in the world.

22. 'When you viewed his Fabergé collection, you were doing *him* a favour'

LATER IN LIFE Malcolm Forbes would be refreshingly candid when asked how to achieve success: 'Sheer ability, spelt, "I-N-H-E-R-I-T-A-N-C-E" . . . If you can pick a parent that owns a business and be sure he's not mad at you when he checks out, it's a surer way to the top than anything else that comes to mind.'[1]

In Forbes's case the parent had been his father, 'B.C.' Forbes, an incisive and resourceful financial journalist who had started the magazine that bore his name in September 1917, a month before the Bolshevik Revolution. Malcolm's inheritance, on B.C.'s death in 1954, was a third share in that magazine, which then had a fortnightly circulation of over 100,000, making it one of the top business publications in the US, behind only *Fortune* and *BusinessWeek*. If there was a complication, it was that Malcolm's older brother Bruce had a matching sharehold-ing, with most of the remainder split between two younger brothers. Malcolm became nominal editor in chief of the maga-zine and took over his father's 'Fact and Comment' column. Here he developed his own writing style: chatty, opinionated and firmly in favour of free market economics. For the first few years of his editorship, however, Malcolm spent much of his time in a vain bid to become Republican governor of New Jersey. Bruce, by contrast, was a hands-on publisher, the magazine's chairman and boss, even after Malcolm finally gave up politics in 1957.

Malcolm's obsession with Fabergé started with a single purchase: a plain gold cigarette case bought in London as a Christmas present for his wife Roberta in 1960. The gift was a success and awoke memories in its purchaser of how during his childhood 'Fabergé was offered as an example of the waste and extravagance of the Imperial Russian Court.'[2] The thought only encouraged him; for Malcolm Forbes, conspicuous consumption would become a way of life. As he later put it, 'One man's decadence is another man's creative art.' The following Easter he bought his first Fabergé egg – which he would later describe as a 'jelly bean', one of the hundreds of small eggs turned out by the Fabergé workshop every Easter – a miniature version of the *Red Cross* eggs given to the two tsarinas in 1915.

Malcolm was becoming hooked, but it was not until 15 May 1965 that he really started to spend. That was the day he attended an auction in New York of items from the collection of Madame Ganna Walska, a Pole who had once been an opera singer but soon found a much more lucrative career as a wife. Her six husbands had included a carpet tycoon once described as the richest bachelor in America and Harold Fowler McCormick, whose father had founded International Harvester, the agricultural machinery manufacturer. With the passing of the years the diva had mellowed and was devoting her energies to her remarkable estate in San Diego, Lotusland, where she was creating a series of botanical gardens. This was an expensive undertaking, and Madame Walska had decided to fund it with the sale of some knick-knacks. It was Lot 326 that had attracted Malcolm's attention:

Important Wrought Gold, Rose and White ENAMEL SERPENT AND EGG ROTARY CLOCK, SET WITH DIAMONDS, BY CARL FABERGÉ Dated 1902

Note: We believe the monogram to be that of Queen

Alexandra, wife of Edward VII. By curious coincidence, the date beneath the clock, 1902, was the year of their coronation and could possibly have been a royal gift. She was an admirer of Fabergé's work, and her collection is now at Sandringham.

In short, Lot 326 was a Fabergé egg, apparently with royal connections. Forbes decided that he had to have it. When the bidding finally stopped – at $50,000 (£18,000, £230,000), three times the egg's pre-sale estimate and almost twice the previous auction record for any Fabergé egg – he was its new owner. It is hardly surprising that, as he later reminisced, 'I didn't sleep at all that night worrying about what auction fever had done to our exchequer.'[3] Forbes's only comfort was that the underbidder, whose counter-offers had pushed the egg's price to such dizzy heights, was someone he had heard of – Alexander Schaffer.

In his native Hungary Schaffer had once been a professional footballer, but in the forty-odd years since his arrival in the United States he had built a reputation as his adoptive country's most important dealer in Russian pre-revolutionary art. In the process he had firmly superseded Armand and Victor Hammer. There was irony in this as Schaffer had once been a Hammer Galleries employee. In 1933 he had set up on his own with the Schaffer Collection of Russian Imperial Treasures, stocked with the judicious purchases he had made on travels to Europe and Russia over the previous decade. By the outbreak of the Second World War he was in a position to sponsor the immigration to the United States of Léon Grinberg and his uncle Jacques Zolotnitsky, the proprietors of A La Vieille Russie in Paris. Having already experienced one war, they had no wish to remain in Europe to witness another, and they brought with them the name of which they were co-owners. Schaffer used it to provide his own business with a far more redolent brand. So A La Vieille Russie, which had been founded in Kiev in 1851

and moved to Paris in 1920, finally arrived on New York's Fifth
Avenue, where it still resides today.

In the 1930s Schaffer's greatest coup had been to buy the
1903 *Peter the Great Egg* from US Customs for around $1,000
(£200, £9,200) after its first, anonymous, purchaser failed to
pay the import duty required to claim it. Other dealers thought
Schaffer insane for handling such a modern piece. His judgement had finally been vindicated in 1942 when he sold the egg
on to Lillian Pratt for $16,500 (£4,100, £130,000) paid in
instalments, the only one of her five eggs that she did not buy
from Armand Hammer. This was a pattern typical of Schaffer.
After buying a piece he was quite happy to hang on to it until
the rest of the market came to its own appreciation of the value
of what he had bought.

It was therefore good news for Malcolm Forbes that Schaffer had been prepared to bid to just under $50,000 for Lot 326.
The dealer's history seemed to show that Forbes's investment in
the egg would eventually, come good. Schaffer would have been
happy at the outcome too. For one thing it established a marker
that set a price for the eggs he still owned, sitting in his vaults
on Fifth Avenue. For another, Malcolm Forbes was now a potential customer. Schaffer's eagerness to make contact with the
auction's victor was all too understandable. As he put it when
introducing himself, 'If Mr Forbes were interested in *important*
pieces of Fabergé, he might like to drop by A La Vieille Russie
that afternoon.'[4] It was the careful emphasis on 'important' that
made his meaning clear: Forbes should realize that, despite its
record-breaking price, Lot 326 did not fall into that category.

Subsequent research by Christopher 'Kip' Forbes – the
second of Malcolm's four sons – would establish the truth behind
Schaffer's insinuation. What Kip now calls 'my first scholarly
discovery' would show that the egg did not have the royal provenance suggested in the auction catalogue. The monogram was
actually that of Consuelo, Duchess of Marlborough, and the egg
was the souvenir she had ordered in St Petersburg so many years

before, the 1902 *Pink Serpent Clock Egg*. In 1926 she had consigned this memento of an unhappy marriage to a charity sale in Paris. Ganna Walska had been its purchaser.

Forbes accepted Schaffer's invitation to 'drop by *A La Vieille Russie*'. That afternoon he bought his first Imperial egg, the gaudy and strangely swollen 1894 *Renaissance Egg*, which Schaffer had bought from the Linskys seven years earlier. Within three months Forbes had bought another, paying a private collector $35,000 (£13,000, £160,000) for Marie Fedorovna's 1911 *Bay Tree Egg*. This egg had the dubious distinction of having been through more owners than any other since it was first brought out of Russia by Emanuel Snowman. Even its purchase by Maurice Sandoz had not stopped its wanderings: his heirs had sold it while choosing to retain his two other Imperial eggs, the 1906 *Swan Egg* and the 1908 *Peacock Egg*.

In 1966 Forbes's relationship with Schaffer moved to another level when the dealer negotiated the sale to the publisher of three Fabergé eggs in one go. All came from the estate of Lansdell Christie, a mining tycoon whose Fabergé collection had previously been on extended loan at the Metropolitan Museum. The museum's acceptance of the loan had aroused the ire of Belle Linsky, who remembered the scornful response of its director to her own collection of Fabergé a few years before. As she later told an interviewer, 'Never again will I ask for or listen to any expert's advice!'[5] Now she could derive grim satisfaction from the sale of Christie's collection to Forbes as it led to the museum losing what was by then a prized Fabergé display.[*]

Forbes believed that two of the three eggs from the Christie estate had Imperial provenance. One, the *Spring Flowers Egg*, was made of red enamel decorated with green gold in a rococo

---

[*] The most surprising aspect of the whole affair is that the Linskys continued with their plan to endow the Metropolitan with a significant collection of more 'mainstream' paintings and other objets d'art.

pattern, and opened to reveal an exquisite flower basket. The egg was small – a little over three inches high – and had only recently appeared in the West, but the brilliance of its workmanship and design was enough to convince observers that it was one of the early eggs presented to Marie Fedorovna by her husband. The other was the massive *Chanticleer Egg*, one of the six Kelch eggs which had first appeared in Paris in 1920. In his 1953 catalogue Kenneth Snowman suggested that this had been Nicholas's Easter gift to his mother in 1903. There was no reason to doubt the attribution. As far as Malcolm Forbes was concerned, he now owned four Imperial eggs.

In November 1966 Forbes's first burst of acquisitions culminated with his purchase of Alexandra's 1911 *Fifteenth Anniversary Egg*. The history of this egg since the Revolution is distinctly murky: it does not appear in either the 1917 or the 1922 inventories, but by 1953 Kenneth Snowman believed that it was in the Kremlin Armoury. It seems to have left Russia later in the 1950s, possibly as a gift – even a bribe – to one of the Soviet Union's American 'friends'. Once again Forbes bought the egg from Alexander Schaffer. Something about its craftsmanship and the detailed miniatures that cover its surface especially appealed to the publisher. Among all the eggs that he would go on to acquire, this one remained his favourite.

In less than two years Malcolm Forbes could claim to have built the largest collection of Fabergé eggs outside the Kremlin: seven, including five Imperial eggs. It had been a remarkable buying spree, of a different order to his previous spending pattern. He could afford it because he was no longer the junior partner in the business his father had founded. On 2 June 1964 Bruce had died, aged forty-eight, from a cancer that had been diagnosed only weeks before. He left a gap at the top of the magazine and Malcolm was the obvious person to fill it. He moved fast to assert both his authority and his free-spending credentials. Within a few months Malcolm had commissioned an expensive refurbishment of the Forbes headquarters in New

York and approved the advertising campaign that would come to define both him and his magazine: '*Forbes* – Capitalist Tool'.

The new air of profligacy that hung about the business had alarmed Bruce's widow, Ruth, the inheritor of her husband's shareholding. She decided to sell her stake while it still had some value. Malcolm was the obvious purchaser. By May 1965 he was firmly established as both chairman and majority shareholder of *Forbes* magazine.

In the space of a few months Malcolm's position had been transformed. Before Bruce's death he had been a moderately wealthy man. Now, although no richer than before, Malcolm could bring the full power of his company's resources to bear on whatever obsession he chose. So the eggs had not in fact been bought by Malcolm Forbes personally, but by *Forbes* magazine. They could hardly be classified as a standard business investment, and the remaining minority shareholders might have objected, but there was little they could do about it or about any of 'Chairman Malcolm's' other extravagances. In time, and with Malcolm's encouragement, his brothers and one other small shareholder would also sell out, leaving him in the same position as their father had once been – 100 per cent owner of *Forbes* magazine and the eggs that it owned.

Forbes may have had little need to justify himself to shareholders, but the US tax authorities were another matter. As time went on, Forbes would succeed in making many of his other extravagances tax-deductible. From parties on the yacht to balloon trips, careful systems ensured that all corporate guests were photographed and logged, as evidence to show that junkets were being used to sell advertising. Why should the eggs not be treated in the same way? In 1967, to celebrate the magazine's golden jubilee, the Forbes Fabergé collection was put on display in the lobby of the Forbes building. Potential advertisers would be treated to a tour of tsarist treasures. Later in the decade a publicity campaign tried to make an explicit connection: 'Carl Fabergé knew his business. *Forbes* magazine knows its business. *Forbes* – Capitalist Tool.' But it was not enough: the authorities insisted the eggs be paid for with the magazine's post-tax income.

Perhaps that is why Malcolm bought no more eggs for a decade. Or perhaps his resources were being absorbed by other projects and purchases: the chateau in Normandy, the town-house in London, the Fijian island or the palace in Tangiers. In 1975 the first of these became the home of the world's first ballooning museum, evidence of another enthusiasm, one that had seen Malcolm become the first man to balloon across the United States. All of this was paid for partly by the increasing success of the magazine – by the end of 1972 its circulation was up to 625,000 from the 200,000 that it had been at Bruce's death – and partly by the cash generated from another of Malcolm's purchases. In 1969 Forbes had paid around $4 million (£1.7 million, £18.5 million) for 174,000 acres of wilderness in Colorado. He had planned to turn it into a hunting preserve but was blocked by the state authorities, who declared that all the wildlife on the land belonged to the people. Perhaps, they enquired sweetly, Forbes would be able to drive all the existing animals off and then restock the preserve with his own game? Forbes had a better idea – give urban easterners the chance to own their own slice of land out west, a five-acre lot sold on easy credit for between $3,500 and $5,000. It was a piece of inspiration; and the mathematics was compelling. In the course of seven years the scheme raised over $30 million (£17 million, £85 million).

So in March 1976 Forbes was able to turn his attention once again to Fabergé, with the acquisition of the 1916 *Cross of St George Egg*, which had been inherited by the Grand Duchess Xenia from Marie Fedorovna. Allowed a grace and favour house near Windsor and buttressed by the money raised from the sale of her mother's jewels, Xenia had been more fortunate than the relations she had left behind in Russia. But as time went on she became an increasingly pathetic figure, living as simply as possible in order to support her seven grown-up children, and eventually confined by illness to a room filled with icons, photographs and souvenirs of Russia. The *Cross of St George Egg* had remained among them, never sold nor even exhibited again after that one occasion in Belgrave Square in 1935. When Xenia died in 1960, aged eighty-five, the egg passed to her youngest son, Prince Vasilii Romanov, who raised award-winning tomatoes in California. It held few memories for him – he had been only ten in 1917 – and in any case the Prince's finances left little room for sentiment. So in 1961 he had put it up for sale, at Sotheby's in London, where it raised £11,000 (£160,000). This was a record until Forbes's purchase of the *Pink Serpent Clock Egg* a few years later and a tidy sum, considering that at Xenia's death her entire estate, split between her seven children, had been valued at £117,272 (£1.8 million).

The 1961 purchaser of the 1916 *Cross of St George Egg* had been another corporation, one which could perhaps justify its acquisition with rather more reason than *Forbes* magazine was ever able to do – Fabergé Inc. By 1961 the toiletries firm founded by Samuel Rubin had achieved nationwide success. What was more natural than that it should have a tangible link to the man whose name had inspired it? In 1964, however, Rubin had sold Fabergé for $25 million (£9 million, £120 million) to Rayette, a cosmetics company.* It had no need for fantastic fripperies, whatever their histories, and the *Cross of St George Egg* was eventually sold again, coming to Forbes via – who else? – Alexander Schaffer and A La Vieille Russie.

The purchase of the egg signalled that Forbes was beginning another phase of Fabergé acquisitions. Nevertheless, he passed

---

* The subsequent chain of ownership of the Fabergé name includes the McGregor Corporation (a clothing company) and the Anglo-Dutch multi-national Unilever plc. In January 2007 the name was bought by Pallinghurst Resources LLP, which plans to develop Fabergé as a brand for luxury goods and gemstones.

on the next one to come up for sale, later in 1976. Its story might have been the most romantic of them all. The egg had only just come to light, after being bought in a Shanghai flea market in the 1920s. This provenance alone seemed to tell a tale of aristocratic émigrés fleeing east from the advancing communists, desperately selling possessions once they arrived in the relative safety of Shanghai. Then there was the egg's design. It had a body of lapis lazuli, studded with inlaid pieces of foil, or *paillons*, in the shape of stars to represent the night sky. It recalled Fabergé's night sky drawings for Alexandra's last egg, the one she never received, and the date on its back – 1917 – only reinforced the notion. This must be that last abortive gift, finally rediscovered after years of obscurity. It was dubbed the *Twilight Egg*, an evocative name for an object that marked the end of the dynasty. Forbes, however, was dissuaded from bidding by the clumsiness of much of the workmanship. It might have begun life in Fabergé's workshop, but it had clearly been finished off elsewhere. It was sold by Christie's in Geneva for 100,000 Swiss francs (£22,000, £110,000).

The *Twilight Egg* had been found in time to appear in a Fabergé exhibition which, in terms of the number of eggs displayed, had never been matched before, even in pre-revolutionary times. From June to September 1977 twenty-six eggs were on display at the Victoria and Albert Museum in London. The occasion was the Silver Jubilee of Queen Elizabeth II, who had inherited the Fabergé collection of her grandmother Queen Mary. The Queen's two Imperial eggs were in the exhibition, along with several others that remained in British hands and every Imperial egg owned by Malcolm Forbes. The show drew more visitors than any previous exhibition at the V.&A., an indication of the extent to which appreciation for Fabergé had now entered the mainstream.

The following January Forbes bought two of the jubilee exhibition's most notable exhibits. The Antikvariat had sold them both to a European dealer in the 1920s. They had then come up for auction at Christie's in 1934, where they were bought by a financier later ennobled as Lord Grantchester. In 1976 he and his wife had died within months of each other, so the eggs were already looking for a long-term owner when they appeared in the exhibition.

Both of the eggs were early examples of Fabergé's work. In fact, one was the first of them all – the 1885 *Hen Egg*, an especially covetable prize whose relative simplicity set it apart from all the other eggs in the series. The other boasted a rare religious theme: a shell of transparent rock crystal through which a sculpture was visible of Jesus rising from the tomb, with two angels kneeling in attendance. This was the *Resurrection Egg* – described in the V.&A. catalogue as 'one of Fabergé's masterpieces . . . essentially a jewel'. Most observers, including Emanuel Snowman, thought this must be an Imperial egg, one of Marie Fedorovna's early Easter gifts from her husband, and Forbes had no reason to doubt the attribution. As far as he knew, his magazine now owned eight Imperial eggs.

The amount Forbes paid for these two eggs was never revealed. It is safe to assume that the Grantchester estate made a decent return on a total investment in 1934 of £195 (£9,200), but as a private seller, especially with death duties involved, it would not have been keen to publicize the fact. The size of Forbes's next transaction, by contrast, soon became public knowledge. Once again two eggs were involved, and once again both had been in the V.&A. exhibition: the *Coronation Egg*, given to Alexandra in 1897, and her *Lilies of the Valley Egg* from the following year. Both had been brought out from Russia by Emanuel Snowman, and although each had subsequently been sold to a British buyer, both were back in Wartski's possession by the end of the 1940s. It had retained them for over thirty years, an investment but also a source of joy to Emanuel's son Kenneth, Wartski's chairman.

Urbane and charming, Snowman had by now been the

world's greatest Fabergé expert for more than a quarter of a century. His fame was such that Ian Fleming had even written him into a James Bond short story, tapping his teeth with a golden pen as a piece of Fabergé went up for auction. He had been both instigator and curator of the V.&A. exhibition, and its success had been a personal triumph. Snowman saw the 1897 *Coronation Egg* as Fabergé's greatest achievement and the 1898 *Lilies of the Valley Egg* as scarcely less remarkable. Wartski would only sell its treasures when the time was right.

In the words of Kip Forbes, negotiations were as protracted as any preceding a cold war nuclear treaty: 'There were times, over a year or two, that Pop and Kenneth didn't speak to each other. Kenneth would name the price. Two years later Pop would call and say, "All right, we're ready to go," and the price would have gone up.' By 1979, however, Snowman needed the money. Wartski's only other shareholder, Hambros Bank, had made a policy decision to sell its stakes in smaller companies. This was Snowman's chance to regain full ownership of the firm his grandfather Morris had founded, but to do so he needed to raise the money. Finally, he was ready to sell his firm's most significant assets. He told Forbes his price. Luckily, as Kip now says, 'We just happened to be having a very good year.'

Forbes paid Snowman £1 million (£3.4 million) for the two eggs. The figure sounds less impressive now, after nearly three decades of asset price inflation, but then, in the words of one Wartski director, it was 'a gasp-making sum'. In 1973, with Forbes uninterested, the 1900 *Cuckoo Clock Egg* had been sold by Christie's in Geneva for 620,000 Swiss francs, or £80,000 (£650,000). In the six years since then, which included one of the worst stock market collapses of the twentieth century, it seemed that the value of Fabergé eggs had gone up by something like a multiple of six.

These are the times when one realizes what a nebulous concept value is. In the end, that was what Malcolm Forbes was prepared to pay, so that was what the eggs were worth.

Apart from that break in the early 1970s, he had been driving the Fabergé market for fifteen years, happily admitting that 'most of the spending records we break are our own'.[6] He was a true obsessive who took simple pleasure in the fact that he could summon his secretary using a Fabergé bell push. As the columnist William Buckley would later put it, 'When you viewed his Fabergé collection, you were doing *him* a favour.'[7]

Forbes had made his ambition clear in 1978 when he wrote the introduction to a catalogue of his collection: 'History is not without its amusing ironies. In September 1917, one month before the Soviets seized power in Russia, B.C. Forbes published the first issue of *Forbes* magazine. Sixty-one years later, the "Capitalist Tool", as *Forbes* is known, owns only two fewer of Fabergé's Imperial eggs than the Soviet Government.'[8] Six months after writing that, the acquisition of the *Coronation* and *Lilies of the Valley* eggs took Forbes level with the Kremlin. Now, he wanted to win.

To BEAT THE Kremlin, however, Forbes needed an Imperial egg to come up for sale. That was becoming an increasingly rare occurrence. By 1979 about forty Fabergé eggs were known to have emerged from Russia since the Revolution. Forbes might have 'only' ten of them, but by far the majority of the remainder were no longer available for purchase. Marjorie Post's last house, Hillwood in Washington DC, had been a museum in all but name, as her last husband was fond of complaining, for years. Her death in 1973 formalized the arrangement: the Hillwood Museum's two eggs would never be sold. Nor would Matilda Gray's three; in 1971 she had left them to her own foundation, to keep on public display. Then there were Lillian Pratt's five eggs, by now cherished exhibits at the Virginia Museum of Fine Arts. The two that Henry Walters had bought from Alexander Polovtsov in 1930 were still in the museum he had established in Baltimore. And in 1965 another American collector, India Minshall, had left Marie Fedorovna's 1915 *Red*

Cross Portraits Egg to the Cleveland Museum of Art in Ohio. Across the Atlantic Queen Elizabeth II seemed unlikely to sell the two eggs bought by her grandmother, and in Switzerland another sort of royalty, the fabulously wealthy Sandoz family, was about to put the 1906 *Swan Egg* and the 1908 *Peacock Egg* under the control of the Fondation Edouard et Maurice Sandoz. Finally, there was a growing recognition that not all the eggs previously classified as 'Imperial' necessarily deserved that status. In the course of the 1980s the debate over the status of several eggs would intensify.

In short, only six unimpeachably Imperial eggs were known to remain in private hands, and several of those had not been seen for decades. Wartski had sold the 1887 *Blue Serpent Clock Egg* to a private Swiss buyer in the early 1970s but had since lost track of it. The 1895 *Rosebud Egg* and 1907 *Love Trophies Egg* remained listed as 'whereabouts unknown', just as they had been when Kenneth Snowman compiled his catalogue in 1953. Most worrying of all perhaps, the 1913 *Winter Egg* had been missing since the death of its British owner, Bryan Ledbrook, in 1975. To Geoffrey Munn, who is now Wartski's managing director, the *Winter Egg* was 'the absolute swansong and greatest masterpiece of all the eggs' – proof that, even as the First World War approached, Fabergé's capacity to astonish remained undimmed. Ledbrook, however, had never looked after it very well. Kenneth Snowman asserted that he used to keep it in a garage close to Victoria Station in London; Geoffrey Munn remembers him bringing it into Wartski in the kind of 'wicker basket that turkeys used to be carried in years ago'. After Ledbrook's death Munn went so far as to place a small advertisement in the classified section of London's *Daily Telegraph* in an attempt to trace what had happened to the egg. Plenty of the eccentric's friends came forward but none was any help in locating the treasure. There was a real possibility that it might have been destroyed.

As for the two remaining locatable eggs, they seemed to be

pretty securely held. Matilda Gray Stream still owned Marie Fedorovna's 1899 *Pansy Egg*, given to her by her aunt Matilda Geddings Gray more than thirty years before, and the 1900 *Cuckoo Clock Egg* was the prized possession of Bernard Solomon, president of Everest Records, who had bought it at that Swiss auction in 1973. It was likely to be some time before Forbes achieved his dream.

THERE WAS of course another way to get hold of a Fabergé egg, although not one that would ever have appealed to Malcolm Forbes. In accordance with the will of Matilda Geddings Gray, her collection had spent the years since her death in 1971 travelling around America, taking Fabergé to places it otherwise might not have reached. On 13 September 1980 it arrived at the Paine Art Center in Oshkosh, Wisconsin for a stay intended to last for three months. During the night of 21 October, however, the run was cut short. In a remarkably successful burglary all three of the Matilda Geddings Gray Foundation's eggs were stolen.

As far as the thieves were concerned, that was the easy part. It soon became clear that their haul of instantly recognizable and unique objects was not going to be easy to sell. The only possible course was to demand a ransom for the return of the collection, so on 27 January 1981, after the director of the Paine Center had inspected the stolen goods and confirmed that they were undamaged, $250,000 (£124,000, £330,000) was left at a designated location. Thereafter, however, things did not go so smoothly for the criminals. The drop point had been staked out by the FBI. The high-speed car chase that ensued crossed several state lines but ended with the arrest of two men and the recovery of the ransom.

Having recovered all its treasures, the Gray Foundation understandably decided that in future they would be more securely displayed in a permanent, and stationary, exhibition. The New Orleans Museum of Art in Matilda's home state of

Louisiana was the chosen partner. In May 1983 the Matilda Geddings Gray Collection went on display in its own dedicated room behind specially strengthened glass.*

FORBES HAD TO wait until 1985 before another Imperial egg became available. The marriage of Bernard and Donna Solomon was coming to an end, and the 1900 *Cuckoo Clock Egg* was being sold as part of the divorce settlement. One hundred years after the first egg was given to Marie Fedorovna, this would be the first time that one of the Imperial eggs had come up for auction in the United States. Bidding soon went beyond the $1 million estimate, but there can never have been much doubt as to who would be the eventual winner. Forbes would later rationalize the cost – $1,760,000 (£1.4 million, £2.8 million) – as something that 'didn't lessen the value of some of the more beautiful and more famed eggs that we already had'.[9] More to the point, the auctioneer had announced as he brought down the gavel, 'The score now stands at the Kremlin – 10, Forbes – 11.'[10] Finally, on behalf of the capitalist West, Malcolm Forbes could declare undisputed victory over the Russians. He insisted on taking the egg away with him there and then. By the next morning it was on display in the Forbes Building.

---

* The foundation moved its collection to a new home, at Cheekwood in Nashville, Tennessee, in March 2007.

23. 'He who dies with the most toys wins'

Soon after he secured the 1900 *Cuckoo Clock Egg*, Forbes was asked if he would continue his 'egg race' with the Kremlin. His reply – 'Eggs usually come in dozens' – was a strong hint that there would be one more acquisition. Negotiations were already underway. In March 1986 Forbes was able to announce the purchase of Alexandra's 1895 *Rosebud Egg*. Missing for something like forty years, the egg was in a condition which suggested that there was some truth to the story that it had been used as a missile in one of the Talbot-Cliftons' marital disputes. In the meantime it had been inexpertly repaired – the yellow enamel of its rosebud surprise has nothing of Fabergé's usual vibrancy – and the crown and pendant the rosebud had once contained were missing. Nevertheless, it was an Imperial egg, the first that Nicholas had given Alexandra. It would be the last purchased by Malcolm Forbes.

There were, however, other extravagances. In 1987 Forbes publicized an exhibition of his Fabergé collection at Baron Thyssen's Villa Favorita in Switzerland with an object that succeeded in combining two of his pleasures. The *Rosebud* balloon was a ninety-foot-high replica of Forbes's final Fabergé acquisition. Costing £30,000, it had taken two seamstresses more than a month to put together from over 1,000 yards of fabric. The large red balloon was no doubt an impressive advertisement for the exhibition as it floated over the Alps. Carl Fabergé, a businessman who appreciated the value of good public relations, might well have approved, but it would be hard to say the same of the egg's original owner, the unnaturally shy Alexandra.

Then in October 1989 came a Fabergé exhibition that made everything that had gone before look second rate. For the first time since the Revolution the Kremlin agreed to let most of its eggs go to the West. Eight of them travelled to the San Diego Museum of Art, where they were combined with the bulk of the Forbes Magazine Collection and other loans from private owners, including Queen Elizabeth II and the Matilda Geddings Gray Foundation, to put twenty-seven eggs on display. In January the following year twenty-three of them went to the Kremlin, where they were joined by the two eggs that had not travelled to San Diego to create another spectacular show.

Between them, the two exhibitions represented a grand reciprocal gesture, one that reflected the remarkable thawing in Russia's relationship with the West that had followed the appointment of Mikhail Gorbachev as general secretary of the Communist Party in 1985. Perestroika and glasnost – reform and openness – had seen the emergence of the first private enterprises in Russia since Stalin replaced the New Economic Policy with centralized planning, and had allowed far greater freedom of expression than at any time since Lenin's death. Only a few years before, the Soviet Union had been, in Ronald Reagan's immortal phrase, 'the evil empire'. Now, the joint exhibition was one more piece of evidence that relations between Russia and the West had moved from conflict to cooperation. More than that, it seemed that the Soviets were finally coming to terms with their country's pre-revolutionary past. Ignored for so many years in his native country, Fabergé was finally being welcomed home.

Malcolm Forbes was an enthusiastic participant in the dual event, displaying the flamboyance that had by now become his trademark. He was delighted to make known the only condition he had placed on his eggs being allowed to go to Moscow: that they should do so in the plane named after the strapline of the magazine that owned it: *Capitalist Tool*. His 'Fact and Comment' column for 5 March 1990 gave his own tongue-in-cheek assessment of the occasion's significance: 'It is the first time in my life that I have been wholeheartedly rooting for the stability and survival of the Russian government as presently constituted – at least, for the duration of the exhibit!'[1]

That column appeared posthumously. On 24 February 1990, while his eggs were still in Moscow and shortly after flying back to his home in New Jersey from a bridge game in London, Malcolm Forbes suffered a fatal heart attack. He was only seventy, but he should have been content. He had spent his life enjoying not just the Fabergé, the balloons, the houses, the island, the yacht and the plane, but also major collections of miniature boats, American presidential memorabilia, Victorian paintings and a fleet of Harley-Davidson motorcycles. One of his favourite quotes was, 'He who dies with the most toys wins.'[2] By that measure, Malcolm Forbes had led a successful life.

If MALCOLM FORBES died after a life well lived, then Armand Hammer could be said to have hung on too long. In December 1990 he finally succumbed to bone marrow cancer, aged ninety-two. He and Forbes had been friends, of a sort. Both were staunch Republicans. Hammer's support for Richard Nixon's Watergate-tainted presidential bid had seen him convicted of making illegal campaign contributions (he was later pardoned), while Forbes's abortive political career had received support from Nixon in his earlier incarnation as Eisenhower's vice-president. More practically, and in direct contrast to their domestic political sympathies, in 1979 Hammer had used his communist connections to facilitate a Forbes motorcycle trip to Moscow. He was hardly returning a favour: in fact quite the reverse. Eight years earlier *Forbes* magazine had lambasted Hammer (then seventy-three) for being too old and frail to continue as chief executive of Occidental Petroleum. Hammer was, however, entirely used to ignoring all such calls for him to

retire. He was still in post on the day he died, exercising extraordinary and capricious power over the major multinational
he had created.

Hammer's reputation suffered serious damage in the years
after his death. It soon became clear that, for Occidental's
shareholders at least, the last years of his leadership had been
distinctly uninspiring. More injurious was the information that
would emerge from the former Soviet Union in the course of
the 1990s. It was not Mikhail Gorbachev's glasnost that was
responsible, more the wholesale repudiation of communism
that followed Gorbachev's fall in December 1991. Within a few
years democratization and freedom of information had opened
up the Kremlin's archives to historians. The story they told of
Hammer's years in the Soviet Union was very different from
his own account in *The Quest of the Romanoff Treasure*. By
1996 Edward Epstein, in *Dossier: The Secret History of Armand
Hammer*, was able to paint a portrait of a man who was not so
much an entrepreneur, taking advantage of the opportunities
created by Lenin's New Economic Policy, as a courier working
for the Russian government, who used the cover of his business
activities to deliver money from Russia to communist organiza-
tions overseas. Conspiracy theorists nowadays have little trouble
believing that Hammer remained a Soviet agent for the rest of
his life. According to this view, whether or not he paid for them,
Hammer's haul of Fabergé eggs, acquired with such aplomb in
1930, can simply be seen as payment for services rendered.

OBJECTS as well as people had their pasts rewritten as a result
of glasnost and the collapse of communism. The opening of the
Kremlin archives meant that researchers were able to supple-
ment the unreliable memories of Eugène Fabergé and his
brothers with contemporaneous documents relating to the eggs.
The trickle of information that had begun in the early 1980s
reached its climax in 1997 with the publication of *Fabergé
Imperial Easter Eggs*. Its authors included Tatiana Fabergé,

Agathon's granddaughter, who had inherited her family's records, and Valentin Skurlov, a Russian researcher who had already spent years tracking down documents in the Russian State Archives. An American dealer, Lynette Proler, completed the trio. Between them, they had succeeded in unearthing Fabergé invoices and Imperial account book entries relating to nearly all the eggs. The few gaps could be filled from other sources. Finally, they were able to give an exact listing of all the eggs and when they were given.

For at least one owner, the archives had already brought a piece of good news. In 1933 Britain's Queen Mary had acquired what appeared to be an egg-shaped basket of enamelled flowers. It may have been a gift, as there is no record of her having paid for it. In any case, it was accorded no great importance. Kenneth Snowman believed it to be the work of a French jeweller, Boucheron. In 1989, however, an eagle-eyed visitor to the San Diego exhibition noticed an egg that looked remarkably like this flower basket in a photograph of the exhibition that had been hosted in 1902 at the von Dervis house in St Petersburg. Two years later a Kremlin researcher confirmed that Nicholas had given the egg to Alexandra in 1901. With the addition of the 1901 *Flower Basket Egg*, the Queen's collection of Imperial eggs had, at a stroke, increased by 50 per cent.

Other collectors were not so lucky. An inevitable corollary of the ability to assign an egg to each year with certainty was the equal ability to demote to non-Imperial status those eggs which did not appear on the list. The Forbes Magazine Collection was the principal sufferer – a consequence of the Soviet Union's implosion which the Capitalist Tool can hardly have expected or appreciated. Three of its eggs had to be reclassified. There was no place in the list of Imperial presents for two of Forbes's smallest acquisitions: the jewel-like *Resurrection Egg* with its representation of Christ rising from the tomb, and the *Spring Flowers Egg*, bought from Landsell Christie's estate in 1966. And another purchase from the Christie estate, the *Chanticleer*

Egg, despite its size and magnificence, had not after all belonged to the Dowager Empress. Alexander Kelch had given it to his wife in 1904, the last egg she was to receive before the collapse of their business interests and their marriage. The provenance of the rest of the magazine's collection might have been recon-firmed by researchers, but that was small consolation. Malcolm Forbes had not won the egg race. He had built a collection that contained only nine Imperial eggs; the Kremlin still had ten.

PERHAPS THE RACE baton would be taken up by the next gen-eration? At least one of Malcolm's sons had inherited his passion for Fabergé. Kip Forbes's identification of the Duchess of Marl-borough's *Pink Serpent Clock Egg* while he was still a schoolboy was hardly happenstance. Even before that, the second edition of Kenneth Snowman's book had awoken a passion evidenced by the hand-illustrated ten-page report Kip produced as an eighth-grade assignment in 1963: 'Carl Fabergé: Life and Art'. This was to be the precursor of many publications, culminating in 1999's lavishly produced *Fabergé: The Forbes Collection*. Bound in lilac, its pages trimmed with silver, if ever there was a book which itself aspired to be a Fabergé egg, then this was it – apparent confirmation of the Forbes family's continuing commitment to Fabergé. The introduction backed this up, high-lighting the purchase of two non-Imperial eggs since Malcolm Forbes's death: the *Nobel Ice Egg* and the *Globe Clock Egg*. After noting what remained to come onto the market, it closed on an optimistic note: 'there are still plenty of eggs which could end up in our basket!'.

That final phrase was disingenuous. Whatever Kip's per-sonal passion for Fabergé, he was only one of the four sons who had inherited the Forbes empire. It was the eldest, Steve, who had been left the controlling interest in the business and its assets, including the Fabergé collection. His enthusiasms lay elsewhere: two bids for the Republican presidential nomination, in 1996 and 2000, would cost a total of $76 million; as a collector he was more interested in Churchilliana. Those two further purchases, therefore, were far from being signs of the family's continuing commitment to the egg race with the Kremlin. Not only did neither have Imperial provenance, the *Globe Clock* 'egg', as its name implies, is a sphere; there is nothing ovoid about it.

More to the point, at least two Imperial eggs had been sold in the years between Malcolm Forbes's death and the publication of his son's book, and the family had not shown any interest in bidding for either of them. The first was the *Love Trophies Egg*, presented to Marie Fedorovna in 1907 as a late celebration of the Tsarevitch's birth. Since the late 1930s this egg had been in a private collection in America. It emerged briefly for the San Diego exhibition in 1989, although it did not subsequently make the trip to Moscow. Then in June 1992 it was auctioned at Sotheby's in New York. The last Imperial egg to come up for sale before that had been the 1900 *Cuckoo Clock Egg*, in 1985, when the occasion was dominated by Malcolm Forbes's showmanship and wallet. This time, however, the Forbes family did not even bid. The egg went from one anonymous American owner to another.*

The 1907 *Love Trophies Egg* came on the market when the Forbes Collection was still believed to have a dozen Imperial eggs. It was arguably a relatively unexciting example of Fabergé's work, especially as it had long since been separated from its surprise. Even if Malcolm Forbes had still been alive he might have decided to pass on it. The same cannot be said, however, of the egg which came up for auction two years later.

In 1994 possibly the greatest of all the Imperial eggs emerged from years of obscurity: the 1913 *Winter Egg*. Its whereabouts since Bryan Ledbrook's death have never been satisfactorily explained, although it is believed to have been found in a London

---

* An article in the *Washington Post*, Saturday, 13 March 2004, p. C01, suggests that the anonymous buyer was Robert M. Lee, the founder of Hunting World, an upmarket luggage company.

safe. It was in surprisingly good condition; Ledbrook had not been as careless with his treasure as had been feared. That November Christie's in Geneva offered it for sale. For this egg, surely, Malcolm Forbes would have been keen to round his collection up to a baker's dozen. Once again, however, his heirs passed on the opportunity. They did so again, in 2002, when the egg came on the market for the second time in less than ten years. By that time it was clear to all that there were only nine Imperial eggs in the Forbes Magazine Collection. Yet, according to Kip, the family was 'not even tempted' to close the gap with the Kremlin.

The death of Malcolm Forbes had closed an era. By paying 'gasp-making' prices that were both extravagant and foolhardy he had almost single-handedly sustained the market for Fabergé. So how did it cope with the absence of its most important purchaser? The auction prices of the Imperial eggs sold since Forbes's death tell their own story. In 1992 the *Love Trophies Egg* fetched the equivalent of £1.8 million, smashing the record established by Forbes's purchase of the *Cuckoo Clock Egg* in 1985; two years later the *Winter Egg* cost its anonymous purchaser £3.6 million; in 2002 it went for £6.4 million to a representative of the Emir of Qatar. Demand for Fabergé's greatest creations had not only survived the death of Malcolm Forbes, it had developed its own momentum, generated by a new breed of purchasers from around the world. The exhibitions, the publications, the romance of the Romanovs and the sheer enthusiasm of Malcolm Forbes: all had done their part. The world's appreciation for Fabergé had come of age.

24. 'Handle it and then question it; that thing is as right as rain'

SOME TIME in the course of 2001 the Fersman Mineralogical Museum in Moscow made a remarkable discovery. A few years before, Tatiana Fabergé had found in her family archives a letter that Fabergé's former designer François Birbaum had written to Eugène Fabergé in 1922. In it he had set down all that he could recollect about those last two eggs made for Easter 1917, but never delivered because of the revolution. Alexandra's was to be 'an egg of dark blue glass incrustated with the constellation of the day of the Tsarevitch's birth . . . supported by silver cherubs and clouds of opaque rock crystal'.[1] Birbaum's description, together with a design signed by Carl Fabergé in 1917, which had first been published in Kenneth Snowman's book in 1953, gave a remarkably clear view of Fabergé's intentions for Alexandra's 1917 egg. The information was enough, eventually, for staff at the Fersman Museum to realize that among the artefacts in its storerooms was an object that looked remarkably like it, the 1917 *Blue Tsarevitch Constellation Egg*.

The Fersman Museum has a long and distinguished history. It moved to Moscow in the 1930s and in 1955 was renamed in honour of its recently deceased director, Alexander Fersman, but before those two events it had been Leningrad's Museum of Geology and Mineralogy. The relic it had found was part of the A. Fabergé Collection, the odds and ends the museum received from Agathon Fabergé in 1925 before he left Russia. It had an egg component exactly as described by Birbaum and an oddly misshapen stand carved from a piece of opaque rock crystal. Roughly worked, the piece was clearly unfinished. Nor was there any evidence of a surprise – Birbaum's letter mentioned a clock – so it is perhaps understandable that, for seventy years, the museum believed the egg to be a lamp stand. That is to under-sell the egg. Despite its shortcomings, it is a strikingly modern object, one which shows that, even in the darkest days of the First World War, with many of his best craftsmen conscripted and subject to ever fiercer budgetary constraints, Fabergé could still produce an egg that broke new ground in both design and materials.

Birbaum's letter to Eugène Fabergé also mentioned a wooden egg 'which was to have been presented in 1917 but which Kerensky did not allow to be delivered to the Tsar'.[2] This seemed to correspond with the memory passed down by Eugène Fabergé of an egg intended for Marie Fedorovna that was made of Karelian birch. For years it had been thought that this egg had been destroyed in the Revolution or perhaps never even completed, so it was especially exciting when another of Tatiana Fabergé's discoveries raised hopes that it might have been fin-ished and subsequently preserved. This time she had found an inventory made only five days after the October Revolution. It listed the treasures expropriated from the Vladimir Palace in Petrograd, which had been built as a home for Grand Duke Vladimir Alexandrovitch, the brother of Alexander III who had been involved in the purchase of the very first Imperial egg. Among the confiscated objects was a 'Wooden egg in gold setting; inside, an elephant, mechanical, silver and gold, with rose-cut diamonds. Fabergé.' Not only did the description of the egg match Birbaum's memory, but the elephant sounded exactly like a suitable surprise for Marie Fedorovna.

Nevertheless, Tatiana could discover nothing about what had happened to the egg found in the Vladimir Palace, and no further confirmation that it might really be Marie Fedorovna's missing present. All the more surprising therefore was the news in November 2001 that the 1917 *Karelian Birch Egg* had been found. It came from the egg's new owner, a group of Russian businessmen, thought to include several oil barons, that for no clear reason called itself the Russian National Museum (RNM). The egg had been made to a design that corresponded exactly to some more sketches found in the Fabergé family archives. It was missing that elephant surprise but still contained a key for its mechanism, monogrammed MF.

The story of where the egg had spent the previous eighty years was less obscure than one might expect for such a late discovery. From the Vladimir Palace it had apparently gone first to the Rumyantsevsky Museum, but when that was closed by the communists in 1927 450 of its exhibits, including the egg, were sold to the West. Since then the 1917 *Karelian Birch Egg* had apparently been sitting in a London vault, its owners – first an anonymous Russian émigré and then his equally nameless descendants – waiting until the time was right for a sale. They judged their moment well; the RNM would not say exactly what it paid for an egg made of wood and gold, but it admitted to 'millions of dollars'.

Remarkably, the egg came with its own documentation – a ready-made and apparently cast-iron provenance. First, there was a letter from Carl Fabergé to Kerensky, in which Fabergé complained at not having been paid and asked for the egg to be sent on to Nicholas. And then there was the invoice, dated 25 April 1917, for 12,500 roubles, a lot given the materials and evidence that Russia's currency was already beginning to suffer from the effects of inflation. Most poignant of all, however, was the invoice's addressee: 'Nicholas Romanov'. Already and even to his most famous supplier, Nicholas was no longer Tsar but a private citizen expected to pay his bills on time.

*

DISCOVERIES like these are the stuff of which dreams are made, and they keep alive the possibility that, some day, somewhere, another missing egg or surprise may turn up. The archival researches of the 1990s have provided a complete listing, with descriptions, of the fifty Imperial eggs presented from 1885 to 1916. With every egg assigned to a year and a recipient, it is easy to identify the remaining gaps. Every one of the twenty eggs given to Alexandra can now be accounted for – an ironic side-benefit of the rapidity with which she and her husband were imprisoned and their possessions secured after Nicholas's abdication. Eight of Marie Fedorovna's eggs, however, are missing, those from 1886, 1888, 1889, 1896, 1897, 1902, 1903 and 1909. Finding one remains the goal and dream of just about every Fabergé researcher.

At least two of the missing eight may have come to the West in the 1920s or early 1930s. In 1889 a manager responsible for Alexander III's valuables listed the first five eggs that the Tsar had presented to Marie Fedorovna. The list, which was first published in 1984, describes the egg from 1888 as an 'Angel pulling a chariot with an egg'.[3] This sounds remarkably similar to the 'miniature silver amour holding wheelbarrow with Easter Egg, made by Fabergé'[4] advertised by Armand Hammer at Lord and Taylor in 1934. It is not in the list of eggs that Hammer bought from the Antikvariat in 1930, but he could have acquired it elsewhere, possibly at a 1933 sale in Berlin, where some eggs may have been sold and which he once admitted to attending. Of course, that begs the question as to why Hammer did not make more of a song and dance about the egg. Perhaps, as an early example, it was relatively small, and Hammer was not aware of its Imperial status.

Another one of Marie Fedorovna's early eggs, from 1889, is described on its invoice as a 'Nécessaire egg, Louis XV style'.[5] This is probably the egg included in an inventory drawn up to keep track of the Tsarina's jewellery as she travelled from Gatchina to Moscow. This refers to 'One item in the form of an egg, decorated with stones, containing ladies toilet articles, thirteen pieces'.[6] Compare that with the catalogue description of Item 20, lent anonymously to the exhibition that Wartski held in 1949 to accompany the publication of Henry Bainbridge's biography of Fabergé: 'A Fine Gold Egg . . . designed as an Etui [a case for holding articles of daily use] with thirteen gold and diamond set implements'.[7] Surely that egg too remains somewhere in the West.

The idea that these two early eggs, at least, may have survived the Revolution is supported by the appearance of eggs with similar descriptions in the inventories made in 1917 when confiscated objects were sent to Moscow, and again in 1922 when the Armoury passed them on to Gokhran. Of the remaining six missing eggs, there are two others that may also have made it as far as the Kremlin Armoury. The egg from 1886, described in that 1889 list as 'The hen taking a sapphire egg out of the wicker basket',[8] may be the 'silver hen, speckled with rose-cut diamonds, on gold stand'[9] that is mentioned in the Armoury's 1922 inventory. And the 1917 inventory includes a 'Nephrite egg on gold stand, with medallion portrait of the Emperor Alexander III'.[10] Is this the same as Marie's Easter gift from 1902: 'Nephrite and gold EMPIRE egg, with two diamonds and miniature'?[11]

The archives hold out no such hopes for the last four missing eggs. We must acknowledge the probability that they were destroyed in the course of 1917, either by casual ransackers after Nicholas's abdication or in the more systematic destruction of Gatchina that was ushered in by the Bolshevik coup. They may have been hidden or squirrelled away by a knowledgeable looter, but, more than eighty years later, the chances are surely against their survival. All we have are the brief descriptions on Fabergé's invoices, and in the case of two of the eggs, grainy black and white photographs taken before the Revolution.

Nevertheless, one researcher, Will Lowes, has suggested that there remains some hope that even these four eggs may one day re-emerge.[12] What if Marie Fedorovna took more than the 1916 *Cross of St George Egg* with her when she left the Crimea on HMS *Marlborough*? The sequence of events is crucial here. Marie Fedorovna spent Easter 1916 in Petrograd, only leaving for Kiev some weeks later. Shortly after Nicholas's abdication she moved further south to the Crimea. There is therefore no particular reason why the *Cross of St George Egg* should have been the only Imperial egg in that infamous jewellery box. She could have packed several of them when she left Petrograd for the last time. After all, Marie was always more devoted to her eggs than Alexandra; to her, Fabergé was an 'unparalleled genius'.

The invoice descriptions of Marie's four missing eggs lend support to this theory. They show that two of them – those from 1896 and 1909 – memorialized her husband, Alexander III, and a third – the egg she received in 1903 – contained portraits of Marie's parents. The fourth missing egg – from 1897 – is described on its invoice simply as a 'mauve enamel egg with three miniatures – 3,250 roubles'.[13] At first reading this is not necessarily a personal gift at all, except that among other Fabergé pieces bought by Malcolm Forbes was a heart-shaped frame of strawberry enamel set with the date 1897. It opens into a three-leaved clover, revealing pictures of Nicholas, Alexandra and a new-born Olga. Surely this is the surprise from the missing egg. It confirms that each of the four missing eggs touched on subjects highly personal to the Dowager Empress – they were exactly the sort of objects that Marie might have always kept by her side.

Documentary evidence for the idea that more than one egg accompanied Marie to the West is no more than circumstantial. There's that elusive Item 32 in the inventory prepared by the valuers when Marie's jewellery box was opened after her death, the 'gold chain set rubies and diamonds with gemset Easter egg'. Removed by the Grand Duchess Xenia, it has since disappeared but it may be a red herring; certainly it is hard to fit that description with any of the four missing eggs.*

Much more intriguing are the frustratingly vague descriptions of the several items lent by the Grand Duchess Xenia to the 1935 Exhibition of Russian Art in London's Belgrave Square. Two entries in the exhibition's catalogue appear to match the invoice descriptions of the surprises from the missing 1902 and 1896 eggs. And a listing that reads 'Easter Egg: Miniature of the Empress Alexandra and the Grand Duchess Olga inserted'[14] might be that missing egg from 1897, inadequately described. All this, however, can only be speculation. None of these catalogue items has surfaced again, and whoever owns them now is either not aware of their significance or does not wish to attract unwelcome attention.

Kip Forbes for one is convinced that most, if not all, of the missing eight eggs will eventually surface. The only risk, as he sees it, is that the eggs may have been destroyed in the Second World War. That would be a sad irony for objects that had already survived one war and a revolution. But there's another danger that all these eggs would now face if they were to emerge undamaged after years of obscurity: who would believe that they were real?

Early forgeries of Fabergé tended to be relatively crude – good enough to fool Armand Hammer's more gullible customers but relatively easy to identify now. The Virginia Museum of Fine Arts now celebrates the undoubtedly genuine eggs and other

---

* It may, however, explain the route to the West of the 1895 *Twelve Monogram Egg*, commemorating Alexander III, that Marjorie Post acquired in 1949. Its surprise is missing, but it could have been a diamond and ruby necklace, considering the short time Fabergé had to prepare that year's Easter gift, only six months after the death of Alexander III. More to the point, the egg does not appear on any Soviet inventory and its history remains distinctly murky. Might the egg have been sold by Xenia to 'Mrs Berchielli', the Italian woman who sold it to Marjorie Post?

Fabergé objects it inherited from Lillian Pratt, but it has also had to come to terms with the fact that some of her purchases were not so astute. It makes the best it can of them by devoting a display cabinet to her collection of 'Fauxbergé'. Visitors learn how early forgers in one sense tried too hard – they placed Fabergé stamps in inappropriate places or made flower fantasies with many stems when Fabergé always confined himself to one – but in another way simply did not try hard enough: the quality of workmanship is never commensurate with what Carl Fabergé would have allowed to leave his shop.

The increase in the price of genuine Fabergé, however, has inevitably brought a rise in the quality of its imitators. Hardstone figurines have proved particularly profitable and a stream of objects emerged from the Soviet Union in the 1960s and 1970s. These were not pre-revolutionary collections that had been preserved down the generations and were now finally being carefully liquidated but – as it eventually turned out – the work of one man, whose skill finally landed him in a Soviet jail.

At the top end of the scale the rewards for forgery have proved truly spectacular. The emergence of Fabergé's designs for Alexandra's last, unfinished egg clearly debunked the claims to Imperial status of the *'Twilight'* egg exhibited at the V.&A. in 1977, even before the Fersman Museum identified the 1917 *Blue Tsarevitch Constellation Egg* in its storerooms. It may have been built around an original piece of Fabergé, but everything that attempted to link it with the Romanovs and to cast it as an unpresented Imperial egg from 1917 was almost certainly a forgery.

At least the *'Twilight'* egg raised a relatively modest 100,000 Swiss francs (£22,000, £110,000) when it was sold by the Geneva branch of Christie's in 1976. One year later, however, an Iranian-born real estate millionaire, Eskandar Aryeh, paid the same auction house $250,000 (£140,000, £600,000) for the *'Nicholas II Equestrian'* egg. In 1953 Kenneth Snowman had suggested, on apparently very little evidence, that this was the only Fabergé egg to have been bought by Alexandra as a gift to Nicholas. So when Aryeh questioned the quality of the piece, he was shown a letter from Snowman to a Christie's director: 'In answer to your question. . . I confirm, without hesitation, that this is undoubtedly a work by Fabergé.'[15] A few years later Aryeh judged that prices had risen far enough for him to make a profit on his investment. He entrusted the egg to Christie's in New York only to find it withdrawn on the eve of the sale. Upon seeing the egg in the flesh for what he said was the first time Snowman had changed his mind. At the very least, he said, the egg had been 'sophisticated' with unwonted Imperial attributes. The resulting court case lasted for three years and ended in Christie's making an out-of-court settlement believed to amount to $5 million. By then the successful claimant was Mr Aryeh's estate: he had died during the litigation, aged only fifty-three.

The odd thing about both the 'Twilight' and the 'Nicholas II Equestrian' eggs is that their workmanship is in places so poor it is amazing that anyone could ever have been fooled. Here was a forger prepared to go to great lengths to improve the value of what may in each case have been an original piece of Fabergé, and to construct an apparently plausible provenance that made it seem like an Imperial egg. Yet the additions had nothing of the quality of true Fabergé. A lone craftsman, however talented, is always going to have difficulty reproducing the output of a team. No one person can be expected to master the full range of techniques – from enamelwork to stone carving – deployed in one of Fabergé's masterpieces. For years after the original business collapsed that limitation provided the ultimate guarantee when it came to authenticating the eggs that emerged from Russia, however obscure the route they had taken to the West.

Yet the value of Fabergé is now such that it would be worth assembling a team of master craftsmen and putting them together with the best designers if the result could pass for a genuine piece. The possibility means that any egg to emerge without indisputable provenance will be subjected to the closest possible scrutiny. Even the *Spring Flowers Egg*, which first came to attention as long ago as 1961, has been challenged. Valentin Skurlov, whose archival discoveries in the 1990s first established that it did not belong in the list of Imperial Easter presents, has since gone even further. He now asserts that it is almost certainly a forgery: 'it costs fifteen thousand dollars to make such an egg'. He has, however, never properly examined it. Kip Forbes has, many times, and has no doubt that it is genuine Fabergé: 'It is too good; it's too modest. . . Forgeries, especially in the 1960s, weren't that good.'

If the challenge to the *Spring Flowers Egg* has been relatively easy to shrug off, more recently discovered eggs have had to endure far more scepticism. For a brief period the RNM claimed to have its own version of the 1917 *Blue Tsarevitch Constellation Egg*, in a more finished state than the object found in the Fersman Mineralogical Museum, but with no published chain of previous owners. Clearly at least one of these eggs cannot be real, with the result that the claims of both to authenticity are undermined. The implication carries over to the RNM's other acquisition, the 1917 *Karelian Birch Egg*. For some its discovery so soon after the information about its design came to light is just too convenient, and the accompanying documents are simply evidence of the lengths to which forgers will now go in their efforts to impart authenticity to their creations. In May 2005 the *Art Newspaper* reported that some Fabergé experts were not convinced by its 'supposed Imperial provenance'. Most were not prepared to go on the record, although Alexander Schaffer's son Peter, a co-owner of A La Vieille Russie, would admit that the wooden egg had stirred up a lot of controversy. Other observers have no doubts about the egg's authenticity. They include Kip Forbes, who has one suggestion for the sceptics: 'Handle it and then question it; that thing is as right as rain.'

Well, it may be, but the debate about the authenticity of the *Karelian Birch Egg* carries its own implication: the excitement that will inevitably greet the apparent discovery of any further Imperial egg will be tempered with equally inevitable cynicism. Craftsmanship and design are no longer the final guarantees of authenticity. Fabergé has ceased to be inimitable.

25. 'You can put all your eggs in one basket'

In January 2004 *Forbes* magazine announced that it had decided to sell the greatest collection of Fabergé remaining in private hands. In doing so, it was following its previous owner's wishes. In a memoir published a year before his death Malcolm Forbes had made his feelings clear: 'I've often told my children I hope that, if they decide to be done with one of my collections, they will put it back on the auction block so that other people can have the same vast fun and excitement that we did in amassing it.'[1] The family had been taking that advice for some time. The island of Laucala in Fiji and the palace in Tangiers had both been sold in the 1990s; so had the collection of orientalist paintings, and over 70,000 toy soldiers. In 2001 an auction of American paintings brought in $6 million (£4.1 million); a year later some of Malcolm's less interesting pieces of Fabergé netted the same amount, while several remarkable American historical documents were sold for $30 million (£20 million). Then, in 2003, a collection of Victorian artworks realized £15 million. Assembling them had been Kip Forbes's especial project; most of the paintings had been bought for next to nothing, and the sale's success was a tribute to Kip's taste and forethought. Not that he necessarily saw it that way. At the time he was quoted as saying that he would not attend the sale as 'it will be too sad'. Nowadays Kip displays a bit more pride in his investment nous: 'I'm no longer the brother who spent money.'

All these sales were to be dwarfed by the auction that the

Forbes family had engaged Sotheby's to hold of its remaining
Fabergé in New York in April 2004. One hundred and eighty
pieces were up for sale, including all nine Imperial eggs. The
1897 *Coronation Egg* alone was estimated at $18–24 million
(£9.8–13.1 million). In total, the collection was expected to
raise $90–120 million (£49–66 million). Commentators sus-
pected that the decision to sell was linked to the family's losses
in the dot-com crash a few years earlier and the advertising
downturn that had followed it. Insiders insisted however – and
still maintain – that estate planning was the prime motivator:
the collection had become so valuable it was starting to distort
the overall value of the business. The death of one sibling might
have necessitated an unplanned, and undesirable, sale of shares.

Whatever the family's real motivation for the sale, its timing
was undoubtedly inspired. Appreciation for Fabergé had continued to grow around the world. From America and Europe it
had spread to Asia, where collectors especially admired the
craftsmanship and – in the words of one Sotheby's expert –
'dinky' nature of the jeweller's work. Moreover, only a few
months before Forbes decided to sell Russia had decided to
scrap a 30 per cent duty on imported artefacts. Any number of
oligarchs enriched by rising commodity prices might now be
expected to bid.

Within days of Sotheby's announcement the Kremlin took an
interest, when Elena Gagarin, the director of the Armoury
Museum and the daughter of cosmonaut Yuri Gagarin, made an
impassioned plea for the eggs to be returned to state museums
in Russia. But less than two weeks later the auction was cancelled; in an almost unprecedented move, a forty-six-year-old
Russian billionaire, Viktor Vekselberg, had pre-empted the
entire sale.

To say that the offer had come out of the blue would be an
understatement. Mr Vekselberg had never seen the collection
and had no particular interest in Fabergé. The Forbes family
knew of him, but only because it could read about him in its

own magazine's ranking of the world's billionaires. He had been new to the list in 2003, brought to the attention of the world's media when Tyumen Oil (TNK), Russia's third-largest oil company, merged with the Russian oil operations of BP. Mr Vekselberg had been a major shareholder in TNK and received a significant slice of the $6.75 billion (£4.1 billion) that BP shelled out. He had made previous fortunes in aluminium, bauxite and oil during a career that had in 1994 encompassed Russia's first successful hostile takeover, of the Vladimir Tractor Company. *Forbes* estimated his wealth at $2.5 billion (£1.5 billion) – enough to fund a lifestyle similar to the Tsar's.

The exact sum Mr Vekselberg paid for the Forbes Fabergé collection has never been revealed, but one of his advisers was at least prepared to admit it was 'more than $90 million [£49 million]. I won't say how much more, but it was more.'[2] A pedant might complain that selling the entire collection in one go would hardly generate the 'vast fun and excitement' that Malcolm Forbes had asked his family to grant to future collectors, but the publisher is unlikely to have turned in his grave. His frivolous purchases of Fabergé had turned out, in the end, to be among his best investments; only the ranches in Colorado yielded a higher return. As Kip puts it, 'He was happy to disprove the old saying – you can put all your eggs in one basket.' It is hard to imagine a better vindication of the big spender's whole approach to life.

The family might even have made more from their Fabergé. Viktor Vekselberg's offer to pre-empt the sale at Sotheby's may have been unusual but it was by no means unique. In fact another, anonymous, billionaire made a similar approach to the Forbes family at the same time. For him too money would have been no object; according to Kip, he figures even more highly in the *Forbes* rich list. His bid was scuppered by his American legal advisers, who insisted on approaching Sotheby's with a seventy-page questionnaire. By contrast, Mr Vekselberg's Swiss lawyers submitted only seven pages of very 'straightforward questions and the deal was done in ten days and to this day the wife of the other gentleman involved complains bitterly'. Kip draws his own moral: 'Yes they probably could have paid more but they had a law firm that was more worried about their billing hours than getting the job their client wanted done.'

So why did Viktor Vekselberg pay an unimaginable sum for objects in which he had never before shown the slightest interest? He has been reticent on the subject, saying little more than he allowed himself on the day the purchase was announced: 'This was a once in a lifetime chance to give my country back some of its treasures.'[3] To discover more in the way of explanation, however, most observers feel the need to look no further back than the previous year. On 25 October 2003 Mikhail Khodorkovsky, Russia's richest man, worth an estimated $15 billion (£9.2 billion), and chief executive of Yukos, Russia's leading oil company, had been arrested at gunpoint on his private jet and jailed on charges of fraud and tax evasion. Few doubted that Khodorkovsky had been singled out for the temerity he had shown in funding a challenge to Vladimir Putin's presidency, but his vulnerability made everyone take notice.

Khodorkovsky's peers had gained so much in the privatizations of the mid-1990s; now it was time for them to start giving something back. How better to do that than by repatriating objects that had once been the extravagant playthings of a decadent court but were now towering examples of Russia's cultural heritage? There's a satisfying symmetry inherent in the idea of eggs that were once ordered by the Tsar, the individual at the apex of an aristocratic society, being brought back to Russia by his modern-day successors, the oligarchs who now bestride the Russian economy.

The eggs and other objects from the Forbes collection were allowed one final exhibition in Sotheby's New York branch. Most of them had been on public display in the Forbes Building for most of the previous three decades. On this occasion, however, thousands queued in the cold to say farewell. The hard cash that confirmed the eggs' enormous value had brought them a whole new audience. Three months later they were in Moscow, on display in the Patriarch's Palace in the Kremlin, only a few hundred yards from the Armoury Museum. It was a conspicuous display of loyalty to Putin's government. Moreover, the collection was now owned by the Link of Times, a foundation established by Vekselberg to 'search for, acquire and bring back home to Russia historically significant works of art'.[4] The world's greatest collection of Fabergé eggs was, it seemed, coming back to the land of the tsars.

Afterword

ON 28 SEPTEMBER 2006, seventy-eight years after her death and to the sound of horns and cannon, Marie Fedorovna returned to St Petersburg. In a pomp-laden ceremony led by the Russian Orthodox patriarch himself, Alexis II, her coffin was finally laid next to her husband's in the royal crypt of the St Peter and St Paul Fortress on the river Neva. Nearby, in the same crypt, lay the remains of her eldest son and his family. Fragments of partially burned bodies had been discovered in a pit outside Sverdlovsk in 1991; by 1994 DNA analysis had tentatively identified them as Romanovs.* On 17 July 1998, in another dramatic ritual, timed to take place exactly eighty years after their massacre, Nicholas and Alexandra, together with three of their children, had been reburied in St Petersburg.‡

The parallels are irresistible. For decades the Romanovs' palaces were neglected and their religion suppressed. In the absence of physical remains, the eggs the family had exchanged at Easter acquired a consequence that no one could have expected when they were first commissioned. They became the most famous surviving symbols of the last years of the tsars.

---

* As Alexandra's great-nephew through his mother and grandmother, the Duke of Edinburgh had provided a crucial sample. His mitochondrial DNA – passed down unaltered, except by random mutation, through the maternal line – showed that he and most of the corpses found near Sverdlovsk shared a common maternal ancestor.

‡ The bodies of the two remaining children, Alexis and one of his sisters, were finally discovered in 2007.

Now, within a few years of each other, both the eggs and the Romanovs have begun returning to their rightful home.

It is an appropriate conclusion to the story, but nothing is ever quite that straightforward, especially in Russia. The Link of Times exhibition in the Kremlin was only a temporary affair. Its Fabergé collection remains firmly under the control of Viktor Vekselberg and is stored in London. He continues to decide where and when it will be exhibited. Since that first exhibition in 2004 the collection has spent more time outside Russia than within. Recently it was in Zurich, a city more famous as a custodian of expatriated wealth than as a centre of cultural appreciation. Crowds did not flood to see it. An exhibition planned for London in 2007 was cancelled, reportedly under pressure from the Russian authorities, hinting that perhaps it was time for the foundation to live up to its stated objectives. It is the kind of messy compromise between competing interests that seems all too appropriate in the realpolitik of modern Russia.

So PERHAPS it is better to look to the past for closure, to what Kip Forbes calls 'my last contribution to the scholarship' and the inspiration that came to him in a moment of serendipity. It arrived with his family's decision to sell their Fabergé collection, and the task Kip took on – to call the director of Oregon's Portland Art Museum to explain that items due to arrive there for a Fabergé exhibition would after all be going to Sotheby's: 'Yes, Lucy, you should get him out of the shower.' All things considered, the director had taken the withdrawal in 'very good grace'.

That evening Kip guiltily took home the Portland exhibition's catalogue to understand how big a gap would be left by the absence of the Forbes family's contribution. In it he saw, for the first time, a high-quality photograph of the Fabergé exhibition held in 1902 at the von Dervis mansion in St Petersburg. A similar print had already produced one eureka moment fifteen years before, with the authentication of the Queen's 1901 *Flower*

Basket Egg. Kip noticed something else: in a display case devoted to Marie Fedorovna's collection of Fabergé was his own family's *Resurrection Egg*, the small rock crystal egg showing Christ rising from the tomb which Malcolm Forbes had bought in 1978. This was an egg whose importance had been heavily discounted over the previous decade, ever since the Kremlin's archives had revealed it did not belong in the list of gifts from the tsars to the tsarinas. Kip's discovery, however, showed that it was, at the very least, a piece of Fabergé that had once belonged to the Dowager Empress.

Kip's next breakthrough came when he found himself 'sitting there reading the Russian book with the descriptions' – *Fabergé Imperial Easter Eggs*, by Tatiana Fabergé, Valentin Skurlov and Lynette Proler. In it he read carefully, again for the first time, the invoice description of another item in his family's collection, the strangely bulbous 1894 *Renaissance Egg*. It was the invoice's reference to pearls that excited him. The *Renaissance Egg* had none; they could only have been on its missing surprise. The shaft of the *Resurrection Egg* consists of a single large pearl, and there are more on its base. Might it have once been the surprise inside the *1894 Renaissance Egg*?

At the time the *Renaissance Egg* was in Seattle. Kip had to wait for its return east before he could test his theory, but when he did he found that the *Resurrection Egg* fitted it 'like a hand in glove'. It did not need any padding, it did not rock; everything about the whole ensemble seemed to fit together. At last Kip could make sense of the outer egg's curious shape, of its casket-like qualities and of its wonderful translucence: 'You can fold it up, and all you see is the figure of Christ', a silhouette just visible through the agate shell.

The idea transforms the *1894 Renaissance Egg* from an also-ran in Fabergé's output, a relatively unexciting member of the sequence, into an original masterpiece. More than that, it imbues it with a religious symbolism that few other eggs can match. But it is the egg's timing that seems especially masterful. Fabergé cannot have known that Marie's husband, Alexander III, would die before he commissioned another egg. Nobody, that Easter in 1894, knew how ill the Tsar was. It must just be happenstance that Fabergé chose this, his tenth commission, to make an egg with such an explicit message of hope, of resurrection itself. Perhaps all genius requires a measure of luck.

Appendix

Full listing of the Imperial eggs

Presented to Marie Fedorovna

Year   *Name (Height/length in millimetres)*
Surprise / Current owner / Comments on provenance

1885   *First Hen Egg* (64)
Golden yolk containing hen; now missing crown and pendant. /
Link of Times Foundation. / Sold by Kremlin in 1920s;
subsequent owners included Lord and Lady Grantchester and
the Forbes Magazine Collection.

1886   *Hen Egg with Sapphire Pendant* (n/a)
Hen taking the egg out of wicker basket. / Whereabouts
unknown. / Apparently sent to Kremlin Armoury for safekeeping
in 1917.

1887   *Blue Serpent Clock Egg* (183)
A clock. / Prince Albert of Monaco. / Sold by Kremlin in 1920s;
subsequently passed through Wartski on a number of occasions.

1888   *Cherub Egg with Chariot* (n/a)
Unknown. / Whereabouts unknown. / May have been advertised
by Armand Hammer in 1930s.

1889   *Nécessaire Egg* (n/a)
Set of thirteen ladies' toilet articles. / Whereabouts unknown. /
Possibly exhibited at Wartski in 1949.

1890   *Danish Palaces Egg* (102)
Ten-panel screen with pictures of Empress's homes and Imperial yachts. / Matilda Geddings Gray Collection. / Sold by Antikvariat to Armand Hammer in 1930.

1891   *Memory of Azov Egg* (93)
Model of cruiser *Memory of Azov*. / Kremlin Armoury. / Was destined for sale in 1933, but subsequently returned to the Armoury.

1892   *Diamond Trellis Egg* (108)
Clockwork elephant (missing). / Private collection. / Sold by Kremlin in 1920s; subsequently separated from its genuine stand by Emanuel Snowman in mistaken belief that this was a later addition.

1893   *Caucasus Egg* (92)
Pictures of Grand Duke George's home in the Caucasus behind panels in egg's surface. / Matilda Geddings Gray Collection. / Sold by Antikvariat to Armand Hammer in 1930.

1894   *Renaissance Egg* (133)
Unknown, but Christopher Forbes now speculates that this may be the *Resurrection Egg*. / Link of Times Collection. / Sold by Antikvariat to Armand Hammer in 1930; subsequent owners include Henry and Lillian de Vere Clifton, Jack and Belle Linsky and the Forbes Magazine Collection.

1895   *Twelve Monogram Egg* (79)
Unknown. / Hillwood Museum, collection of Marjorie Merriweather Post. / Apparently never sent to the Armoury, the route by which this egg left Russia remains unclear.

1896   *Alexander III Portraits Egg* (n/a)
Six miniatures of Alexander III. / Whereabouts unknown, apparently never sent to the Armoury. / The egg's surprise may have been lent by the Grand Duchess Xenia to an exhibition in 1935.

1897   *Mauve Egg with Three Miniatures* (n/a)
A heart-shaped frame containing miniatures of Nicholas, Alexandra and their eldest daughter. / Egg is missing; surprise is in the Link of Times Collection. / Egg apparently never sent to the Armoury; surprise was formerly part of the Forbes Magazine Collection.

1898   *Pelican Egg* (102)
Egg unfolds to create screen of pictures showing educational institutions. / Virginia Museum of Fine Arts, collection of Lillian Thomas Pratt. / Sold by Antikvariat to Armand Hammer in 1930.

1899   *Pansy Egg* (146)
Easel with eleven miniatures of family members. / Matilda Gray Stream, a wedding present from her aunt, Matilda Geddings Gray. / Sold by Antikvariat to Armand Hammer in 1930.

1900   *Cuckoo Clock Egg* (203)
Singing bird that rises from top of the egg when a button is pressed. / Link of Times Collection. / Sold to Emanuel Snowman in 1920s; later part of Forbes Magazine Collection.

1901   *Gatchina Palace Egg* (127)
Model of Gatchina Palace. / Walters Art Gallery. / The egg's route out of Russia is not clear; sold to Henry Walters by Alexander Polovtsov in 1930.

1902   *Alexander III Medallion Egg* (n/a)
Medallion portrait of Alexander III. / Whereabouts unknown. / Egg may have been sent to Armoury in 1917; its surprise may have been lent by the Grand Duchess Xenia to an exhibition in 1935.

1903   *Royal Danish Egg* (*c.* 275)
Double-sided miniature screen with pictures of Marie's parents. / Whereabouts unknown.

1904 and 1905   No eggs presented because of Russo-Japanese War.

1906   *Swan Egg* (100)
Clockwork swan. / Fondation Edouard et Maurice Sandoz. /
Sold to Emanuel Snowman in 1920s; subsequent owners included
King Farouk.

1907   *Love Trophies Egg* (146)
Miniature of the Imperial children (missing). / Private collection. /
Apparently never sent to the Armoury, the route by which the egg
came to the West is not clear.

1908   *Peacock Egg* (190)
Clockwork peacock. / Fondation Edouard et Maurice Sandoz. /
Sold to Emanuel Snowman in 1920s.

1909   *Alexander III Commemorative Egg* (95)
Gold bust of Alexander III. / Whereabouts unknown. / Apparently
never sent to the Armoury.

1910   *Alexander III Equestrian Egg* (155)
Gold miniature statue showing Alexander III on horseback. /
Kremlin Armoury.

1911   *Bay Tree Egg* (273)
Singing bird that emerges from top of tree when a jewel is
pressed. / Link of Times Collection. / Sold to Emanuel Snowman
in 1920s; numerous owners, most recently the Forbes Magazine
Collection.

1912   *Napoleonic Egg* (117)
Six-panel octagonal folding screen with pictures of Dowager
Empress's regiments. / Matilda Geddings Gray Foundation. /
Sold by Antikvariat to Armand Hammer in 1930.

1913   *Winter Egg* (142)
Basket of flowers. / Emir of Qatar. / Sold to Emanuel Snowman
in 1920s; missing for a number of years before re-emergence in
1994.

1914 *Catherine the Great Egg* (121)
Wind-up sedan chair containing Empress Catherine the Great
(missing). / Hillwood Museum, collection of Marjorie
Merriweather Post. / Sold by Antikvariat to Armand Hammer in
1930.

1915 *Red Cross Portraits Egg* (76)
Hinged folding screen with miniature portraits of Imperial women
serving as Red Cross nurses. / Virginia Museum of Fine Arts,
collection of Lillian Thomas Pratt. / Sold by Antikvariat to
Armand Hammer in 1930.

1916 *Cross of St George Egg* (90)
Pictures of Nicholas II and Alexis behind panels on egg's surface. /
Link of Times Foundation. / Left Russia with Marie Fedorovna;
subsequent owners include Fabergé, Inc. and the Forbes Magazine
Collection.

1917 *Karelian Birch Egg* (n/a)
Possibly a mechanical elephant (missing). / Russian National
Museum, a Moscow-based group of private individuals. /
Apparently sold to a Western buyer in 1920s; questions over
authenticity.

Presented to Alexandra Fedorovna

1895 *Rosebud Egg* (74)
Yellow rosebud; the crown and pendant it contained are
now missing. / Link of Times Foundation. / Sold to Emanuel
Snowman in 1920s; it has since been damaged and lost its
last two surprises; previous owners include Henry and Lillian
de Vere Clifton and the Forbes Magazine Collection.

1896 *Egg with Revolving Miniatures* (248)
Twelve miniatures of Empress's homes, mounted on six panels
around central shaft. / Virginia Museum of Fine Arts, collection of

Lillian Thomas Pratt. / Sold by Antikvariat to Armand Hammer in 1930.

1897 *Coronation Egg* (127)
Model of coronation coach. / Link of Times Foundation. / Sold to Emanuel Snowman in 1920s; bought back by Wartski in 1930s and held for forty years until its sale to the Forbes Magazine Collection in 1979.

1898 *Lilies of the Valley Egg* (151)
Miniatures of Nicholas, Olga and Tatiana that emerge from top of egg. / Link of Times Foundation. / Sold to Emanuel Snowman in 1920s; bought back by Wartski in 1948 and held for forty years until its sale to the Forbes Magazine Collection in 1979.

1899 *Madonna Lily Clock Egg* (270)
A clock. / Kremlin Armoury.

1900 *Trans-Siberian Railway Egg* (260)
Model train. / Kremlin Armoury.

1901 *Flower Basket Egg* (230)
Flower basket. / HM Queen Elizabeth II. / Sold by the Antikvariat in 1933 and acquired in the same year by Queen Mary; for a long time it was not believed to be a genuine Fabergé egg.

1902 *Clover Leaf Egg* (98)
Clover leaf with four miniature portraits (missing). / Kremlin Armoury. / Was destined for sale in 1933 but subsequently returned to the Armoury.

1903 *Peter the Great Egg* (111)
Miniature statue of Peter the Great. / Virginia Museum of Fine Arts, collection of Lillian Thomas Pratt. / Sold by Antikvariat in 1933 and eventually purchased from US Customs by Alexander Schaffer.

1904 and 1905   No eggs presented because of Russo-Japanese War.

1906   *Moscow Kremlin Egg* (361)
       Interior of egg is decorated to resemble Uspenski Cathedral; also a
       musical bòx. / Kremlin Armoury.

1907   *Rose Trellis Egg* (77)
       Diamond chain with miniature of Alexis (missing). / Walters Art
       Gallery. / The egg's route out of Russia is not clear; sold to Henry
       Walters by Alexander Polovtsov in 1930.

1908   *Alexander Palace Egg* (110)
       Model of the Alexander Palace. / Kremlin Armoury.

1909   *Standart Egg* (153)
       Model of *Standart* yacht. / Kremlin Armoury.

1910   *Colonnade Egg* (286)
       The egg is also a clock. / HM Queen Elizabeth II. / Sold to
       Emanuel Snowman in the 1920s; acquired by Queen Mary and
       given to George V in 1931.

1911   *Fifteenth Anniversary Egg* (132)
       Miniature paintings on surface of egg. / Link of Times
       Foundation. / The egg's route out of Russia is not clear; sold by
       A La Vieille Russie to Forbes Magazine Collection in 1966.

1912   *Tsarevitch Egg* (125)
       Miniature easel with picture of Alexis. / Virginia Museum of Fine
       Arts, collection of Lillian Thomas Pratt. / Sold by Antikvariat to
       Armand Hammer in 1930.

1913   *Romanov Tercentenary Egg* (190)
       Sphere, of which one half shows the territory of Russia in 1613
       and the other half shows it in 1913. / Kremlin Armoury.

1914   *Mosaic Egg* (95)
       Oval screen showing profiles of Imperial children. / HM Queen
       Elizabeth II. / Sold by Antikvariat in 1933 and acquired by King
       George V and Queen Mary the following year.

1915   *Red Cross Triptych Egg* (86)
       Egg unfolds to show triptych of orthodox icons. / Cleveland
       Museum of Art, collection of India Early Minshall. / Sold by
       Antikvariat in 1930.

1916   *Steel Military Egg* (101)
       Easel with picture of Nicholas and Alexis with group of officers.
       Kremlin Armoury.

1917   *Blue Tsarevitch Constellation Egg* (n/a)
       Egg was intended to be a clock. / Fersman Mineralogical Museum
       (may have been transferred to Kremlin Armoury). / Given by
       Agathon Fabergé to the museum in 1925 and only recently
       identified as an unfinished egg.

Glossary

agate – A striped version of *chalcedony quartz* which has formed in layers of different colours or textures.

alloy – A mixture of two or more metals, combined when they are melted together.

amber – A translucent fossilized tree resin, typically dark orange, but also yellow red, white, black and blue.

amethyst – A relatively common form of *quartz*, usually a shade of purple. Its name derives from the Greek for 'not drunken', based on the belief that the stone prevented intoxication.

aquamarine – A *porous semi-precious* stone, a transparent, light blue or sea-green form of *beryl.*

archimandrite – In the Russian Orthodox Church a priest ranking just below a bishop.

art nouveau – A style of decorative art popular from the end of the nineteenth century until the First World War characterized by curves and naturalistic designs of plants and flowers.

assay – A test of the precious metal content in an alloy.

baroque – A style of art, architecture, music, theatre and even philosophy particularly popular in the seventeenth century. It typically combined exaggerated forms or motion with clearly rendered detail to achieve an exuberant effect.

base metal – Any non-precious metal such as copper, lead or zinc.

beryl – Aluminium beryllium silicate ($Be_3Al_2Si_6O_{18}$), a glassy mineral that occurs in hexagonal prisms.

bloodstone – An inexpensive and soft form of *chalcedony*, green with red highlights caused by iron oxide. Also known as heliotrope.

Bolshevik – The more radical wing of the Russian Social Democratic Party, first formed by Lenin in 1903 and devoted to achieving a Marxist state through revolution and dictatorship.

bowenite – A pale milky-green form of *serpentine* resembling *nephrite*, named after George Bowen, the American mineralogist who first analysed it in 1822.

cabochon – A gem which has been rounded off on one or more sides.

caftan – A full-length open gown with long wide sleeves.

cameo – A shell or stone carved in relief so that the design protrudes from the surface.

carat – A measure of weight used for gemstones, equivalent to 200 milligrams, also a synonym for *karat*.

chalcedony – A form of *quartz* which is *translucent* and *porous* and includes a family of *semi-precious* stones; often milky, grey, or bluish.

chased – Used to describe metal that has been decorated by use of a hammer and *punch*.

choker – A type of necklace that fits tightly around the neck.

corundum – A crystalline form of aluminium oxide (Al_2O_3) which includes rubies and sapphires.

diadem – A curved piece of jewellery worn on the head.

diamond – A *precious stone* consisting of tightly compressed carbon, colourless in its pure form but occurring naturally in many colours as a result of impurities.

emerald – A green *precious stone*, a form of *beryl*, coloured by chromium and some vanadium impurities.

enamel – A hard decorative surface created by fusing powdered glass onto metal using heat.

étui – French for 'case', therefore a small, usually ornamental, container for articles such as needles, scissors, tweezers and other articles of toilet or daily use, similar to *nécessaire*.

garnets – A group of *semi-precious silicate* stones that occur in any colour except blue.

glasnost – Russian for 'openness'; used to describe the policy of greater candour initiated by Mikhail Gorbachev in the 1980s.

guilloche – A repetitive pattern etched into a metal surface, usually with machine tools; in guilloche *enamel* the pattern is then visible through the transparent enamel.

hallmark – A mark stamped onto a precious metal by a legally appointed official to denote the amount of precious metal contained in a piece, a form of consumer protection against fraud that dates back to the Middle Ages.

hardstone – A general term used to describe any opaque stone capable of being carved for use in jewellery-making.

jade – A *semi-precious* stone, usually green but also white, lilac, brown or almost black.

karat – Used to define the proportion of gold in any different item on a 24-point scale. Thus 24-karat gold is pure and (say) 14-karat gold is an *alloy* containing 14 parts of gold to every 10 parts of another metal.

lapis lazuli – A rich blue opaque *semi-precious* stone.

Maltese cross – A cross whose arms are all of an equal length and widen from the centre point, the badge of the Knights of Malta.

monogram – A design composed of one or more letters, typically the initials of a name, used as an identifying mark.

mother-of-pearl – The common name for iridescent nacre, a blend of minerals lining the shells of oysters and other molluscs.

nécessaire – French for 'necessary', therefore a receptacle for items such as pens and matches or, as in the case of the 1889 *Nécessaire Egg*, ladies' toilet articles, similar to *étui*.

nephrite – A soft form of *jade*, green and often slightly veined.

opal – A *semi-precious* stone, an iridescent type of *quartz*.

opalescent – Semi-opaque and with a rich milky appearance.

pearl – A hard smooth round object produced by certain molluscs, primarily oysters, valued as a gemstone.

pendant – A hanging ornament, usually worn on a chain around the neck.

perestroika – Russian for 'reconstruction'; used to describe the restructuring of the Russian economy and bureaucracy initiated by Mikhail Gorbachev in the 1980s.

porous – Describes stones containing tiny holes so that they can be penetrated by water, oils and other substances. This can lead to their appearance changing over time.

portrait diamond – A flat-cut diamond through which a design or miniature can still be clearly seen.

precious stone – A stone that is valuable and rare such as a diamond, emerald, ruby or sapphire.

punch – A tool used for stamping or for perforating holes in metallic plates and other substances.

quartz – A crystalline material that comes in many forms, some of them very common.

quatre-couleur – An eighteenth-century technique for colouring gold by alloying it with other metals.

red – The colour that has come to symbolize Communism since 1917, hence Red Army and Red Guards; contrast with *white*.

rock crystal – The purest form of *quartz*, absolutely transparent.

rococo – A style of especially architecture and decorative art that originated in France in the early eighteenth century, marked by elaborate but loosely rendered ornamentation, such as scrolls, foliage and animal forms.

ruby – A *precious stone*, a member of the *corundum* family, coloured by chromic oxide. Rubies are classically deep red, but also pink, purple and brown.

sapphire – A *precious stone*, a member of the *corundum* family, colourless in its pure form but more typically blue and many other colours as a result of impurities.

sautoir – A long necklace frequently with an ornament at its end.

semi-precious – Describes a gem that has commercial value but is not as rare or valuable as a precious stone.

serpentine – A group of mineral rocks said to be named either for their serpent-like patterns or because of an ancient belief that they provided protection from snakebite.

silicate – A generic term applying to the large group of common minerals made up of silicon and oxygen with one or more other elements.

soviet – Russian for 'council', used initially to describe the ad hoc group of workers who directed the general strike in 1905 and later extended to imply a workers' government.

staretz – A holy man in the Russian orthodox church, not necessarily a priest.

translucent – Describes a material that allows light to pass through it, but scatters it so that it is not transparent.

troika – A Russian vehicle, either a carriage or a sled, pulled by three horses.

turquoise – A *porous* opaque *semi-precious* stone originally believed to come from Turkey, hence its name which is now applied to the stone's typical colour.

white – A generic label for Russians opposed to communism, whether in exile as White Russians or fighting in the civil war against the *Red* Army.

Notes

The following references show the sources for most quotations used in the text. Full publication details may be found in the Bibliography.

Introduction

1 Bainbridge, *Peter Carl Fabergé*, p. 110
2 *Sun*, London, 7 March 2006, 'Kate's Off Her Egg', p. 1

1. 'Christ is risen!'

1 Stoliza y Usadba, 15 January 1914, quoted in Snowman, *Carl Fabergé, Goldsmith to the Imperial Court of Russia*, p. 11
2 Hamilton, *The Vanished World of Yesterday*, p. 412
3 von Habsburg & Lopato, *Fabergé: Imperial Jeweller*, p. 58
4 Fabergé, Proler & Skurlov, *The Fabergé Imperial Easter Eggs*, pp. 16–17
5 Mikhailovitch, *Once a Grand Duke*, pp. 60–1
6 Maylunas & Mironenko, *A Lifelong Passion*, p. 7
7 Lothrop, *The Court of Alexander III*, pp. 156–7
8 von Habsburg & Lopato, *Fabergé: Imperial Jeweller*, p. 56

2. 'As precious as an egg on Christ's own day'

1 Vorres, *The Last Grand-Duchess*, p. 30
2 Ibid. p. 46
3 *Apollo, The Magazine of the Arts*, London, January 1984, 'Fresh Insight on Carl Fabergé', p. 44

4 Unpublished notes by Léon Grinberg, quoted in Lowes & McCanless, *Fabergé Eggs*, p. 198

5 Memoirs of François Birbaum, quoted in von Habsburg & Lopato, *Fabergé: Imperial Jeweller*, p. 446

3. 'A continuation of the long funeral ceremonies'

1 Maylunas & Mironenko, *A Lifelong Passion*, pp. 6, 15

2 Bing (ed.), *The Letters of Tsar Nicholas & Empress Marie*, p. 75

3 Hough (ed.), *Advice to a Grand-daughter*, p. 55

4 Bing (ed.), *The Letters of Tsar Nicholas & Empress Marie*, p. 76

5 Nicolas II, *Journal Intime*, p. 55

6 Bing (ed.), *The Letters of Tsar Nicholas & Empress Marie*, p. 77

7 Tisdall, *The Dowager Empress*, p. 163

8 Ibid. p. 173

9 Nicolas II, *Journal Intime*, p. 125

10 Vyrubova, *Memories of the Russian Court*, p. 21

11 Memoirs of François Birbaum, quoted in von Habsburg & Lopato, *Fabergé: Imperial Jeweller*, p. 446

12 Mikhailovitch, *Once a Grand Duke*, p. 132

13 Maylunas & Mironenko, *A Lifelong Passion*, p. 115

14 Buxhoeveden, *The Life & Tragedy of Alexandra Fedorovna*, p. 44

15 Maylunas & Mironenko, *A Lifelong Passion*, p. 111

16 Bing (ed.), *The Letters of Tsar Nicholas & Empress Marie*, p. 74

4. 'Utterly different in character, habits and outlook'

1 Vorres, *The Last Grand-Duchess*, p. 72

2 Radziwill, *My Recollections*, p. 308

3 Radziwill, *Nicholas II*, p. 103

4 Mouchanow, *My Empress*, p. 43

5 Tisdall, *The Dowager Empress*, p. 168
6 Hall, *Little Mother of Russia*, p. 141
7 Vorres, *The Last Grand-Duchess*, p. 82
8 Ibid. p. 40
9 Ibid. p. 80
10 Bing (ed.), *The Letters of Tsar Nicholas & Empress Marie*, p. 116
11 Bainbridge, *Peter Carl Fabergé*, p. 33

5. 'The warm and brilliant shop of Carl Fabergé'

1 Crankshaw, *The Shadow of the Winter Palace*, p. 288
2 'Rapport du Jury International (Joaillerie)', 1902, quoted in von Habsburg, *Fabergé*, p. 40
3 Bainbridge, *Peter Carl Fabergé*, p. 38
4 Fabergé, Proler & Skurlov, *The Fabergé Imperial Easter Eggs*, p. 52
5 Eagar, *Six Years at the Russian Court*, p. 11
6 *The Spectator*, London, 25 November 1949, 'Marginal Comment', p. 737
7 Snowman, *The Art of Carl Fabergé*, Appendix B, p. 134
8 Nabokov, *Speak Memory*, p. 87
9 Bainbridge, *Peter Carl Fabergé*

6. 'The ancestor who appeals to me least of all'

1 Bing (ed.), *The Letters of Tsar Nicholas & Empress Marie*, p. 144
2 Buxhoeveden, *The Life & Tragedy of Alexandra Fedorovna*, p. 58
3 Mossolov, *At the Court of the Last Tsar*, p. 16

7. 'We shall have to show dirty nappies'

1 Bing (ed.), *The Letters of Tsar Nicholas & Empress Marie*, p. 176
2 Ibid. p. 207

3 Figes, *A People's Tragedy*, p. 202
4 Memoirs of François Birbaum, quoted in von Habsburg & Lopato, *Fabergé: Imperial Jeweller*, p. 455

8. 'A good, religious, simple-minded Russian'

1 Madol, *The Private Life of Queen Alexandra*, p. 212
2 Mossolov, *At the Court of the Last Tsar*, p. 247
3 Dehn, *The Real Tsaritsa*, p. 39
4 Maylunas & Mironenko, *A Lifelong Passion*, p. 129
5 Vorres, *The Last Grand-Duchess*, pp. 142–3

9. 'The little one will not die'

1 von Habsburg & Lopato, *Fabergé: Imperial Jeweller*, p. 62
2 Memoirs of François Birbaum, quoted in ibid., p. 454
3 Kokovtsov, *Out of My Past*, p. 131
4 Bing (ed.), *The Letters of Tsar Nicholas & Empress Marie*, p. 229
5 Kokovtsov, *Out of My Past*, p. 304
6 Maylunas & Mironenko, *A Lifelong Passion*, p. 331
7 Massie, Robert K., *Nicholas and Alexandra*, p. 199
8 Bing (ed.), *The Letters of Tsar Nicholas & Empress Marie*, p. 272
9 Vyrubova, *Memories of the Russian Court*, p. 92
10 Gilliard, *Thirteen Years at the Russian Court*, p. 29
11 Vyrubova, *Memories of the Russian Court*, p. 93
12 Ibid. pp. 93–4
13 Ibid. p. 94
14 *The New York Times*, 10 November 1912, p. C1

10. 'An unparalleled genius'

1 Narishkin-Kurakin, *Under Three Tsars*, p. 206
2 Kokovtsov, *Out of My Past*, p. 471
3 Ibid. p. 470

4 Tillander et al., *Carl Fabergé and his Contemporaries*, p. 45
5 Ibid. p. 46
6 Snowman, *Fabergé – Lost and Found*, p. 25
7 von Solodkoff, *Fabergé*, p. 24
8 Bainbridge, *Peter Carl Fabergé*, p. 60

11. 'Fabergé has just brought your delightful egg'

1 Narishkin-Kurakin, *Under Three Tsars*, p. 179
2 Russian Central State Historical Archives f472 op68 del120, quoted in von Habsburg & Lopato, *Fabergé: Imperial Jeweller*, p. 29
3 Hanbury-Williams, *The Emperor Nicholas II as I Knew Him*, pp. 89–90
4 'Dnevniki Imperatora Nikolaya II' Fond 601 GARF; Orbita, Moscow 1992, quoted in von Habsburg, *Fabergé: Treasures of Imperial Russia*, Chapter 11
5 Hanbury-Williams, *The Emperor Nicholas II as I Knew Him*, p. 94
6 Bing (ed.), *The Letters of Tsar Nicholas & Empress Marie*, p. 296
7 Fuhrmann (ed.), *The Complete Wartime Correspondence of Tsar Nicholas II and the Empress Alexandra*, p. 449
8 Maud, *One Year at The Russian Court*, p. 209
9 Maylunas & Mironenko, *A Lifelong Passion*, p. 487
10 Vorres, *The Last Grand-Duchess*, p. 98
11 Yusupov, *Lost Splendour*, p. 229

12. 'Everything seems sad'

1 Grabbe, *The Private World of the Last Tsar*, p. 167
2 Maylunas & Mironenko, *A Lifelong Passion*, p. 517
3 Buchanan, Sir George, *My Mission to Russia and Other Diplomatic Memories*, II p. 46
4 Kokovtsov, *Out of My Past*, p. 478
5 Muntian, *Fabergé, Jeweller of the Romanovs*, p. 130

13. 'Guard it well. It is the last'

1 Narishkin-Kurakin, *Under Three Tsars*, pp. 224–5
2 Churchill, *The World Crisis, The Aftermath*, p. 73
3 Benckendorff, *Last Days at Tsarskoe Selo*, p. 98
4 Gilliard, *Thirteen Years at the Russian Court*, p. 255
5 Ibid.
6 Vyrubova, *Memories of the Russian Court*, p. 336
7 Avdeev, quoted in Alexandra, *The Last Diary of Tsaritsa Alexandra*, p. 121

14. 'This is life no more'

1 Mikhailovitch, *La Fin du Tsarisme*, p. 242
2 Trotsky & Eastman (trans.), *The History of the Russian Revolution*, p. 46
3 Bainbridge, *Peter Carl Fabergé*, p. 34
4 von Habsburg & Lopato, *Fabergé: Imperial Jeweller*, p. 84
5 Muntian, *The World of Fabergé*, p. 23
6 Bainbridge, *Peter Carl Fabergé*, p. 36
7 Ibid.
8 Polovtsov, *Les Trésors d'Art Sous le Régime Bolsheviste*, pp. 22–3
9 Ibid. p. 101
10 Lukomsky, *Châteaux et Palais de Russie*, p. 161
11 Figes, *A People's Tragedy*, p. 526
12 Ulyanov & Peshkov, *Lenin and Gorky*, p. 278

15. 'You will have all of it when I am gone'

1 Yusupov, *Lost Splendour*, p. 263
2 Ibid. p. 264
3 Mikhailovitch, *Once a Grand Duke*, p. 306
4 Vorres, *The Last Grand-Duchess*, p. 157
5 Van der Kiste & Hall, *Once a Grand Duchess*, p. 147
6 Vorres, *The Last Grand-Duchess*, p. 180
7 Ponsonby, *Recollections of Three Reigns*, p. 340

16. 'Determining their fate irrevocably in a few moments'

1 Ulyanov & Peshkov, *Lenin and Gorky*, p. 179
2 Iljine & Semyonova, *Selling Russia's Treasures*, p. 17
3 Bainbridge, *Peter Carl Fabergé*, p. 62
4 Fabergé, Proler & Skurlov, *The Fabergé Imperial Easter Eggs*, p. 64
5 Iljine & Semyonova, *Selling Russia's Treasures*, Appendix III, p. 283
6 Moscow Kremlin Armoury Archive, stock 20, inv. 1917 file 5, and stock 20, file 23, quoted in Fabergé, Proler & Skurlov, *The Fabergé Imperial Easter Eggs*, p. 255
7 Benckendorff, Count Paul, *Last Days at Tsarskoe Selo*, Appendix, p. 119
8 Lukomsky, *Châteaux et Palais de Russie*, p. 159
9 Ulyanov & Peshkov, *Lenin and Gorky*, p. 194
10 Larsons & Rappoport (trans.), *An Expert in the Service of the Soviet*, p. 65
11 Pipes (ed.), *The Unknown Lenin*, p. 150
12 von Solodkoff, *Masterpieces from the House of Fabergé*, p. 43
13 Lancaster, *Homes Sweet Homes*, p. 64
14 Reminiscence of 'Countess M', quoted in von Habsburg & Lopato, *Fabergé: Imperial Jeweller*, p. 153
15 Bainbridge, *Peter Carl Fabergé*, p. 17

17. 'Pick out gold, silver and platinum . . .'

1 Iljine & Semyonova, *Selling Russia's Treasures*, p. 46
2 von Solodkoff, *Masterpieces from the House of Fabergé*, p. 124
3 Department of manuscripts, printed, and graphic stores of Kremlin State Museum, store 20, inv. 1929/30, p. 125, quoted in Mukhin, *The Fabulous Epoch of Fabergé*, p. 67
4 Department of manuscripts, printed, and graphic stores of Kremlin State Museum, store 20, inv. 1929/30, pp. 27–8, quoted in ibid., p. 67

5 Fabergé, Proler & Skurlov, *The Fabergé Imperial Easter Eggs*, p. 84

6 *Times*, London, 4 June 1931, 'Russian Art Experts Arrested', p. 13

18. '. . . May was passionately fond of fine jewellery'

1 Bainbridge, *Peter Carl Fabergé*, p. 16
2 Ibid. p. 83
3 Vorres, *The Last Grand-Duchess*, p. 184
4 Pope-Hennessy, *Queen Mary*, p. 225
5 *Times*, London, 16 March 1934, 'Sale Room: Carl Fabergé's Work', p. 16

19. 'Department stores – try the department stores'

1 Hammer, *Hammer: Witness to History*, pp. 190–1
2 Ibid. p. 88
3 Blumay, *The Dark Side of Power*, p. 104
4 Hammer, *Hammer: Witness to History*, p. 196
5 *New Yorker*, 23 December 1933, 'Innocents Abroad', p. 20
6 Hammer, *Hammer: Witness to History*, p. 175
7 Ibid. p. 189
8 Ibid.
9 Ibid. p. 198
10 Ibid. p. 202
11 Ibid. p. 204
12 Ibid. p. 205
13 Ibid. p. 206
14 Ibid. p. 197
15 Blumay, *The Dark Side of Power*, p. 104

20. 'Old civilisations put to the sword'

1 Rubin, *American Empress: The Life and Times of Marjorie Merriweather Post*
2 Hammer, *Hammer: Witness to History*, p. 214

3 Curry, *Fabergé: Virginia Museum of Fine Arts*, p. 15
4 Hammer, *Hammer: Witness to History*, p. 221

21. 'Turn of the century trinkets'

1 Snowman, *Carl Fabergé, Goldsmith to the Imperial Court of Russia*, p. 128
2 Snowman, *The Art of Carl Fabergé*, p. 23
3 *The Connoisseur*, June 1983, *The Natural*, p. 90
4 Ibid.

22. '. . . you were doing *him* a favour'

1 Forbes & Clark (ed.), *More than I Dreamed*, p. 36
2 Ibid. p. 220
3 Ibid. p. 221
4 von Solodkoff, *Masterpieces from the House of Fabergé*, p. 12
5 *The Connoisseur*, June 1983, 'The Natural', p. 90
6 Forbes & Clark (ed.), *More than I Dreamed*, p. 206
7 Winans, *Malcolm Forbes*, p. 9
8 Forbes, *Fabergé Eggs: Imperial Russian Fantasies*, p. 5
9 Forbes & Clark (ed.), *More than I Dreamed*, p. 206
10 *Times*, London, 13 June 1985, 'Forbes Goes to Work on $1.7m Fabergé Gold Egg', p. 12

23 'He who dies with the most toys wins'

1 *Forbes*, New York, 5 March 1990, 'Fact and Comment', p. 20
2 Winans, *Malcolm Forbes*, p. 206

24. 'Handle it and then question it . . .'

1 Lowes & McCanless, *Fabergé Eggs*, p. 145
2 Ibid. p. 144
3 *Apollo, The Magazine of the Arts*, London, January 1984, 'Fresh Insight on Carl Fabergé'

4 Lord & Taylor catalogue 4524, 1933, p. 11, quoted in Fabergé, Proler & Skurlov, *The Fabergé Imperial Easter Eggs*, p. 100

5 Fabergé, Proler & Skurlov, *The Fabergé Imperial Easter Eggs*, p. 101

6 Ibid.

7 Wartski, *A Loan Exhibition of the Works of Carl Fabergé*, 1949, p. 10

8 *Apollo, The Magazine of the Arts*, London, January 1984, 'Fresh Insight on Carl Fabergé'

9 Fabergé, Proler & Skurlov, *The Fabergé Imperial Easter Eggs*, Appendix 4, p. 256

10 Ibid.

11 Ibid. p. 159

12 Lowes & McCanless, *Fabergé Eggs*, pp. 6–7

13 Fabergé, Proler & Skurlov, *The Fabergé Imperial Easter Eggs*, Appendix 4, p. 256

14 Russian Art, *Catalogue of the Exhibition of Russian Art*, p. 108

15 *Sunday Times*, London, 20 March 1988, 'Lawyers go to work on an egg', p. C9

25. 'You can put all your eggs in one basket'

1 Forbes & Clark (ed.), *More than I Dreamed*, p. 223

2 *The Times*, London, 5 February 2004, 'Fabergé eggs are restored to Russia', p. 21

3 Ibid.

4 von Habsburg, *Fabergé: Treasures of Imperial Russia*, Preface

Bibliography

Key Texts

Bainbridge, Henry Charles, *Peter Carl Fabergé: His Life and Work*, Batsford, London, 1949 – The first biography and the only one based on personal acquaintance.

Clarke, William, *The Lost Fortune of the Tsars*, Weidenfeld & Nicolson, London, 1994 – A journalistic study of what happened to the Romanovs' jewels and other wealth following the collapse of the Imperial regime.

Fabergé, Tatiana, Lynette Proler and Valentin Skurlov, *The Fabergé Imperial Easter Eggs*, Christie's, London, 1997 – The breakthrough book containing archival research on the Imperial eggs.

Figes, Orlando, *A People's Tragedy: The Russian Revolution 1891–1924*, Jonathan Cape, London, 1996 – Magisterial study of the Russian Revolution.

Lowes, Will and Christel Ludewig McCanless, *Fabergé Eggs: A Retrospective Encyclopedia*, Scarecrow Press, London, 2001 – The best single source about all known Fabergé eggs.

McCanless, Christel Ludewig, *Fabergé and His Works: An Annotated Bibliography of the First Century of His Art*, Scarecrow Press, London, 1994 – A work of scholarship giving details of numerous newspaper articles and other sources.

Massie, Robert K., *Nicholas and Alexandra*, Victor Gollancz, London, 1968 – Continues to overshadow all subsequent books about Russia's last tsar.

Maylunas, Andrei and Sergei Mironenko, *A Lifelong Passion:*

Nicholas and Alexandra – Their Own Story, Weidenfeld & Nicolson, London, 1996 – A very readable digest of primary sources.

Snowman, A. Kenneth, *The Art of Carl Fabergé*, Faber and Faber, London, 1953 – Largely superseded but important as the first proper study of Carl Fabergé.

von Habsburg, Géza and Marina Lopato, *Fabergé: Imperial Jeweller*, Thames & Hudson, London, 1993 – Includes a number of interesting articles and much new research.

von Solodkoff, Alexander, *Fabergé*, Pyramid, London, 1988 – Another book that, when first issued, contained much new research.

Other Sources

Albright-Knox Art Gallery, *The Armand Hammer Collection, Four Centuries of Masterpieces*, The Gallery, Buffalo, NY, 1978

Alexandra, Tsarina, and Vladimir Kozlov and Vladimir M Khrustalëv (eds), *The Last Diary of Tsaritsa Alexandra*, Yale University Press, London, 1997

Alice, Grand Duchess of Hesse, *Letters to Her Majesty the Queen*, John Murray, London, 1885

Bainbridge, Henry Charles, *Twice Seven: The Autobiography of H.C. Bainbridge*, Routledge, London, 1933

Balsan, Consuelo Vanderbilt, *The Glitter and the Gold*, Heinemann, London, 1953

Baring, Maurice, *A Year in Russia*, Methuen, London, 1907

Baring, Maurice, *The Mainsprings of Russia*, Thomas Nelson, London, 1914

Baylen, Joseph O., *The Tsar's Lecturer-General: W. T. Stead and the Russian Revolution of 1905*, School of Arts and Sciences Research Papers, Georgia State College, Atlanta, GA, July 1969

Benckendorff, Count Paul and Maurice Baring (trans.), *Last Days at Tsarskoe Selo. Being the Personal Notes and Memoirs of*

*Count Paul Benckendorff Telling of the Last Sojourn of the
Emperor and Empress of Russia at Tsarskoe Selo from March 1
to August 1, 1917*, Heinemann, London, 1927

Bill, Valentine T., *The Forgotten Class: The Russian Bourgeoisie
from the Earliest Beginnings to 1900*, Frederick A. Praeger, New
York, 1959

Bing, Edward J. (ed.), *The Letters of Tsar Nicholas and Empress
Marie*, Ivor Nicolson & Watson, London, 1937

Blumay, Carl, with Henry Edwards, *The Dark Side of Power: The
Real Armand Hammer*, Simon & Schuster, New York, 1992

Bolitho, Hector (ed.), Mrs J. Duchay and Lord Snelley (trans.),
*Further Letters of Queen Victoria from the Archives of the House
of Brandenburg-Prussia*, Thornton Butterworth, London, 1938

Botkin, Gleb, *The Real Romanovs*, Putnam, London, 1932

Brokhin, Yuri, *Hustling on Gorky Street: Sex and Crime in Russia
Today*, W.H. Allen, London, 1976

Buchanan, Sir George, *My Mission to Russia and Other Diplomatic
Memories*, Cassell, London, 1923

Buchanan, Meriel, *Recollections of Imperial Russia*, Hutchinson,
London, 1923

Buxhoeveden, Baroness Sophie, *The Life and Tragedy of Alexandra
Fedorovna, Empress of Russia*, Longmans, London, 1928

Buxhoeveden, Baroness Sophie, *Before the Storm*, Macmillan,
London, 1938

Cantacuzène, Princess Julia and Terence Emmons (ed.),
Revolutionary Days, R.R. Donnelley & Sons, Chicago, 1999

Cerwinske, Laura, *Russian Imperial Style*, Barrie & Jenkins,
London, 1990

Charques, Richard, *The Twilight of Imperial Russia*, Oxford
University Press, London, 1965

Christie's Sale Catalogue, *Gold Boxes, Important Miniatures, Highly
Important Works of Art by Carl Fabergé, Russian Objects and
Paintings*, Geneva 15–16 November 1994

Christie's Sale Catalogue, *The Winter Egg by Carl Fabergé*, Geneva,
16 November 1994

Churchill, Winston, *The World Crisis*, Thornton Butterworth, London, 1929

Clifton, Harry, *Dielma and Other Poems*, Duckworth, London, 1932

Clifton, Harry, *Flight*, Duckworth, London, 1934

Clifton, Harry, *Gleams Britain's Day*, Duckworth, London, 1942

Considine, Bob, *Larger Than Life: A Biography of the Remarkable Dr Armand Hammer*, W.H. Allen, London, 1976

Crankshaw, Edward, *The Shadow of the Winter Palace: The Drift to Revolution, 1825–1917*, Macmillan, London, 1976

Curry, David Park, *Fabergé: Virginia Museum of Fine Arts*, Virginia Museum of Fine Arts, Richmond, 1995

Davies, Joseph E., *Mission to Moscow*, Victor Gollancz Ltd, London, 1943

de Basily, Nicolas, *The Abdication of Emperor Nicholas II of Russia*, Kingston Press, Twickenham, 1984

de Guitaut, Caroline, *Fabergé in the Royal Collection*, Royal Collection, London, 2003

de Stoeckl, Baroness and George Kinnaird (ed.), *Not All Vanity*, John Murray, London, 1950

Dehn, Lili, *The Real Tsaritsa*, Thornton Butterworth, London, 1922

Dolgorouky, Princess Stéphanie, *La Russie Avant la Débâcle*, Eugène Figuiere, Paris, 1926

Eagar, M., *Six Years at the Russian Court*, Hurst & Blackett, London, 1906

Epstein, Edward Jay, *Dossier: The Secret History of Armand Hammer*, Random House, New York, 1996

Erickson, Carolly, *Alexandra: The Last Tsarina*, St Martin's Press, New York, 2001

Fabergé Fantasies: The Forbes Magazine Collection, Electa, Milan, 1987

FitzLyon, Kyril, *Before the Revolution: A View of Russia under the Last Tsar*, Allen Lane, London, 1977

Fitzpatrick, Sheila, *The Commissariat of Enlightenment: Soviet Organization of Education and the Arts under Lunacharsky*

October 1917–1921, Cambridge University Press, Cambridge, 1970

Forbes, Christopher, *Fabergé Eggs: Imperial Russian Fantasies*, Abrams, New York, 1980

Forbes, Christopher et al., *Fabergé: The Imperial Eggs, San Diego Museum of Art*, Prestel, Munich, 1989

Forbes, Christopher and Robyn Tromeur-Brenner, *Fabergé: The Forbes Collection*, Hugh Lauter Levin Associates, New York, 1999

Forbes, Malcolm and Tony Clark (ed.), *More than I Dreamed*, Simon & Schuster, London, 1989

Foster, Roy, *W. B. Yeats, A Life, Volume II: The Arch-Poet*, Oxford University Press, Oxford, 2003

Fry, A. Ruth, *Three Visits to Russia 1922–25*, James Clarke & Co, London, 1942

Fuhrmann, Joseph T. (ed.), *The Complete Wartime Correspondence of Tsar Nicholas II and the Empress Alexandra, April 1914–March 1917*, Greenwood Press, London, 1999

Galitzine, Prince George, *Imperial Splendour: Palaces and Monasteries of Old Russia*, Viking, London, 1991

Galitzine, Princess Nicholas, *Spirit to Survive*, William Kimber, London, 1976

Gattey, Charles, *The Incredible Mrs Van der Elst*, Leslie Frewin, London, 1972

Geifman, Anna (ed.), *Russia under the Last Tsar: Opposition and Subversion, 1894–1917*, Blackwell, Oxford, 1990

George, Grand Duchess, *A Romanov Diary: The Autobiography of Her Imperial and Royal Highness Grand Duchess George*, Atlantic International Publications, New York, 1988

Gilliard, Pierre and F. Appleby Holt (trans.), *Thirteen Years at the Russian Court; A Personal Record of the Last Years and Death of Czar Nicholas II and His Family*, Hutchinson, London, 1921

Grabbe, Alexander, and Paul and Beatrice Grabbe (eds), *The Private World of the Last Tsar: In the Photographs & Notes of General Count Alexander Grabbe*, Collins, London, 1985

Grosvenor, Loelia, *Grace and Favour: The Memoirs of Loelia Grosvenor, Duchess of Westminster*, Weidenfeld & Nicolson, London, 1961

Hall, Coryne, *Little Mother of Russia: A Biography of the Empress Marie Fedorovna (1847–1928)*, Shepheard-Walwyn, London, 1999

Hamilton, Lord Frederick, *The Vanished World of Yesterday*, Hodder & Stoughton, London, 1950

Hammer, Armand, *The Quest of the Romanoff Treasure*, William Farquhar Payson, New York, 1932

Hammer, Armand with Neil Lyndon, *Hammer: Witness to History*, Simon & Schuster, London, 1987

Hanbury-Williams, Sir John, *The Emperor Nicholas II as I Knew Him*, A.L. Humphreys, London, 1922

Harcave, Sidney, *Years of the Golden Cockerel: The Last Romanov Tsars, 1814–1917*, Robert Hale, London, 1968

Hardinge of Penshurt, Lord, *Old Diplomacy*, John Murray, London, 1947

Hastings, Patrick, K.C., *Cases in Court*, William Heinemann, London, 1949

Hawley, Henry, *Fabergé and His Contemporaries: The India Early Minshall Collection of The Cleveland Museum of Art*, Cleveland Museum of Art, Cleveland, OH, 1967

Hill, Gerard (ed.), *Fabergé and the Russian Master Goldsmiths*, Hugh Lauter Levin, New York, 1989

Hodgetts, E. A. Brayley, *Moss From a Rolling Stone*, J. M. Dent, London, 1924

Hough, Richard (ed.), *Advice to a Grand-daughter: Letters from Queen Victoria to Princess Victoria of Hesse*, Heinemann, London, 1975

Iljine, Nicolas and Natalya Semyonova, *Selling Russia's Treasures: The Story of the Sale of Russian National Art Treasures Confiscated from the Tsarist Royal Family, the Church, Private Individuals and Museums in the USSR in 1918–1937*, Trefoil Press, Moscow, 2000

Ingham, Robert, *What Happened to the Empress: The Visit to Malta of H.I.M. The Dowager Empress of Russia*, The Red Tower, Hamrun, Malta, 1949

Johnston, William R., *William and Henry Walters, The Reticent Collectors*, Johns Hopkins University Press, London, 1999

Jones, Arthur, *Malcolm Forbes, Peripatetic Millionaire*, Harper & Row, London, 1977

Kedzie Wood, Ruth, *The Tourist's Russia*, Andrew Melrose, London, 1912

Keefe, John Webster, *Masterpieces of Fabergé: The Matilda Geddings Gray Foundation Collection*, New Orleans Museum of Art, 1993

King Waddington, Mary, *Letters of a Diplomat's Wife, 1883–1900*, Smith, Elder & Co, London, 1903

Kleinmichel, Countess Marie and Vivian Le Grand (trans.), *Memories of a Shipwrecked World*, Brentano's, London, 1923

Kokovtsov, Vladimir Nikolaevich, H.H. Fisher (ed.) and Laura Matveev (trans.), *Out of My Past: The Memoirs of Count Kokovtsov*, Stanford University Press, Stanford, CA, 1935

Kurth, Peter, *Tsar: The Lost World of Nicholas and Alexandra*, Madison Press, Toronto, 1995

Lancaster, Osbert, *Homes Sweet Homes*, John Murray, London, 1953

Larsons, M.J. and Angelo S. Rappoport (trans.), *An Expert in the Service of the Soviet*, Ernest Benn, London, 1929

Latimer, Robert Sloan, *Under Three Tsars: Liberty of Conscience in Russia, 1856–1909*, Morgan Scott, London, 1909

Lothrop, Almira and William Prall (ed.), *The Court of Alexander III: Letters of Mrs Lothrop*, J.C. Winston, Philadelphia, 1910

Lukomsky, Georgy, *Châteaux et Palais de Russie: Leurs Sort et Histoire, Leurs Richesses et Trésors d'Art*, Lukomsky, Vicence, 1925

MacArthur, John R., *The Selling of 'Free Trade': NAFTA, Washington and the Subversion of American Democracy*, Hill and Wang, New York, 2000

McNeal, Shay, *The Plots to Rescue the Tsar: The Truth Behind the Disappearance of the Romanovs*, Century, London, 2001

Madol, Hans Roger, *The Private Life of Queen Alexandra, as Viewed by Her Friends*, Hutchinson, London, 1940

Marie, Grand Duchess, *Things I Remember*, Cassell, London, 1931

Massie, Robert K., *The Romanovs, The Final Chapter*, Jonathan Cape, London, 1995

Massie, Suzanne, *Land of the Firebird*, Hamish Hamilton, London, 1980

Maud, Renée Elton, *One Year at The Russian Court: 1904–1905*, John Lane, London, 1918

Meshcherskaya, Ekaterina, *Comrade Princess: Memoirs of an Aristocrat in Modern Russia*, Doubleday, New York, 1990

Mikhailovitch, Grand Duke Alexander, *Once a Grand Duke*, Cassell, London, 1932

Mikhailovitch, Grand-Duke Nicolas, *La Fin du Tsarisme: Lettres inédites à Frédéric Masson 1914–18*, Payot, Paris, 1968

Monkswell, Lady Mary, and the Hon. E.C.F. Collier, (ed.), *A Victorian Diarist: Later Extracts from the Journals of Mary, Lady Monkswell, 1895–1904*, John Murray, London, 1946

Moore, Andrew (pseudonym), *Theo Fabergé and The St Petersburg Collection*, Dauphin and the St Petersburg Collection, London, 1989

Mossolov, A. A., A. A. Pilenco (ed.) and E. W. Dickes (trans.), *At the Court of the Last Tsar: Memoirs of A. A. Mossolov, Head of the Court Chancellery 1900–1916*, Methuen, London, 1935

Mouchanow, Marfa, *My Empress: Twenty-three Years of Intimate Life with the Empress of All the Russias from Her Marriage to the Day of Her Exile*, Bodley Head, London, 1918

Mukhin, Vyacheslav, *The Fabulous Epoch of Fabergé, St Petersburg-Paris-Moscow: Exhibition at the Catherine Palace in Tsarskoye Selo*, Nord, Moscow, 1992

Munn, Geoffrey C., *Tiaras: A History of Splendour*, Antique Collectors Club, Woodbridge, 2001

Muntian, Tatiana, *The World of Fabergé*, Red Square Publishers, Moscow, 1996

Muntian, Tatiana, *Fabergé, Jeweller of the Romanovs*, Europalia, Brussels, 2005

Nabokov, Vladimir, *Speak Memory: An Autobiography Revisited*, Weidenfeld & Nicolson, London, 1967

Narishkin-Kurakin, Elizabeth, René Fülöp-Miller (ed.) and Julia Lössei (trans.), *Under Three Tsars: The Memoirs of the Lady-in-Waiting Elizabeth Narishkin-Kurakin*, E. P. Dutton, New York, 1931

Nicolas II, Emperor and A. Pierre (trans.), *Journal Intime de Nicolas II*, Payot, Paris, 1925

Niet (pseudonym), *La Russie d'Aujourd'hui*, Paris, 1902

Paleologue, Maurice and F. A. Holt (trans.), *An Ambassador's Memoirs*, Hutchinson, London, 1923

Paley, Princesse, *Souvenirs de Russie, 1916–1919*, Librairie Plon, Paris, 1923

Pipes, Richard, *Russia Under the Old Regime*, Weidenfeld & Nicolson, London, 1974

Pipes, Richard (ed.), *The Unknown Lenin: From the Secret Archives*, Yale University Press, London, 1996

Pless, Princess Daisy and D. Chapman-Huston (ed.), *The Private Diaries of Daisy Princess of Pless, 1873–1914*, John Murray, London, 1950

Poliakoff, Vladimir, *The Empress Marie of Russia and Her Times*, Thornton Butterworth, London, 1926

Polovtsoff, Alexandre, *Les Trésors d'Art en Russie sous le Régime Bolcheviste*, Société Française d'Imprimerie et de Librairie, 1919

Ponsonby, Sir Frederick, *Recollections of Three Reigns*, Eyre and Spottiswoode, London, 1951

Pope-Hennessy, James, *Queen Mary*, Allen and Unwin, London, 1959

Pridham, Arthur Francis, *Close of a Dynasty*, Allen Wingate, London, 1956

Radzinsky, Edvard and Maria Schwartz (trans.), *The Last Tsar: The Life and Death of Nicholas II*, Doubleday, London, 1992

Radziwill, Princess Catherine, *My Recollections*, Isbister, London, 1904

Radziwill, Princess Catherine, *Those I Remember*, Cassell, London, 1924

Radziwill, Princess Catherine, *Nicholas II: The Last of the Tsars*, Cassell, London, 1931

Romanovsky-Krassinsky, Princess and Arnold Haskell (trans.), *Dancing in Petersburg: The Memoirs of Kschessinska*, Victor Gollancz, London, 1960

Ross, Marvin C., *The Art of Karl Fabergé and His Contemporaries*, University of Oklahoma Press, Norman, 1965

Rothschild Archive, *Review of the Year April 2004 to March 2005*, Rothschild Archive, London, 2005

Rubin, Nancy, *American Empress: The Life and Times of Marjorie Merriweather Post*, Villard Books, New York, 1995

Russian Art, *Catalogue of the Exhibition of Russian Art, 1 Belgrave Square*, London, 1935

Snowman, A. Kenneth, *Fabergé, 1846–1920, Goldsmith to the Imperial Court of Russia: An International Loan Exhibition Assembled on the Occasion of the Queen's Silver Jubilee and Including Objects from the Royal Collection at Sandringham*, Debrett's, London, 1977

Snowman, A. Kenneth, *Carl Fabergé: Goldsmith to the Imperial Court of Russia*, Debrett's, London, 1979

Snowman, A. Kenneth, *Fabergé – Lost and Found: The Recently Discovered Jewelry Designs from the St Petersburg Archives*, Thames and Hudson, London, 1993

Sotheby Parke-Bernet Sale Catalogue, *Louis XV, Louis XVI and Other Furniture, Important Objets d'Art*, New York, 15 May 1965

Spiridovitch, General Alexandre and M. Jeanson (trans.), *Les Dernières Années de la Cour de Tzarskoie-Selo*, Payot, Paris, 1928

Stopford, Albert, *The Russian Diary of an Englishman: Petrograd, 1915–1917*, William Heinemann, London, 1919

Tillander, A., *Carl Fabergé and his Contemporaries*, Museum of Applied Arts, Helsinki, 1980

Tisdall, E. E. P., *The Dowager Empress*, Stanley Paul, London, 1957

Trotsky, Leon and Max Eastman (trans.), *The History of the Russian Revolution*, Pluto Press, London, 1977

Trufanoff, Sergei Michailovich, *The Mad Monk of Russia: Iliodor*, Century Co., New York, 1918

Ulyanov, Vladimir and Alexei Peshkov, *Lenin and Gorky: Letters, Reminiscences, Articles*, University Press of the Pacific, Honolulu, 2003

Van der Kiste, John and Coryne Hall, *Once a Grand Duchess: Xenia, Sister of Nicholas II*, Sutton Publishing, Stroud, 2002

Vladimirovitch, Grand Duke Cyril, *My Life in Russia's Service – Then and Now*, Selwyn & Blount, London, 1939

von Habsburg, Géza, *Fabergé*, Habsburg, Feldman Editions, Geneva, 1987

von Habsburg, Géza, *Carl Fabergé*, Abrams, New York, 1994

von Habsburg, Géza, *Fabergé Fantasies and Treasures*, Aurum, London, 1996

von Habsburg, Géza, *Fabergé in America*, Thames & Hudson, London, 1996

von Habsburg, Géza, *Fabergé: Treasures of Imperial Russia*, Link of Times Foundation, 2005

von Hoffman, Nicholas, *Capitalist Fools: Tales of American Business from Carnegie to Malcolm Forbes*, Chatto & Windus, London, 1993

von Solodkoff, Alexander, *Masterpieces from the House of Fabergé*, Abrams, New York, 1984

von Solodkoff, Alexander, *Fabergé, Juwelier des Zarenhofes*, Edition Braus, Heidelburg, 1995

Vorres, Ian, *The Last Grand-Duchess: Her Imperial Highness Grand-Duchess Olga Alexandrovna*, Hutchinson, London, 1964

Vyrubova, Anna, *Memories of the Russian Court*, Macmillan, London, 1923

Wartski, *A Loan Exhibition of the Works of Carl Fabergé, Jeweller and Goldsmith to the Imperial Court of Russia*, 8–25 November 1949, London

Wartski, *Fabergé and the Russian Jewellers*, 10–20 May 2006

Waterfield, Hermione and Christopher Forbes, *Fabergé: Imperial Eggs and Other Fantasies*, Thames & Hudson, London, 1979

Weinberg, Steve, *Armand Hammer: The Untold Story*, Ebury Press, London, 1989

Welch, Frances, *The Romanovs and Mr Gibbes: The Story of the Englishman Who Taught the Children of the Last Tsar*, Short Books, London, 2002

Williams, Robert C., *Russian Art and American Money, 1900–1940*, Harvard University Press, Cambridge, MA, 1980

Witte, Count Sergei and Abraham Yarmolinsky (ed. and trans.), *The Memoirs of Count Witte*, Documentary Publications, Salisbury, NC, 1977

Winans, Christopher, *Malcolm Forbes: The Man Who Had Everything*, Peter Owen, London, 1991

Yusupov, Prince Feliks, and Ann Green and Nicolas Katkoff (trans.), *Lost Splendour*, Jonathan Cape, London, 1953

Recommended Websites

Russian History

http://www.alexanderpalace.org/palace/mainpage.html
  – 'The world's most popular website for Russian and Romanov history' includes several online books and gives access to numerous primary sources.

http://www.angelfire.com/pa/ImperialRussian/index.html
  – 'A celebration of the Romanov Dynasty in Word and Photographs' includes biographies of every major Romanov and is sponsored by Gilbert's Royal Bookshop.

Fabergé Specialist Sites

http://www.mieks.com/Faberge2/index2.htm – Includes
    descriptions and photographs (where available) of every major
    Fabergé egg.
http://home.hiwaay.net/~christel/index.html – Includes
    comprehensive bibliography, details of forthcoming exhibitions
    and much else.

Fabergé Collections and Museums

http://www.cheekwood.org/ – Cheekwood Botanical Gardens and
    Museum of Art.
http://www.clevelandart.org/ – Cleveland Museum of Art.
http://www.fmm.ru/ – Fersman Mineralogical Museum.
http://www.hillwoodmuseum.org/ – Hillwood Museum.
http://www.kreml.ru/ – The Kremlin Armoury Museum.
http://www.treasuresofimperialrussia.com – Online version of book
    about the Link of Times Collection by Geza von Habsburg.
http://www.royalcollection.org.uk/ – The Royal Collection of Queen
    Elizabeth II.
http://www.vmfa.state.va.us/ – Virginia Museum of Fine Arts.
http://www.thewalters.org/ – Walters Art Museum.

Other

http://www.forbes.com/collecting/2004/02/27/cx_cd_0224soc.html
    – A column about the sale of the Forbes Magazine Collection
    to Viktor Vekselberg. The sidebar contains links to several
    interesting articles.
http://www.stpetersburgcollection.com/history.asp – Information
    about Theo and Sarah Fabergé.

Archives Consulted

Faber and Faber, London
Hillwood Museum, Washington DC
Wartski of Llandudno, London

Index

Ai Todor, 161, 162

Albert Victor (Eddy), Duke of Clarence, 195–6

Alexander I, Tsar, 101

Alexander II, Tsar, 12–13, 20, 23

Alexander III, Tsar: accession, 12; accession manifesto, 14; children, 17; coronation, 17–18; death, 35, 99, 260n, 273; Fabergé's first egg.4, 5, 11, 18–19, 21; famine during reign, 31, 171; father's death, 12; illness, 35–6; lifestyle, 15; marriage, 16–17; memorials, 94; politics, 13–14; relationship with wife, 11, 16–17, 36, 110; sons' travels, 27–9; terrorist threats to, 18; train crash, 20

Alexander Mikhailovitch (Sandro), Grand Duke, 12, 38, 160–1, 163, 167

Alexander Palace: after revolution, 134, 138–9, 158, 221; after WWII, 220–1; *Alexander Palace Egg*, 83–4; Alexandra's mauve boudoir, 41–2, 84, 142, 172; communist school, 158; daily life at, 86–7, 138–9; decorations, 41, 83; Nicholas and Alexandra in, 41–2, 50, 83; picture of, 50; Rasputin at, 101

Alexandra, Queen: death, 194; Fabergé patronage, 190–2, 194, 196; Hvidore villa, 109; ill health, 166; marriage, 15; sister's letters, 113; sister's visits, 109, 166; widowhood, 194

Alexandra Fedorovna, Tsarina (Alix of Hesse): appearance, 33, 86, 94; body, 270; character, 33, 44–5, 49, 67, 85, 127; children, 51, 66, 78–9, 88–9, 94, 141; children's illness, 134, 138; coronation, 52, 53–5; death, 147–9, 165; Easter eggs, 279–82; education, 44; in Ekaterinburg, 145–6, 164; engagement to Nicholas, 33–4, 35–6, 44; family background, 32–3, 42, 44, 50, 141; government role, 126; haemophilia in family, 80–1; health, 86; jewels, 35, 142, 146, 148; journey to Siberia, 141–2; lifestyle, 86–7; marriage, 97; miscarriage, 54–5; in Moscow, 65; political judgement, 98, 126; portraits, 94, 259; reburial, 270; relationship with husband, 39, 42, 66, 86–7, 97, 105, 109, 121–2, 125–6; relationship with mother-in-law, 42, 43–4, 49–50, 109, 119; relationship with Rasputin, 90–1, 100–1, 126–7, 130; religion, 33–4, 36, 44, 65–6, 78–9; Revolution (February 1917), 134–6; son's haemophilia, 80–1, 82, 89–91, 104; in Tobolsk, 142–5; unpopularity, 44–5, 51, 53, 121, 126, 127; war effort, 119–21; wedding, 36–7, 182

Alexei Alexandrovitch, Grand Duke, 176

Alexeiev, Michael Vasilevitch, 121

Alexis II, Patriarch, 270

Alexis, Tsar, 68

Alexis, Tsarevitch: at army HQ, 124; birth, 79–80, 95, 109, 185, 254; body, 270n; character, 124; childhood, 112; death, 147–9; education, 124, 143; in Ekaterinburg, 146; father's abdication, 135; haemophilia, 80–1,

Acknowledgements

I am extremely grateful to all the people who were generous with their time and knowledge while I was writing this book.

Christopher Forbes, of *Forbes* magazine, and Geoffrey Munn, of Wartski, deserve particular thanks, both for being informative and entertaining interviewees, and for allowing me to reproduce pictures controlled by their companies. So does Christel McCanless, co-author of *Fabergé's Eggs: A Retrospective Encyclopaedia*. She read an early draft of this book. Her comments greatly improved it and she has since been a consistently encouraging friend.

I enjoyed meeting Kristen Regina, librarian at Hillwood; her colleagues Karen Kettering and Heather Corey searched the Hillwood archive on my behalf. Vic Gray and Erica Somers did the same with the Faber and Faber archive; and so did Carol Leadenham at the Hoover Institution archive. Yelena Harbick, of Christie's, and Joanna Vickery, of Sotheby's, gave me helpful interviews. Nic Iljine and Natalia Semenova, co-authors of Selling Russia's Treasures, provided me with an English translation of their excellent book and with some of the images that it contains. William Clarke, author of *Lost Fortune of the Tsars*, helped me with sources. Wartski's Kieran McCarthy was with me when I looked through most of the firm's stock books, and he himself continues to uncover new revelations about Fabergé. Annemiek Wintraecken has created a website (www.mieks.com) which is the best introduction to Fabergé's eggs available on the internet.

Elizabeth Nisbet gave me copies of newspaper articles about her Wartski ancestors. George and Dora Zolnai looked after me when I was in Moscow. Peter Crawley trawled his memories on my behalf. Gideon Todes brainstormed titles. Tracey Crawford typed up my interviews. At Christies Images, Laura Nixey, Stella Calvert-Smith and Emma Strouts were all kind and helpful.

The staff at the British Library, where I found most of my sources, were always ready to assist; and my one visit to the Library of Congress was made enjoyable and successful by the flexibility of the staff in the European Reading Room.

The lovely Caroline Dawnay, now of United Agents, encouraged me to write this book. In the UK it was originally commissioned by Jason Cooper at Macmillan. He has moved on to better things, but I am grateful to Richard Milner for taking over so smoothly, to Lorraine Baxter for being an exemplary editor and to Georgina Difford for her meticulousness as an editorial manager. Jacqueline Graham publicised my last book and I am looking forward to working with her on this one too. In the US, Zoe Pagnamenta has been a supportive agent and I am very pleased to be published by Random House, where Susanna Porter has been a perceptive and sympathetic editor, assisted by Jillian Quint, and where London King is an excellent, and russophilic, publicist.

Within my family, my stepmother, Dr Liesbeth van Houts, made insightful comments on an early draft and my siblings have all been interested and encouraging at appropriate moments. My daughter, Lucy, gave me a decorated egg a few Easters ago, that may have been the germ of an idea.

I am indebted to all these people. Above all, however, I want once again to thank my wife, Amanda. She has shared in my excitement, lifted me out of despondency, been a critical and forthright reader of numerous drafts, and has always been there when I needed her. If this book reads well then that is largely because of her. If it does not, or if it contains errors, then the fault is, of course, all mine.